PRAISE FOR *Dream College*

"Dr. Ezeze has written one of the most comprehensive college guides I have read in my 30+ years as a college admissions professional. Using the wisdom and knowledge acquired over his impressive career, he has taken what can be a daunting process and broken it down into manageable and achievable pieces. This is a must-read not only for the parents of high school students but for those parents with children in middle school as well. *Dream College* is a valuable addition to the home reference library."

Sharon M. Alston, Executive Director for Enrollment Management,
American University

"*Dream College* is one of the most comprehensive guides to the college admissions process presently on the market. It goes so much further than other guides because Dr. Ezeze shares information about admission practices that he has gained by having personal and up-front conversations with admissions professionals at colleges across the country. The information in this book will be invaluable to students and parents as they begin the quest to not just college but to their 'Dream College.'"

Norma Paige, Guidance Counselor, Scotch Plains Fanwood High School

"*Dream College* is unmatched in the quality of its information, scope, and timeliness. I have known Dr. Ezeze for about two decades, and he really knows the college admissions business through and through—from research to application to making college dreams come true. This is a comprehensive and useful resource for all readers. This is a great book!"

Audrey T. Hill, Transfer Counselor,
Montgomery College, Maryland

"As a college student, I lament that I could not have Dr. Ezeze's book in my hands a few years ago. The emphasis on early planning would have eliminated misguided decisions. The chapters on college athletics and financial aid would have been indispensable during my college selection process. Fortunately, Dr. Ezeze also provides valuable information about what to expect while in college, which has been invaluable."

Erik Torenberg, University of Michigan, Class of 2012

"As a student I see *Dream College* as offering many routes to a single destination. Its comprehensive nature makes this book a must-read for high school students, college students, parents, and even counselors alike."

Nnamdi Obodo, University of Virginia, Class of 2012

Dream
COLLEGE

**How to Help
Your Child Get
into the
Top Schools**

Second Edition

Kpakpundu Ezeze, Ed.D.

Dream College: How to Help Your Child Get into the Top Schools | Second Edition

By Kpakpundu Ezeze

Published by SuperCollege, LLC
2713 Newlands Avenue
Belmont, CA 94002
www.supercollege.com

Credits: Cover: Kris Taft Miller
Layout: The Roberts Group, www.editorialservice.com

Trademarks: All brand names, product names and services used in this book are trademarks, registered trademarks, or tradenames of their respective holders. Super-College is not associated with any college, university, product, or vendor.

Disclaimers: The author and publisher have used their best efforts in preparing this book. It is sold with the understanding that the author and publisher are not rendering legal or other professional advice. The author and publisher cannot be held responsible for any loss incurred as a result of specific decisions made by the reader. The author and publisher make no representations or warranties with respect to the accuracy or completeness of the contents of the book and specifically disclaim any implied warranties or merchantability or fitness for a particular purpose. The accuracy and completeness of the information provided herein and the opinions stated herein are not guaranteed or warranted to produce any particular results. The author and publisher specifically disclaim any responsibility for any liability, loss or risk, personal or otherwise, which is incurred as a consequence, directly or indirectly, from the use and application of any of the contents of this book.

ISBN13: 978-1-61760-116-3

Manufactured in the United States of America

10 9 8 7 6 5 4 3 2 1

Library of Congress Cataloging-in-Publication Data
Names: Ezeze, Kpakpundu, author.
Title: Dream college : how to help your child get into the top schools / Kpakpundu Ezeze, Ed.D.
Description: Second edition. | Belmont, CA : SuperCollege, 2016.
Identifiers: LCCN 2016015724 (print) | LCCN 2016017174 (ebook) | ISBN 9781617601163 (paperback) | ISBN 9781617601170 | ISBN 9781617601187
Subjects: LCSH: Universities and colleges--United States--Admission. | College choice--United States. | BISAC: STUDY AIDS / College Entrance.
Classification: LCC LB2351.2 .E94 2016 (print) | LCC LB2351.2 (ebook) | DDC 378.1/61--dc23
LC record available at https://lccn.loc.gov/2016015724

DEDICATION

I dedicate this book to my sister, Michelle Rose Hairston.

ACKNOWLEDGEMENTS

A CONFLUENCE OF PROFESSIONAL EXPERIENCES laid this project's foundation. The origins of this guide span three decades of service in secondary and higher education. In various capacities, I had the honor of learning from caring mentors at Lexington, Wellesley, and Washington-Lee high schools, respectively. I expanded my experience as an educator in my service as an administrator with the Upward Bound programs at Boston College, Worcester State College, and Howard University. At Wellesley College I held the position of Head of House-Academic Advisor, and at the University of Pennsylvania I was an Assistant Dean and a Residential Dean in the College of Arts and Sciences; in these two positions I was fortunate to interface with undergraduates on a daily basis. In many ways how I think about education in general and about urban secondary education in particular has been informed by those many discussions among students, faculty, and administrators. In 1989, I launched my own educational consulting firm, Future Quest, Inc., offering guidance to primarily first-generation college-bound youth, who otherwise could not afford to pay for private consulting services but had the greatest need of guidance and support. The company has been in existence for twenty years and has assisted thousands of students with the educational planning and college placement process. Of particular interest has not simply been getting admitted to one's top-choice college, but also the importance of thriving academically and socially once in college and graduating on time. This book tried to catalog the insights I acquired through working with students and education industry professionals in the aim to benefit future generations of college-bound youth and their families.

A number of individuals have imparted invaluable advice and support during the course of this project. For their genuine friendship, fellowship, and direction on many aspects of this assignment, I am especially grateful to Sharon M. Alston, Donna Atkinson, Kevin Carlstein, Carol Cromer, DD Eisenberg, Audrey T. Hill, Andrea Hines, Steve Hines, Vera Faulkner, Michael Ferby, Bernadine Francis, Joyce Hemmons, Rebecca Lamb, Marie Lindsay, Norma Paige, Joe Steele, Glenn Tunstull and Regiie Van Lee. The insight of colleagues and valuable perspectives of former clients speak in the interview contributions that frame each chapter. To my copy editors, Ellen Olmstead and Stephanie Harzewski, I extend special thanks for their exacting eye, advice, and encouragement.

I am also indebted to countless former students, without whom this project could not have been possible. I wish to thank all of my students for their energy and vitality. That youthful spirit has enabled me to feel young, when the reality is I am in the winter of my life. Among those students from whom I have learned and hopefully I have inspired, some stand out among the many: Tanique Adell, Chancellor Agard, Tyler Brooks, Christian Calloway, Derric Daniels, Jasmine Drake, Helena Edwards, Nicole Falls, Neferteneken Francis, Sarah Greenberg, Christina Harastock, Patrick Jefferson, Aaron Jenkins, Constance Lindsay, Nnamdi Obodo, Allen Pinkney, Justin Silvey, Jasmine Smith, Erik Torenberg, Frank White, Jr., and Joshua Williams.

To my sister, Patricia Ann Holland, who passed away in 1975, I give a special acknowledgement for her unconditional love and support throughout our childhood and young adult years. In many ways, her untimely death inspired me to make contributions to the field of education; in certain positions I aimed to contribute to the lives of those who were less fortunate, a trait which she admired most in my character. Through my work in general with young people, and with this project in particular, her love of life and the values for which she stood live on bittersweetly. Over the decades, students' development and hope for the future have continuously affirmed life in the face of challenges. I would be honored if she finds this energy, which was very much a part of her own character, reincarnated here.

And finally I want to thank any individuals whose names I may have unintentionally omitted; I can only hope that they see their insights reflected through the course of this book.

PREFACE

MY FIRST INTRODUCTION TO DR. Ezeze was in 1998 when a mutual friend suggested I contact him about mentoring my budding career as an independent counselor. I drove to Washington, DC, to observe his weekly Tuesday evening vigil at the Martin Luther King, Jr. Memorial Library where he volunteered to meet students who needed college advising but who couldn't afford to pay for it. It was encouraging to witness these kids coming long after nightfall to wait their turn for a follow-up visit with Dr. Ezeze. Students would leave with a to-do list to accomplish before the next meeting and a noticeable sense of empowerment.

There is something recognizably confident in the stride of a teenager who can envision the opportunities before him and carry out a plan with purpose to meet them. Dr. Ezeze helps students approach this pivotal time in their lives by presenting the tools they need to make good decisions and advises them within the framework of their accomplishments, their aspirations, and their potential. I have learned from him over the years that this is the ideal role a counselor plays for the college-bound student—not only to inform and guide, but also to encourage ownership on the part of the student. This piece is critical to their development, and the appropriate tone to set as they move into early adulthood.

For the parents who read this book, one that has been writing itself in Dr. Ezeze's experience these last 25 years, I can attest to the grace and skill Dr. Ezeze brings to his interaction with students and their families. Telling someone what they need to do is very different from assisting them in understanding their options and creating a plan of action. Through each stage of the selection process, long before applications are due, there is much to understand about how admissions will evaluate their applicants, and how students can fully leverage their experience in high school as they anticipate applying to college. And then, of course, there is the shopping to do for the right campus and decisions to be made in the larger context of academic and financial considerations at least. Completing applications can seem like the least complex step in the larger picture. The trick is to help the student move through these stages efficiently, setting goals and managing the path to meeting them, all while nurturing the student to be in charge of their future. The added benefit is better control of anxiety the student and their family feel in this exciting but daunting step in a developing student's life.

Dr. Ezeze doesn't promise manageable stress levels, but I know he delivers his expertise with the kind of composure that generates confidence, and this is worth so much in the tension-laden process we call college planning. Dr. Ezeze offers a smooth path toward the greatest rite of passage in a young person's life—the transition to college.

Parents, while you may get caught up in the worry over where your child might "get in," how to pay for it, or even how you might feel when your student leaves home, remember how important this stage is in your son or daughter's life. They'll go to college and get the education they need because you will work that out together. More importantly, they'll learn to become responsible adults while they're away. What better way to get them and yourself started than to make it possible for your student to begin this evolution by creating an atmosphere in which he is at the center of the process—front and center.

—Rebecca M. Lamb
Independent College Advisor

CONTENTS

INTRODUCTION

THE PATH TO AND THROUGH college is exciting, enriching, tax-ing, and nerve-racking, but one of the greatest experiences of your teen's life! There are so many materials to prepare, so many options to consid-er, and so many new challenges to confront, yet, the challenges and the rewards do not end upon entering college. While getting your teenager into college is accomplishing one milestone, surely, getting her or him through college is achieving another.

The importance of a college education to one's career opportunities need not require a long defense. Still, there are a number of alarming trends that are making many college hopefuls and their parents a bit anxious. For instance, gaining admissions into the college of one's choice continues to be increasingly competitive. Unfortunately, many high school counselors lack the time and resources to adequately address the needs of their ever-growing and complex constituency. In addition, the price tag of today's higher education continues to escalate. Even if your teen clears the first few hurdles of planning for, applying to, and getting into college, has he or she chosen a place where they will be happy and productive?

As a former guidance counselor with fifteen years' experience and as an Independent College Advisor with twenty years' experience, I con-tinue to recognize these trends and address them in *Dream College: How to Help Your Child Get into the Top Schools* in a clear and concise format for the parent who wants to be informed early. Because of the nature, inten-sity, and long duration of assisting teens with planning for, applying to, and getting through college, parents cannot simply be front and center; they have to stay front and center. By teaching parents what they need to know and to do to get their teen into and through college, the guide aims to overcome the "guidance gap," the "financial fright," and the "competi-tive crunch." Furthermore, by knowing how to confront the key elements of educational planning and an effective college search, parents will be more equipped to help their teenager choose a college where he or she is most likely to thrive. Few parents can afford to hire a private consultant to help them with the process, but most parents can afford to buy a book, or certainly access a book through their public library. The point is, my experiences as a college advisor have repeatedly proven that proper and timely guidance can give your teen a significant competitive advantage.

Dream College is divided into nine chapters plus appendices. Generally, the chapters address three principal areas: planning for college throughout the high school years, applying for college in the senior year, and getting through the college years. While much of the information contained here addresses all students independent of ethnicity, gender, or class, there are some chapters that speak to specific categories, for example, athletes, first-generation college-bound students, students with disabilities, and students of color.

Each chapter has its own glossary and bibliography and opens and closes with a passage from either a former student or a parent. Through these retrospective voices readers can learn from those who have gone before them and hopefully be able to relate to some of the experiences that have been revealed. If not, that is okay too, since everyone has a unique path. What is for everyone, of course, is understanding the how to and when of the college admissions process.

As a guide, *Dream College* is designed to assist you and your teenager through the many stages from planning for to graduating from college. While you might find it interesting to read from cover to cover, it can also work as a reference book, directing you to a particular section that addresses a specific question you have up front. In short, at each of the various stages, the guide is designed to supply you and your family with the information you need in a timely fashion.

Most important of all, however, is the continual re-evaluation of expectations. Planning for and experiencing a college education can generate an equally various set of pleasures, rewards, even frustrations. What is presented in *Dream College* is a comprehensive road map of those considerations that inform college planning and a student's choice of an institution, along with her or his staying power once that choice has been made. You as the parent play a key role at all stages, but as with most experiences, there must be clarity of purpose. What do you expect your teen to gain from the process? How engaged do you need to be in assisting her or him? What do you hope her or him to gain from her or his undergraduate education? What kind of individual do you want her or him to become? This will not be a static process, but rather one that is constantly changing and evolving.

I invite you to enjoy both the reading about and the process of helping your teen plan for college, apply to college, and soar.

CALENDAR
of College and Financial Aid Events

SEPTEMBER

Grade 9
- ❑ Outline high school courses to take for the next four years
- ❑ Sign up for extracurricular activities
- ❑ Identify community service opportunities
- ❑ May need to sign up for the PSAT

Grade 10
- ❑ Sign up for extracurricular activities
- ❑ Sign up for the PSAT with counselor
- ❑ Identify community service opportunities

Grade 11
- ❑ Sign up for extracurricular activities
- ❑ Sign up for the PSAT
- ❑ Parents: See guidance counselor and make sure that your child is in at least five academic classes and that he or she is on schedule for graduation
- ❑ Identify community service opportunities

Grade 12
- ❑ Pre-register for Achievement Tests, SAT, or TOEFL
- ❑ Register for the SAT and ACT
- ❑ Go to Collegeboard.com and access the CSS Profile—you need to determine if any of the schools to which you are applying require that you complete that form
- ❑ Know each college's application and financial aid deadlines
- ❑ Speak to teachers and counselors about recommendations. Give teachers the Teacher Evaluation Form. Give the counselor the Counselor Evaluation Form. Sometimes the form is called High School Evaluation Form, or Secondary School Report Form.
- ❑ Athletes: File your NCAA registration form
- ❑ Identify community service opportunities

CALENDAR
of College and Financial Aid Events

OCTOBER

Grade 9
- ❏ PSAT administered

Grade 10
- ❏ Take the PSAT

Grade 11
- ❏ Take the PSAT
- ❏ Attend college fairs

Grade 12
- ❏ Beginning October 1 complete FAFSA
- ❏ Start composing college essays
- ❏ Complete application and essay for Early Decision or Early Action

NOVEMBER

Grade 12
- ❏ Take one or two SAT Subject Tests. (If you have already taken at least three SAT Subject Tests, you may not need to take any more.)
- ❏ Take SAT or TOEFL
- ❏ Submit Early Decision and Early Action applications
- ❏ Continue filling out college applications
- ❏ Research scholarships
- ❏ Complete the CSS Profile by November 1, if applying under the Early Decision and/or Early Action Plan

DECEMBER

Grade 9
- ❏ Research Summer Enrichment Programs, internships, and/or jobs

Grade 10
- ❏ Research Summer Enrichment Programs, internships, and/or jobs

Grade 11
- ❏ Research Summer Enrichment Programs, internships, and/or jobs

Grade 12
- ❏ Take SAT and SAT Subject Tests
- ❏ Take ACT if applicable

CALENDAR
of College and Financial Aid Events

❏ Check with teachers and counselors to make sure their recommendations are complete—they may need to be sent out by January 1
❏ Finish completing college applications

JANUARY

Grade 9
❏ Start applying for Summer Enrichment Programs and/or jobs

Grade 10
❏ Start applying for Summer Enrichment Programs and/or jobs

Grade 11
❏ Start applying for Summer Enrichment Programs and/or jobs

Grade 12
❏ Mail out all college applications by January 1 if you have not previously done so

FEBRUARY

Grade 11
❏ Start thinking about the college application process.
❏ Meet with the counselor to review academic and non-academic achievements and discuss financial aid

Grade 12
❏ Continue researching private scholarships

MARCH

Grade 9
❏ Schedule classes for following year

Grade 10
❏ Research SAT prep programs (optional)
❏ Schedule classes for following year

Grade 11
❏ Pre-register for the SAT, ACT, and TOEFL
❏ Develop a list of colleges; check schools' SAT Subject Test requirements
❏ Schedule classes for the following year

CALENDAR
of College and Financial Aid Events

APRIL

Grade 9
- ❏ Register for the SAT Subject Tests if applicable

Grade 10
- ❏ Register for the SAT Subject Tests if applicable

Grade 11
- ❏ Pre-register for two or three SAT Subject Tests; check college SAT Subject Test requirements
- ❏ Take the ACT
- ❏ Review graduation requirements

Grade 12
- ❏ You will be hearing from most colleges this month
- ❏ Send thank-you notes to people who wrote you recommendations
- ❏ Review financial aid packages
- ❏ Try to visit one or two colleges before making your final decision

MAY

Grade 9
- ❏ Pre-register for summer school or new/make-up work

Grade 10
- ❏ Pre-register for summer school or new/make-up work

Grade 11
- ❏ Take the SAT
- ❏ Research scholarships

Grade 12
- ❏ Notify school of your choice by May 1

JUNE

Grade 9
- ❏ Start building your recommendations file; ask teachers for recommendations for the classes in which you excelled
- ❏ Research scholarships
- ❏ Take SAT Subject Tests if applicable

CALENDAR
of College and Financial Aid Events

Grade 10
- ❏ Take SAT Subject Tests
- ❏ Ask for recommendations
- ❏ Research scholarships

Grade 11
- ❏ Take SAT Subject Tests
- ❏ Ask for recommendations
- ❏ Search for potential colleges
- ❏ Request applications from colleges

Grade 12
- ❏ Meet with the counselor to discuss college retention issues

JULY/AUGUST

Grade 9
- ❏ Visit colleges: you don't need to have a formal visit

Grade 10
- ❏ Visit colleges: you don't need to have a formal visit

Grade 11
- ❏ College visits: call to schedule a formal visit
- ❏ Apply for private scholarships

Grade 12
- ❏ You may need to register for fall classes
- ❏ Attend Freshman Orientation

WHAT TO DO EARLY IN HIGH SCHOOL TO PREPARE FOR COLLEGE

It was not only important for me to say that education was important; I had to show them that it was important by my actions. Waiting until they were teens would be too late. I did not have much faith in the DC public schools though, in retrospect, I would have tried to get my daughters in private schools by applying for financial aid. However, I was able to come up with educational and cultural programs that augmented their public schooling. In elementary school, they were introduced to classical music. I enrolled them in the DC Youth Orchestra where they learned how to play a musical instrument. Sometimes, I would take them to museums and arboretums, and they would keep a journal about their experiences. Each summer, they were required to read several books and to take tennis lessons. A friend introduced me to a program called the SRA Reading Kit, which I used to help improve their reading skills. It had modules for other academic areas like math, writing, science, and history. These modules were grouped according to grade level, and I always kept my girls two grade levels ahead. By the time they took the SAT in eighth grade for a gifted and talented program at Johns Hopkins University, they had already been exposed to algebra and geometry.

During summer recess, they had to work on academics for four hours each day, and then afterwards, they were allowed to play for four hours. When it came to the school year, they knew I had a job and they had a job: their job was to go to school and come home and study; my job was to go to work and come home and facilitate their studies. If the school did not give them enough homework, which was the case in the earlier years, then they had to complete the homework I would assign. Once they completed their homework, they were allowed to watch thirty minutes of television a night, but it had to be age appropriate. When attending parent-teacher conferences, I would always take them along because I wanted to make sure everyone was at the table and that we were all hearing the same message, whatever the message. In that way, there would be no miscommunication. I knew all of the teachers for all of my four daughters, and I knew how to reach them. For many years, I would sit at the dining room table with them at night until they completed their homework. One year, during my third child's senior year, I recall falling asleep at the table. Around 1 a.m. my daughters awoke me and said, "Ma, Go to sleep. We got this," and they had.

—**Bernadine Francis**
Washington, DC

EDUCATIONAL PLANNING

Your teen's experience over the next four years in high school will be filled with many rewards, both academically and socially. This chapter aims to equip you with the information as to how to position your teen to take full advantage of all the opportunities that await her. As planning early is crucial to your child's advantage, what follows is an overview of the seven areas that define educational planning. Each of the seven key planning areas—**courses, college entrance exams, extracurricular activities, community service, summer enrichment, recommendations, and early financial aid research**—is important to the college placement process.

COURSES

The courses your teen will take in high school and the grades he will receive in those courses are the most important and influential part of his college application. That having been said, your child should take on challenges when the opportunity presents itself and work hard and intelligently to get the best grades possible. Please note that all high schools do not offer a slate of comprehensive courses, but you need not worry. With respect to course offerings, students will not be held accountable for what their schools do not offer, but they will be held accountable for not taking advantage of what their schools do offer. In short, students are encouraged to take advantage of the most challenging curriculum available to them.

Below you will find two outlines for four-year high school courses of study. One is for the regular college-bound student and the second is for the accelerated college-bound student.

REGULAR COLLEGE-BOUND

Grade Nine
English I
Algebra I
World History
Physical Science
Foreign Language I
Elective
Elective

Grade Ten
English II
Geometry
World Geography
Biology
Foreign Language II
Elective
Elective

Grade Eleven
English III
Algebra II/Trigonometry
US History
Chemistry
Foreign Language III
Elective
Elective

Grade Twelve
English IV
Pre-Calculus
US Government
Physics
Foreign Language IV
Elective
Elective

ACCELERATED COLLEGE-BOUND

Grade Nine
Honors English I
Geometry
Biology
World History
Foreign Language II
Elective
Elective

Grade Ten
Honors English II
Algebra II/Trigonometry
Chemistry
AP European History
Foreign Language III
Elective
Elective

Grade Eleven
AP English III
Pre-Calculus
Honors Physics
AP US History
AP Foreign Language
Elective
Elective

Grade Twelve
AP English IV
AP Calculus
AP Biology
AP US Government
AP Foreign Language
Elective
Elective

You already understand—but it is worth repeating—that in addition to the quality of your child's academic program, the grades that she receives in her courses are the most important part of her academic record when applying to college. Please note that colleges are most interested in the end-of-year grades, i.e., your child's final grades. This only applies to grades from freshman through junior year. (See Appendix F for a sample high school transcript.) In the senior year, the school counselor will also submit the first and second quarter grades. These are the grades, then, that will make up most of what is called the academic profile. The other piece of information that your child will need to complete that profile is the College Entrance Exam.

COLLEGE ENTRANCE EXAMS

Throughout your teen's high school career, you will hear a great deal of discussion about standardized tests. Indeed, these tests are an important part of the college application, but the degree of their importance varies from school to school. In fact, there are some very competitive colleges that do not require entrance tests while others make them optional. However, since most colleges still require some testing, your teen has to prepare for the exams.

Types of College Entrance Exams

A College Entrance Exam is a standardized test that most colleges require students to submit as part of their application. There are two standard tests with which you need to be familiar: the SAT and the ACT.

The **SAT** is a three-hour test in Evidence-Based Reading and Writing and Math, with a 50-minute optional essay. The lowest score for each subtest is 200 and the highest is 800. Therefore, if your child had a perfect score, it would be 1600.

The **ACT** is a series of subtests of three hours and twenty-five minutes total that measure achievement levels in four basic areas: English, Math, Reading, and Science. The essay is an additional section that is optional, but I would advise that your child take it, especially as most competitive schools require it since they want to have some standardized baseline data upon which to evaluate a student's writing abilities. The test, 40-minutes, consists of one writing prompt that will describe an issue and present three different perspectives. Students are asked to evaluate and analyze the given perspectives, state and develop their own perspective, and explain the relationship between their perspective and those given. Also, since most colleges will accept the ACT or the SAT, it would give the ACT comparable weight to the SAT when judging an applicant. Each of the four major subtests is graded on a 1-36 scale. There is also a composite score for all of the subtests ranging from 1-36. The essay is graded on a scale from 2-12. Therefore, a perfect score on the ACT would be a composite score of 36 and a score of 12 on the essay.

Most colleges today will accept the ACT or the SAT. If your teen chooses to submit both, they will take the higher of the two. In addition to the ACT and the SAT, some of the more selective colleges require at minimum two Subject Tests, sometimes referred to as the SAT II.

The **SAT Subject Tests** are one-hour achievement tests in one of several academic areas that measure your teen's knowledge base in a particular subject, e.g., Spanish, Math Level I or Math Level II, US History or World History, Biology, or Chemistry. The lowest score is 200 and the highest is 800.

For students who speak English as a second language, it is advisable that they take the **Test of English as a Foreign Language (TOEFL)**.

If your child takes **Advanced Placement (AP)** classes, he will also be expected to take the AP exam. The AP Exam is a college-level exam which measures a student's level of proficiency in the knowledge which he has gained from his AP class. These exams are three hours, and they are administered at the high school. The score range for AP exams is 1-5, with 5 being the highest.

The **Preliminary Scholastic Aptitude Test (PSAT)** is a practice test for the SAT, which was originally designed for 11th graders. Today the PSAT for 10th graders is offered, and the PSAT 8/9 was introduced in the 2015-16 school year.

The **PSAT 8/9** is a test that will assist teachers in determining on what students need to focus in order to be college ready. It tests the same skills and knowledge as the SAT, PSAT/NMSQT, and PSAT 10, specific to the students' grade level.

How Does My Teen Prepare for Standardized Tests?

There are several ways that one can prepare for these tests. Educational Testing Service, the administrator of most of these exams, and American College Testing Program, the administrator of the ACT, have developed two exams that are designed to assist students in their preparation for the SAT and ACT, respectively.

The **Preliminary Scholastic Assessment Test (PSAT)** is the practice test for the SAT and, like the SAT, it comes with its own practice test booklet. So, before taking the PSAT, a student can study on his own or in a small group. The PSAT is a three-hour exam that measures Critical Reading and Writing and Math. The score range for each subtest is 160-760. The highest possible score, then, would be 1520.

The **PLAN** is the practice test for the ACT and, like the PSAT the ACT, has its own practice test booklet.

Both the **SAT Subject Tests** and the **TOEFL** also have practice test booklets that your teen should review well in advance before taking the test.

Other options for your teen when preparing for these exams include the following:

- Take an SAT and/or ACT preparation class at the high school. Many high schools offer them as an elective.

- Enroll in a private SAT and/or ACT preparation class with a local educational consulting group. While these preparation classes can be costly, many of them will offer a reduced rate for families with low to modest incomes.

- Take advantage of the Khan Academy resources on the College Board website: https://www.khanacademy.org/test-prep.

- Purchase practice test booklets and/or CDs at any major book-store. These practice tests are much more comprehensive than the practice tests mentioned earlier.

When Should My Teen Take the Test?

That depends on the test and it also depends on your teen. However, most students would follow this schedule:

Test	Year in School	Date
PSAT	Ninth	October
PSAT	Tenth	October
PSAT	Eleventh*	October
SAT	Eleventh	May/June
SAT	Twelfth	October/November
ACT	Eleventh	April
ACT	Twelfth	October/November
SAT Subject Tests	Ninth	June
SAT Subject Tests	Tenth	June
SAT Subject Tests	Eleventh	June
SAT Subject Tests	Twelfth	December
TOEFL	Eleventh	May/June
TOEFL	Twelfth	October/November
AP	Tenth-Twelfth**	May

While the PSAT was designed for juniors, many schools introduce the exam to freshmen and sophomores to give them a competitive advantage

*** The AP exams are administered at your teen's high school in May. If your child takes an AP course in the tenth grade, he or she would take the corresponding AP exam in May.*

When and How Often Should My Teen Take the Test?

How often your teen takes the test is an individual decision. Most students take the SAT and ACT at least twice; some take these tests three times. It is to their advantage to take them more than once since they may do better with more experience and colleges today will take the best score. Note the table below.

Year in School	SAT	EBRW	Math
Grade Eleven	May	**550**	500
Grade Twelve	October	520	**560**

The scores that the colleges will record are EBRW 550, Math 560. Colleges use the best scores from each section of the test even if the scores are from different exam dates.

How Much Does It Cost for My Teen to Take the Test?

The SAT with the essay costs $54.50; the SAT without the essay is $43.00. The registration fee for the Subject Test is $26.00 (this covers one test date, on which you can take one, two, or three Subject Tests). The Language and Listening Test is $26.00 and all other Subject Tests cost $20.00 (per test). The PSAT costs $15.00 dollars. The ACT costs $39.50, and the ACT with Writing costs $56.50. The TOEFL and the AP exams are the most expensive. The TOEFL has a price tag of $170. The AP has a basic fee of $92.

Please be advised that, in most cases, students who qualify can obtain a fee waiver that would pay for either the total or partial cost for all of the aforementioned exams. The college advisor or guidance counselor will inform students how this process works.

Fee Waivers

The College Board Fee Waiver Service assists qualified, economically disadvantaged students who plan to take the following exams : SAT, SAT II Subject Test, PSAT/NMSQT, and AP. The American College Testing Program also offers Fee Waivers for qualified students who choose to take the ACT.

How Are These Exams Used?

With the exception of the PSAT, these exams are used for admissions purposes. Please be aware that while most colleges require at least the ACT or the SAT, some do not. For example, there are some very competitive schools out there that do not require college entrance exams as part of their application process.

For those that do, you should think of it this way: your child's ACT and/or SAT score is only one part of her application, and she may be interested in a college where the average combined SAT score is 1200 but your child's combined score is 1000. Does that mean your child will not be admitted to that school? Not necessarily. The good news is that there are many other aspects of the college application, and any one of those pieces or a combination of such could render the decision in your child's favor. In short, these exams give the admissions office just one indication of how successful your teen might be in that particular college from an academic perspective, but remember, it is just one indicator, and in all cases, it is not the most important. Again, the courses your teen takes in high school and the grades she receives in those courses are the best indicators of how successful she will be in college.

Remember this rule when your child applies to college: she is more likely to get into a selective school with high grades in solid academic classes and low to average SAT scores than with poor grades in solid academic classes and a high SAT or ACT score. Why? Admissions officers read high scores and low grades as a student who is not working up to her potential, whereas they read a student with high grades and a low test score as someone who may not test well on standardized tests but who works hard. Who would you want on your team? Someone who is lazy, or someone who works hard?

The SAT Subject Tests are required by many selective colleges, but not all of the Subject Tests. They are used to determine a student's academic strengths in a particular subject area, and with a high enough score, your child could be placed out of a college-level class that would satisfy one of the required courses in college.

The AP test, unlike the ACT, SAT, and SAT Subject Tests, is not used for college admissions, but it can certainly help your child gain admission to a college since the AP test indicates that she took on challenging courses in high school. Generally, if your child scores 4 or 5 on an AP exam, she can not only place out of certain lower-level college classes, but she can also receive college credit. Whether or not your child should always accept the credit and move up to a higher-level class depends on the course and on your teen. The college advisor or guidance counselor at your child's high school is the best person to advise her or she can wait until enrolling in college and consult her academic dean.

Finally, the TOEFL is a test that admissions officers use to determine a student's proficiency in reading, writing, and speaking English. It is important to note that at most colleges this score would be used with the Math score from the SAT to determine if your child is admissible. So, it is advisable that your teen take the TOEFL if she speaks English as a second language.

How Is the PSAT Used?

While the PSAT is not used for college admissions purposes, it is, however, important to know who uses it and how.

- Students use it to prepare for the SAT.

- The National Merit Scholarship Program uses it to determine if a student is eligible to receive a scholarship.

● Colleges use the scores as a recruitment tool. In other words, once colleges receive your child's scores, they will start sending materials in the hope that your child will at least consider applying to their school. Their goal is to get your teenager to apply and ultimately enrolled if admitted.

Up until this point, the guide has focused a great deal on what college admissions officers call the quantitative side of your teen's academic record, i.e., courses, grades, and tests. However, while test scores are an important part of the application, there is more to a student than numbers. For example, often a student makes a contribution to his local community in a number of ways; a way that he does so is getting involved with extracurricular activities.

EXTRACURRICULAR ACTIVITIES

An extracurricular activity is anything that takes place outside of a formal classroom setting. No matter how much time your teenager spends on his studies, he certainly should have a life outside of the classroom. He should not be afraid to experience some of the wonderful activities his school and community offer. If his school does not offer an activity in which he has an interest, he should ask the principal if he can initiate a new club. In this way, he creates an opportunity for himself as well as for others and shows leadership skills.

Colleges are interested in creating a diverse student population whose individual backgrounds and interests vary. Participation in extracurricular activities is an excellent way to show a college that your teen is more than just a one-dimensional person. Extracurricular activities also help your teen develop teamwork and leadership skills. Best of all, they are fun and rewarding.

How Colleges See Your Teen's Involvement in Activities

Extracurricular activities cannot compensate for poor grades or low test scores, but they can render your child a more attractive candidate, especially when compared with a student who has similar grades and test scores. However, a student should not let these activities become more important than his school studies.

Bottom line: your teen should get involved, stay involved, and have fun. Extracurricular activities are a good way to augment his academic life in high school. It will also give admissions officers another indication of your teen as a total human being and the activities may even suggest how he might contribute to his college.

COMMUNITY SERVICE

Getting involved with community service is another way students can distinguish themselves in the college application process, and they can start this activity early in their high school career. Some high schools require that students participate in a community service activity as part of their graduation requirement. There are also some scholarships available to students who have been involved in community service. Whether or not your teen's high school requires community service, it may be to his advantage to participate in these programs throughout high school. In addition to the support your teen will be giving to a community organization, he will also feel the personal reward of helping his fellow citizens.

SUMMER ENRICHMENT

There are a number of summer opportunities in which your teen can become involved throughout his years in high school. Whether he is between freshmen and sophomore or junior and senior year, there is a summer program out there for him.

Some of these programs are expensive, but some are free. Those that have a price tag attached to them often offer financial assistance to students who qualify. For example, both Phillips Academy at Andover and Exeter's Summer Session offers partial scholarships to qualified students, while the Massachusetts Institute of Technology's MITES Program for rising seniors offers full scholarships.

For students of color interested in business, The Lead Program, offered at several universities across the country within their business schools, is essentially free; students attend the program at the end of their junior year in high school. The Annenberg Scholars Program at the University of Southern California is a program for rising juniors that spans two summers. Students attend the program at the end of their sophomore and junior years in high school and take two college classes each year; for those who qualify, it comes with a $5,000 scholarship for each summer. A final example of a summer enrichment experience is called the MS^2 Program. This program is housed at Phillips Academy in Andover, Massachusetts, and is free. It is for students of color, mostly first-generation college-bound, who have an interest in math and science. Students receive a full scholarship that pays for their participation in the program for three summers.

Participating in summer enrichment programs or elected summer school is one way for your teen to enhance his college application. Like extracurricular activities, a summer enrichment program embellishes a student's college application, but will not necessarily offset a poor academic record. Taking summer school classes can be a vehicle to accelerate into more challenging classes. Enrollment in a summer program at a college can also give him a taste of college life while still in high school.

Internships and work experience during summers can also be considered a plus for the college applicant. In some cases, your teen may want to turn his community service project into an internship.

RECOMMENDATIONS

A recommendation is a written letter that describes in detail a student's academic performance and/or character for an admissions officer. From the very start of high school, your teenager should begin thinking about how he wants the recommendation to read. Whether or not he realizes it, he has control over how people view him and by extension what a teacher or counselor will be able to say about him in the recommendation.

One can assume that, because your teen is a well-mannered student, the teacher and counselor will present him in a favorable light, but that does not necessarily make for a compelling recommendation. There are a lot of nice people in the world, but simply knowing that doesn't tell an admissions officer a great deal. That means your teen has to be more deliberate about letting people at his school know who he is. For example, your teen may have overcome a challenge or may have had a unique experience that changed his life. Your teen can choose to participate in class, show leadership, and support other classmates. In other words, he should give the teacher and counselor something substantial to work with so that they can write more than just, "Rafael is a great kid." They need to show with supporting examples that Rafael is a great kid, and only Rafael can give them the information to do so.

Although recommendations are not given the same weight as grades and test scores, they can inform a student's application by explaining something irregular in his application. This is why a student should give his teacher and counselor every opportunity to know who he is in and out of class. The more they are familiar with your teen as a total person, the better they will be able to write an accurate and compelling recommendation. If all qualifications are equal between two applicants but your teen's recommendations are stronger, then your teen has the greater chance of being admitted. Remember, also, that your teen most likely will need a recommendation before he applies to college if he intends to participate in a summer program, job, or internship. Quite often, your teen will be required to submit a recommendation for these opportunities.

EARLY FINANCIAL AID RESEARCH

One of the basic keys to effective financial aid research is to start early. You want your teen to have the option of attending the college of his choice, regardless of cost. In order to do this, it is important that your teen begin researching financial aid opportunities earlier rather than later in high school.

Take, for example, Devin. He wanted to apply for a city newspaper scholarship. In order to be eligible for the scholarship, he would need to satisfy three qualifications: have a 3.0 Grade-Point Average (GPA), be a resident of that city, and deliver the newspaper for two years in high school. If he had waited until he was a senior to research this particular scholarship, it would have been too late. Fortunately, he conducted his research in his freshman year, so he was perfectly aware of what he needed to do throughout high school to satisfy the qualifications of this scholarship and others, as well.

There are many resources to start exploring financial aid options.

- One set of options available to your child can be found in local libraries. Some libraries even have an entire section devoted to planning for college and financial aid.

- Bookstores are another great resource; they have a wealth of information on financial aid in general and on scholarships specifically.

- College advisors or guidance counselors are also a great resource. They will routinely receive information about scholarship opportunities. While most of them are for seniors, not all are.

- The Internet is another resource (Appendix H) that lists detailed information on scholarships. Your teen can find information about scholarships for which he might qualify on a state and federal level.

- Other resources available may be at your place of employment, church, and other civic/social organizations in your community.

Chapter VII contains a comprehensive section on financial aid, but for right now, all you need to know is that there are two major classifications of financial aid: need-based and merit-based. **Need-based** is dependent on your income, while merit-based is, for the most part, independent of your income. **Merit-based** aid is money your teen can apply for because he possesses a particular talent. It is crucial to research merit-based scholarships early rather than late in high school to know what to do to qualify for them before the senior year.

Chapter I took you through seven key areas of educational planning. By effectively planning your teen's high school years, you and he will be better prepared to take the next steps toward college. As you read on, it will become even clearer how these early steps can impact your teen's future.

Now, we're ready to approach the college application process in earnest, starting with the college search.

● ● ● ●

Both David and Dana were introduced to the concept of college while they were in elementary school. I always told them that it was important for them to do well in elementary school and that would determine what types of classes they could take in middle school, also that they needed to do well in middle school to be able to take advanced classes in high school, and that they had to do well in high school in order to get into a good college. By the time they were in middle school, they knew the speech; it was ingrained in their mind.

Although the kids were in a good school system, I still felt compelled to get involved and stay involved, so I was always at the guidance office when it came time to choosing David and Dana's courses. This process started in elementary school where they took the most advanced math class in sixth grade; this then determined the math courses they took in middle school, and then in high school. I encouraged them to have four years of one language—Spanish—and four years of science, including Biology, Chemistry, and Physics, in addition to other required academic subjects. I also encouraged them to take Advanced Placement (AP) classes and International Baccalaureate (IB) classes in subjects of interest to them or in subjects that would help them with college courses, such as (IB) English. It was relatively easy to encourage them since they were inclined to take these courses anyway and the sequencing of classes they started earlier led to these advanced classes in high school.

—Donna Atkinson, Parent

GLOSSARY

ACT: American College Testing. The ACT is a college entrance exam consisting of four academic sub-tests, Math, English, Reading, and Science. The essay is an optional fifth section.

ACT Program: The American College Testing Program. A non-profit agency that designs and administers tests, including the ACT, for use within the college admissions process.

AP: Advanced Placement. A college-level class offered in high school is referred to as an AP course. Each course has a corresponding AP exam administered at your child's high school in May of each academic year.

CEEB: College Entrance Examination Board. The CEEB develops the policies and practices for many tests such as the PSAT, SAT, SAT Subject Tests, and AP. They also provide other services, for example, a Fee Waiver Program for the SAT and the SAT Subject Tests.

CEEB Code: A six-digit code number assigned by the CEEB to each high school that your child will use when registering for certain tests. The college advisor or guidance counselor will have the CEEB Code.

College-Bound: A high school student enrolled in a college preparatory course and who intends to apply for admission to college.

College Catalogue: A publication describing the academic programs with the associated courses for all of the college majors and minors offered at that particular college or university. This publication also discusses graduation requirements for each major and minor. Today, catalogues also come in electronic versions.

College Fair: A program organized to allow you and your child to meet and talk with representatives from different colleges and universities. Your child may attend these fairs at any point during high school. He or she does not have to be a senior.

College View Books: Publications developed by individual colleges and universities to promote and present information about their respective institutions: campus settings, academic programs, student life, and related campus features.

College Visit: A visit to a college by students to observe firsthand the academics, student life, and related campus activities. You are encouraged to visit colleges with your child. There are many types of campus visits. The college advisor at your child's school will inform you of such at the appropriate time. Your child can visit colleges at any point during his or her high school years. He or she does not have to be a senior.

Class Rank: Your child's standing in his or her graduating class. Rank is based on grade-point average and is usually presented in numerical order. For example, a class of 200 students would be ranked from 1-200, with number 1 being the highest rank in the class.

ETS: Educational Testing Service. ETS is a non-profit organization that develops and administers the test for the College Board, e.g. it administers the PSAT, SAT, and AP tests. It also provides additional services, such as a Fee Waiver Program for the PSAT and TOEFL exams.

GPA: Grade-Point Average. An average of your child's academic achievement as measured by grades. Computed by adding the number of quality points assigned to each grade and then dividing the number of courses into the sum of the quality points. Typically, students are assigned 4.0 quality points for an A, 3.0 for a B, 2.0 for a C, and 1.0 for a D.

GPA/Weighted: GPAs that provide extra quality points for more advanced classes. In most high schools, AP classes are assigned an extra quality point of 1.0. For example, if a student receives an A in regular Calculus they would earn 4.0 quality points. For a class in AP Calculus, they would receive 5.0 quality points.

GPA/Unweighted: GPAs that do not assign extra weight for accelerated courses.

NACAC: The National Association for College Admissions Counseling is a professional organization of secondary school counselors, independent counselors, university admissions officers, and financial aid counselors who assist students with the transition from high school to higher education.

NCAA: The National Collegiate Athletic Association is an organization through which the nation's colleges and universities speak and act on athletic matters at the national level. The NCAA Clearinghouse reviews academic records of prospective Division I and Division II athletes.

PLAN: Preliminary American College Test. A standardized test offered to high school sophomores who are considering a college education. It is designed to familiarize your child with the ACT, taken later, and to provide an assessment of his or her career interests and study skills.

PSAT/NMSQT: The Preliminary Scholastic Assessment Test/National Merit Scholarship Qualifying Test is a practice test designed to prepare your child for the SAT. It is also used in the awarding of merit scholarships for qualifying students. Colleges do not use PSAT scores as part of admissions criteria.

SAT: Scholastic Assessment Test. A test used widely by college and university admissions offices. The test has two sections: Evidence-Based Reading and Writing and Math, with an optional essay section.

SAT Subject Tests: Scholastic Assessment Test Subject Tests. One-hour standardized achievement tests in specific subject areas. Required by some colleges. Some colleges will ask for three, while others will require two. Some none at all.

TOEFL: Test of English as a Foreign Language. A test given by the Educational Testing Service to determine a child's proficiency in speaking, reading, writing, and listening in English. Students who speak English as a second language are encouraged to take this exam.

RESOURCES

Beryer, S. (2006). *College planning for gifted students*, 3rd edition. Waco, TX: Prufrock Press.

Channing Bete Company. (n.d.). *Studying for success: Tips to help build effective study habits.* South Deerfield, MA. shop.channingbete.com/onlinestore/storeitem.html?iid=174891

The College Board. (2016). *The college handbook.* www.collegeboard.org.

Haigler, K. and Nelson, R. (2005). *The gap-year advantage: Helping your child benefit from time off before or during college.* Boston: St. Martin's Griffin.

Levin, S. (1995). *Summer on campus: College experiences for high school students.* New York: The College Board.

McIntire, R. W. (1998) *College keys: Getting in, doing well, and avoiding the four big mistakes.* Columbia, MD: Summit Crossroads Press.

Peterson's. (2009) *Summer opportunities for kids and teenagers.* Albany, NY: Peterson's Guides.

CHAPTER II

THE COLLEGE APPLICATION PROCESS

The college application process can be a stressful and daunting process for most college-bound students and parents. However, it is a process that, if entered with the right temperament and preparation, will help set the tone for the rest of your academic career. If you are planning to start the process the first day of your senior year, you are too late and will exhaust yourself trying to catch up. Begin in your freshmen year developing a strong academic profile by enrolling in college preparatory classes, and prepare and sit for the PSAT, SAT, and ACT administrations at the appropriate times during your high school years. If you are taking classes under the aegis of the AP and/or IB Programs, you will be expected to take the respective exams upon completion of each class. Although most colleges are leaning towards a test-optional policy, many are still using these test scores to determine on-campus scholarship opportunities.

Research summer enrichment opportunities, such as on-campus academic or talent specific programs, internships, or job placements. Establish a strong rapport with your college/guidance counselor and secure a copy of your unofficial transcript at the end of your junior year to verify its accuracy. Use your summer wisely. Keep your recommenders and counselor updated with your summer activities, and provide them with materials for your letters of recommendation. Visit many colleges, both near and far, and request information through their mailing lists. Browse through previous application packets and begin drafts of your college essays. When you return for your senior year, you should be prepared to share with your counselor five to ten colleges which you are interested in attending, drafts of your essays, and the names of all your recommenders.

Take advantage of colleges visiting your high school during the fall and attend college fairs in your area. Think nationally and out of the box when investigating your college choices. Consider schools that have a strong alumni network, which are looking to enhance a skill-set you may possess, which have affiliated graduate or professional schools, and those that can assist generously with financial aid. Do not be afraid to investigate themed schools, such as Historically Black Colleges or Universities, single gendered schools, religious institutions, or Ivy League schools. Pay attention to deadlines and details. Your application can be overlooked if you submit materials late or ignore guidelines for submission. If you are convinced that your personality and abilities are best articulated in person, then it is imperative that you establish relationships with admissions representatives.

Parents, you can assist your child by filing your income taxes and meeting other financial requests before the established deadlines. However, allow your son or daughter to take onus of his or her process. Help him or her through the process, but do not take over the process for your child. Listen to your child. Do not force him or her into a major, a college, or a program because you think it is best for your son or daughter. Allow your child to explore what he or she would like. This is a decision that he or she will have to live with for potentially four years. Your child will have to adjust and mature at whatever college he or she chooses, not you. Parents, if your teenager follows these guidelines, he or she will be an effective consumer and successfully cross the path into the college of his or her choice.

—Sanjay Mitchell,
Independent counselor and retired guidance counselor

SECTION I
THE COLLEGE SEARCH

HOW DOES YOUR TEEN FIND the right school? She wants a place to be happy and productive. She wants a place to grow and develop a more profound sense of identity—and remember that she will be spending four years there. Also, with price tags running up to $280,000 for four years at a private school and over $160,000 at many public colleges, your teen should spend time to take the college selection process seriously.

With over 3,000 colleges and universities in the United States, your teen has a wide variety of schools from which to choose. She can use *The College Handbook*, which she will find in the college advisor's office or at the library, to select some schools worth exploring. Other resources include her counselor, teachers, family, friends, websites, college catalogues, and general college guidebooks.

When your teen starts the college search, there are two questions she should ask. The first is: What do I want in a college? Clearly identifying her needs is an important part of the process in finding a school that's right for her. The second question is: What qualities can I bring to a college? An honest evaluation of her strengths and weaknesses is important to finding a college that is a good "fit"; after all, she wants a college where she has a realistic chance of getting in and then fitting in once she is there.

CHOOSING A COLLEGE

What Does Your Teen Want in a School?

In answering this question, your teen should think about who she is and what she needs. She should not assume that her best friend's choice will be a good fit for her. The list of considerations below will help your teen select a college that will well match her needs, wants, and potential contributions:

- A school that offers her or his major
- One that is near or far from home
- One that is in a particular geographical region of the country
- A school that is in a particular setting, e.g., suburban
- Cost of school
- Size of student enrollment
- Size of average class
- Student/faculty ratio
- On- and off-campus housing options
- Greek life
- Athletics
- Public vs. private schools
- Diverse students and faculty
- Predominantly white colleges
- Historically black colleges
- Women's colleges
- All-male schools
- Religious affiliated schools
- Schools offering services for students who have learning disabilities

- Schools that don't require the SAT nor the ACT

- Study-abroad programs

WHAT QUALITIES AND STRENGTHS DOES YOUR TEEN BRING TO A COLLEGE?

After your teen thinks about what she wants in a college, she should think about what she can offer the college. In evaluating herself, she should not be shy; her competition won't be. On the other hand, your teen should not overestimate her accomplishments. If she has attended one meeting of the Chess Club, it's not a good idea to list it as one of her extracurricular activities on her application.

Before answering the list of questions below, it is highly recommended that your teen go to Appendix A and devote at least an hour to completing the Student Self-Evaluation. After this exercise, she will be able to respond to the questions below more objectively:

- Are you a good, average, or below-average student?

- How do you compare with other students in your class?

- What are your GPA and Class Rank?

- How good are your writing, reading, and math skills?

- What are your strongest and weakest subjects in school?

- Which subjects do you enjoy most and least?

- Have you taken challenging courses in high school?

- Have you taken any college admissions tests?

- If so, how do your scores compare with those of admitted students to the colleges in which you have an interest?

- Do you enjoy learning for the sake of learning or do you see it as a means to a career?

- Do you learn best in small classes where you can engage more often in classroom discussion?

- Do you learn best on your own or do you enjoy working in groups?

- What clubs, sports, committees, or cultural groups do you participate in actively?

- Have you ever held an office, obtained other leadership positions, or received an award or prize?

- What activities, hobbies, or other interests have been important to you either in or out of school?

- What do you want to do right after high school?

- What are your career and professional goals?

After your teen has explored what she wants from a college and what she can bring to one, she can now decide which colleges she wants to research. The goal is for her to come up with eight to ten schools ranging from Safe Schools to Reach Schools. Once she has identified the schools and has the applications in hand, she is ready to approach the college application process in earnest.

COLLEGE FAIRS

One efficient way to get an introduction to a college is through a college fair. College fairs take place throughout the country at some point during the academic year, though usually they will come to or near your community in the fall or spring. Some of the fairs are sponsored by major organizations such as the National Association of College Admissions Counseling, and local churches, schools, sororities, and fraternities may sponsor other college fairs.

It is also important to note that often when there is a college fair in your area, the admissions representative may also visit your teen's school. If this is the case, your teenager may want to meet with the admissions representative, particularly if the representative is from a college in which your teen has an interest. In short, the tips that are recommended for the college fair also apply in that scenario.

- Attend a College Fair at least twice in your high school career, in the spring of your junior year and in the fall of your senior year.

- As a junior, you can use this opportunity to conduct some exploratory research and may even decide to visit a few of the schools during the summer that are represented at the fair. As a senior, you can use it to establish a contact or another contact, assuming that you have already visited the school. It may also give you a last option to add a few more schools to your list.

- Be prepared. Find out ahead which schools will be represented and have your questions ready. In the hour that you may be at the fair, you will probably only have time to speak with five or six schools; so, you have to manage your time wisely. At the fair, there will be other people competing with you for the attention of the college spokesperson; so, you have to be prepared and be succinct.

- Think of this as an interview—the only difference is that you will be asking most of the questions.

- Bring an unofficial copy of your transcript, and SAT and ACT scores, along with a copy of your résumé. If you have the opportunity, ask the admissions officers to glance at your records. In that way, they are more able to give you some indication of your chances of being admitted.

- When speaking with the college representative, don't become distracted by your peers around you. Stay focused and maintain good eye contact.

- Ask if they offer fee waivers.

- If you are a junior, ask if the college offers any summer enrichment programs and, if so, ask if they are free. If not, find out if you can apply for financial aid.

- Whether you are a junior or senior, ask if the college has any visitation programs for students of color. Often schools will pay for your visit if you have the right grades.

- Before leaving, ask each admissions officer for a business card and follow up with an email or card thanking each one for her time.

CAMPUS VISITS

While college fairs offer an affordable and time-efficient forum to glean an initial impression about a college, nothing compares to a campus visit for a more thorough assessment. There are several ways that students can visit a campus, and they do not have to wait until they are seniors. In fact, it is advisable that they don't wait that long. Most students begin visiting colleges in earnest in their junior year. Spring of the junior year is ideal, though the summer preceding senior year is another option, though not the ideal, since the regular students are not on campus. There may even be times when the student is invited to visit a campus with all expenses paid. Under these circumstances, the school is clearly interested in the student and that is why it is willing to invest dollars in either getting the student to apply or getting the student to attend after she has been admitted.

Visiting colleges is a must, but it can also be expensive. This is where involvement in an after-school college access program or summer program can help the student. Many of these programs have a budget to take students on college tours. One can also find this feature in some of the summer programs. Additionally, some high schools and church communities will sponsor college tours for students. Typically, students will pay a nominal fee for church-sponsored tours, while school-sponsored tours usually are free. As a parent, you will also find that if your teen has performed well throughout high school, some colleges will invite her for an all-expense-paid visit, and, here again, this is where having an asset works in her favor.

You do not need to feel compelled to visit every college that your teen visits, but you must visit the college she ultimately chooses to attend. It will be hard enough to let her go emotionally when you are familiar with where she is going, but it will be much more difficult to let her go if you don't know where she is going. Moreover, you want to be there for her when she leaves home, and knowing where she is, what the environment looks like, as well as something about the resources and support systems at the college, will increase your comfort level and provide you with greater confidence to help your child navigate her college years.

Regardless of when or how your teen visits, here are some tips for campus visits:

Plan Ahead

- Call in advance to schedule an appointment. You may not always need a formal appointment, but you will not know until you inquire.

- Sign up for a tour and information session.

- Ask if you can visit classes.

- Schedule meetings with coaches if applicable.

- Leave your name and address so that you can be added to the school's mailing list.

Tour

- Take an official tour; then, take your own tour. Spend at least two to three hours on each campus.

- Evaluate the resources and physical plant.

- Assess the cleanliness, comfort, noise level, privacy, and safety of campus housing.

- Eat a meal on campus.

- Speak to campus security and obtain statistics on crime.

- Assess if it is easy for you to gain access into the dorms. If you can get in without an ID, so can others.

- Pick up a college newspaper.

- Evaluate computer facilities.

- Go to the student center and speak to students randomly when touring on your own.

- Visit the athletic center.

- Make sure you visit the library and science labs.

Special Interest Areas

- If you are planning on participating in sports, you should speak to the coach and a few student athletes.

- Students interested in visual arts should visit the art facilities. You may want to meet with one of the art professors and, at some point, you need to determine if you need a portfolio.

- Students interested in performing arts need to visit the performing arts studios and concert halls. Find out whether or not you need an audition.

- Students who have a learning disability need to inquire if there are specific labs and services to assist students with their needs.

Talk to Students

Ask the tour guide questions, but, more importantly, ask questions of other students as well, such as all or some of the following:

- Why did you decide to attend this school?

- What do you like about the school?

- What do you dislike about it?

- How demanding is the workload?

- How would you describe the social life?

- How would you evaluate the quality of the relationships with the surrounding community?

Observe Students

- Try to get a sense if students have positive attitudes, are happy, and in general appear to enjoy their school.

- If diversity is important, find out how diverse the school is.

- If intellectual inquiry is important to you inside and outside of the classroom, listen to what students talk about as you visit the library, student center, cafeteria, etc.

- Some campuses are very friendly and others are not. You need to assess what is important to you.

- Do students seem to have lots of energy?

Reflect

Immediately after you visit, write down your impressions for future reference. Remember every college has its imperfections.

- What was distinctive about the college?

- Were its students the kind of people whom you would like to get to know?

- Is this an environment where you would feel happy and intellectually challenged for the next four years?

- Trust your instincts.

SECTION II

YOUR TEEN'S APPLICATION

WELCOME TO THE COLLEGE APPLICATION process. Your teen will realize that this process requires a great deal of organization and attention to detail. To assist her with this endeavor, this guide includes, besides the four-year Calendar of College and Financial Aid Events that follows the book's Introduction, a College Application Process Checklist that will help her stay on track and hopefully prevent her from missing any deadlines (Appendix E). When your teen thinks of deadlines, she should think of beating the deadlines, not just simply meeting them. In that way, she will be certain that her paperwork is correctly submitted, professionally presented, and, finally, is in on time.

The first step in making sure that your teen understands this next stage is to be certain that she is familiar with the terminology associated with the application process. There's a glossary of all the terms she needs to understand throughout this process at the end of this chapter.

WHAT, WHO, AND WHEN FOR REGULAR ADMISSION

Upon receipt of each of your teen's applications, it is important that she reads them carefully. She needs to know what is in the application, who is responsible for each section, and when each is due. In other words, she needs to be able to answer the above questions for each application. While some of what she will need to do will be consistent across schools—for example, all schools will require a high school transcript, some information is specific to a particular school. The bottom line: make sure your teen knows what is required of each.

THE APPLICATION

There are many types of applications to which your teen has access. Most schools today give students the option of using the traditional paper version but would prefer that they apply online using the electronic one. More than 500 schools use what is called the Common Application, which also has an electronic version, and allows students to apply to several schools by completing one application. With this application, your teen has to pay close attention to the supplements that some colleges use to gather additional information.

Whether the Common Application, regular paper version, or electronic, most have several sections with which your teen needs to be familiar. Each section needs to go to a particular person, and it is your teen's responsibility to make sure the particular person receives the forms and that the forms are mailed to the colleges by the due date. In some cases, your teen will collect all the information and have it sent out under one mailing, but in most cases, she will mail her section of the application and counselors and teachers will mail theirs separately.

Student's Section of the Application: This is the section where your teen is asked to provide information about herself and her family. It will also ask her to list her classes, test scores, extracurricular interests, summer experiences, and awards. College applications tend to also ask if the applicant has decided on a major. If your teen has not, she can check "undeclared."

Essays are also a common part of an application. They can be short answer essays or they can be one- or two-page essays based on an assigned topic. Other times, your teen may be asked to write a personal statement or be allowed to choose her own topic.

School Report Form or Secondary School Report Form: This form is completed by your teen's school counselor and is sent to the colleges with the high school's profile—a document that outlines the demographics of the high school, its academic programs, grading scale, average SAT and ACT scores, and any special features of the school. Also, in this mailing, the counselor would include a recommendation that she has written for your teen along with your teen's high school transcript and test scores. It is important to note here that many colleges will want the test scores sent directly from the testing agencies, either from Educational Testing Service if your teen took the SAT or from American College Testing Program if your teen took the ACT.

The Secondary School Report Form will ask for other kinds of information, e.g., first-quarter grades, the classes she is taking the first half of their senior year and a list of those she will take the second half (assuming they change), her SAT and ACT scores, class rank, and GPA. These forms usually include a checklist of qualities ranking the student from average to above average to outstanding. Some of those qualities include: respected by faculty, respected by peers, creativity, sensitivity to others, a sense of humor, and more.

If the college has not provided a return envelope, your teenager should provide one for your counselor. Make sure your teen includes the deadline when the form and supporting documents are due and make sure she addresses the envelope and provides a stamp unless otherwise instructed.

Mid-Year School Report Form: This form is similar to the School Report Form and also goes to the counselor. The difference is that it is mailed to the college during the mid-year after the second-quarter grades are available. Here colleges want to make sure that seniors are still in good academic standing or in some cases, whether or not their grades might have improved since the first quarter. Usually, a recommendation would not accompany this form.

Teacher Report Form: Like the counselor, the teacher is asked to evaluate students, but the teacher's recommendation is based on classroom performance; thus, colleges are looking for an academic recommendation from teachers, whereas from counselors they are expecting a character recommendation. Make sure that your teen pays attention to that distinction. Many colleges will ask for two academic recommendations from teachers and one character reference from a school counselor or perhaps from someone in the community. Like the previously mentioned forms, the Teacher Report Form also has a checklist, ranking the student in several areas similar to those mentioned earlier. If your teen needs to do so, provide a stamped, addressed envelope for the teacher. Here again, your teen should make sure the teachers know when the recommendations are due.

Transcript Release Form: Applications that do not require recommendations from your teen's counselor or teacher will include what is called a Transcript Release Form that your teen would give to her counselor. The counselor completes and signs the form, attaches your teen's transcript and test scores, and sends them to the college either in an envelope provided by the college or, if not by the college, then by the student.

Application Fees and Fee Waivers: While your teen may be able to have her application fee waived, most require an application fee. She should make sure she mails the application fee, particularly if your teen is sending her application electronically. Schools will generally accept checks or money orders.

If your teen qualifies, she can receive at least four application Fee Waivers, a service sponsored by the College Board. However, please note your teen cannot receive the application fee waivers unless she has used one of the SAT Fee Waivers within the same academic year in which she is requesting the application fees. She should speak to her counselor to find out if she qualifies for the Fee Waiver Program.

THE PROCESS

By now, you should have a detailed understanding of what your teen can expect to find once she receives her applications. It is time for her to organize her paperwork and develop a schedule to address all that she needs to do to deliver her applications to the various colleges on time. Below, I have outlined a step-by-step process. There are several ways to organize this process. Your teen may elect to develop her own system. That's okay; just make sure that she does not take this exercise for granted.

Step One: August

Write colleges to request an application and other relevant information. You may do so electronically, if you choose. (See Appendix C for a sample materials request letter.)

Step Two: August–September

Read each application to determine what is expected of you. You should pay close attention to deadline dates. Lastly, record each of your schools on your College Application Checklist (Appendix E). Do not forget to register for the SAT and ACT. If applicable, you should also register for the SAT Subject Tests and the TOEFL.

Step Three: September

Go online and access the College Board Website (www.collegeboard. com). Once you are there, go to College Scholarship Service and find the CSS Profile. You need to know if the colleges to which you are applying require the CSS Profile. While you will not be completing the actual financial aid form until January, you can register for the service in the fall.

Step Four: September

Set up a file and label it with the name of each college. If you are applying to ten schools, you should have ten folders. Whatever information you have that pertains to a school, file it in the appropriate folder.

Step Five: September–October

Give the School Report Form to your counselor and the Teacher Report Forms to your teachers. Make sure you write on the form when the recommendations are due. In most cases, you will be sending the recommendations to the school directly. In some cases, your counselor will instruct you to bring the application and supporting documents to school, and the counselor will send out everything from the office.

Step Six: September–October

Where required, contact schools to set up either an on-campus or alumni interview. At the end of this timeline, you will find a section with a series of "Sample Questions and Tips" that you should review before your interviews. If possible, you should interview with your least favorite school first and save your favorite one for last.

Step Seven: October

You should begin filling out applications. You should not wait until the last minute. A last-minute application looks like a last-minute application, and here is where you have to pay attention to the way you represent yourself. See "Tips on Filling Out the Application" later in this chapter.

Step Eight: October–November

Review all of the essay questions for each application. You may have ten applications but only need to write four essays. If this is your scenario, then you could have less work, unless you have one of those very abstract essay topics. Once you understand the scope of the work, you can begin developing your first drafts. You should allow at least two months to complete all of the essays. You should plan on writing three to four drafts for each essay. Make sure that you have someone, preferably your English teacher, review your essays. See "Tips on the Essay" later in this chapter.

Step Nine: October–November

It is now time for your teen to contact colleges to schedule visits. In some cases, you may have already visited colleges and decided to apply to some of those schools because you had a great visit. In other cases, you may not have visited a campus but may decide to do so at a later time. In a few instances, you may wait to visit until after you have been admitted.

Keep in mind that some colleges may have special visitation programs, and you certainly want to take advantage of them. What is important is that, if you can, visit the school before you decide to enroll. See "Tips on Visiting Colleges" later in this chapter.

Step Ten: October–November

Attend at least one college fair in the fall of your senior year. Most of the fairs will take place either in October or November. See "Tips on the College Fair" later in this chapter.

Step Eleven: November–December

Speak with your teachers and counselors to make sure they have completed their recommendations. Also, make sure your counselor has your most recent transcript ready to be mailed off with his or her recommendation. Remember that it is your responsibility to follow up with the people from whom you are requesting information.

Step Twelve: December

Review all of your applications and essays. Before mailing them, you should make copies of everything and keep copies for your files, just in case the college loses your paperwork. It does not happen often, but when it does, having copies will save both time and stress.

Step Thirteen: December–January

Mail off all of your applications before January 1. Now that you have completed that process, you can focus more earnestly on researching and submitting applications for private scholarships.

Tips and Sample Questions

To help students further navigate the process, I have included a series of tips that they will find helpful as they are completing their application, writing their essays, and preparing for the interview.

TIPS FOR YOUR APPLICATION

The college application will consist of three major areas: academic, personal, and supporting documents. Earlier, you read about what those supporting documents are. You will not have any control over what a counselor or teacher writes on an evaluation form, but you do have control over your own presentation in the application. Here are some tips for you to consider so that you can present an application that will make you stand out, that is, for the right reasons.

- Pay attention to the details of the application. Be sure to answer questions succinctly and directly, without overcompensation.

- Be sure to answer all questions. If a question does not apply to you, you can use the acronym N/A (Not Applicable).

- Maintain consistency in format. When citing dates, either use May-June, 2016, or 9-6-2016. Choose one form, but don't mix them.

- Maintain parallelism in sentence structure and tense usage, where appropriate.

- Try to account for consistency. If French is your intended major or you love swimming, your application should reflect your interest.

- Augment your application with additional information, where appropriate.

- You may want or need to attach a résumé. (See Appendix G for a sample.)

- If you are using a paper version, copy the application and develop a draft for review by a parent, counselor, or teacher. After you receive the feedback, you are ready to complete the actual application.

- If you are applying online, make sure someone reviews your application before you send it through.

- Even if there is not space for it, don't leave out a part of yourself that you consider to be integral. Here is where a résumé could work.

- To maintain continuity of thought, only work on one application at a time.

- Make a schedule for yourself so you won't be rushed to comply with the application deadline.

- Don't wait until the last minute. A last-minute application looks like a last-minute application.

THE ESSAY

The purpose of the essay is to allow your teen to present a dimension that reaches beyond grades, recommendations, and test scores. It also allows an insight into who that student is and what is important to her or him. Finally, it demonstrates your teen's abilities for insight, awareness, honesty, and self-evaluation. Here are some tips to think about before starting the essay. I have also provided an example of an outline for the student's review. Various sample essays appear at the end of the essay section ("Essays That Work").

TIPS FOR WRITING THE COLLEGE ESSAY

Dos

- Think small. Write about something with which you are familiar and that has been significant in your own life.

- Reveal yourself in the writing. Come across as a genuine and valuable person. The best way to do that is to allow your writing to reflect who you are.

- Choose words carefully. If a simple word will convey the message, use a simple word. However, don't settle for the little word if the big one will convey what you really mean.

- Be modest. You don't want to sound like you are tooting your own horn. Instead, tell your story simply and in a way that portrays your feelings, perceptions, values, commitments, and interests.

- All winning essays bear in mind the creative writing adage "Show, don't tell."

Telling: "I love basketball. I play basketball some days alone after basketball practice. It is a good team sport, and I hope to continue playing this sport once in college."

Showing: "We enter the game at the end of the second quarter. My favorite team is down by two points. If my cousin had picked me up when he was supposed to, we would have been on time for the game. We hurry to find our seats through the excitement of the half-time event. Before we know it, we are here, with popcorn in one hand and a coke in the other. A guy to the left of me says, 'Third quarter's about to begin. Georgetown enters from the right, St. Johns from the left; they are down by two points.'"

You can see how showing is more captivating than telling!

- Perform a grammar and mechanics check. Review each sentence and eliminate unnecessary words or phrases. Check punctuation, spelling, capitalization, hyphenations, etc.

- Ask someone to read your essay drafts. If that person can't understand it, neither will the admissions officer.

Don'ts

- Don't use big words to impress your reader. "In my early teens, my grandfather tragically died" is better than, "in my early teens, my grandfather tragically perished."

- Avoid clichés. Don't say, "What I have learned is to strike while the iron is hot." Better to write, "I learned to take advantage of opportunities when they present themselves."

- Don't use a flowery, pretentious style. Don't say, "I visited your school and was impressed by the beauty of the campus, all of the excellent facilities, and the welcoming students and faculty." Better to write, "When visiting Swarthmore, I was impressed by the diversity of the students and faculty."

- Don't ramble; get to the point. Don't say, "I really love my job and, moreover, enjoy going to work every day. It has really had a positive impact on my life." Better to write, "I love my job because I am able to work with kids who have disabilities. This experience inspired me to give back to my community."

- Avoid abstractions and unsupported generalizations. "Everyone who owns a house must pay a mortgage," is better than "Everyone who owns a house has a lot of money."

- Do not patronize schools.

TIPS ON OUTLINING YOUR ESSAY

Choosing a Topic

- Colleges will either give you one or let you choose your own.

- Narrow the topic, and be as specific as possible.

- Don't write about basketball because it's too broad.

- Do write about an experience you had at a particular basketball game. That narrows the topic and will help you focus the essay.

Preparing to Write

- Organize your thoughts.

- Develop a framework for your essay.

- You may decide to write about a game you lost and what you learned from that experience. What your audience will read is a story that you have shared through your voice about that game and what it means to you.

- Or, you can write about a game you attended and why that particular game resonates with you.

- In both cases, you also need to decide whether you want your story to be linear (start at the beginning, go to the middle, and move to the end) or whether you want it to be non-linear.

- You can have a dialogue between two people.

- You can open or close your essay with a poem; there are numerous examples.

- Whether you are telling a story about a game in which you played or one that you attended, you need to be very deliberate about how you are going to format your essay.

Writing the Essay

- Your first draft does not have to be the perfect essay; in fact, it probably won't be, so don't put pressure on yourself.

- Write your first draft. Tell your story. Don't think about it; just get your ideas on paper. Then, put the draft aside for one or two days.

- Your second draft is where you begin to focus on style, grammar, tone, and spelling. At this stage, share the essay with your English teacher and/or a counselor. If you have a friend who writes well, you might share it with him or her.

Take full advantage of the opportunity to let this writing define you beyond your GPA and ACT/SAT scores. The final product should be your voice and not sound like your teacher's. You don't have to be a genius to write a good essay. The key ingredients are time and sweat. Take the time to think thoroughly about your subject. A good essay is achieved through attention to detail and successive drafts.

ESSAYS THAT WORK (SAMPLE COLLEGE ESSAYS)

These unabridged student essays represent college admission essays that exceed a prose version of a résumé and instead reveal a sense of person not otherwise obvious from the application. They are peer models intended to inspire, not intimidate, your teen.

AARON J., WILLIAMS COLLEGE

He was a white guy, plain and simple. To me, that is what he was. He was just a white guy. I was not trying to be offensive, but when Pierantonios asked me what his race was, I said that he was "white". I soon saw him change from a nice, friendly person to a run-for-cover Greek who looked as though he had been slapped in the face not once, not twice, but thrice. His face turned crimson red and his tone changed dramatically.

"Listen, Aaron," he said, trying to keep his composure. "The color of my skin is white. In that observation you are correct. But my race or ethnicity, or who I am, that is Greek. And I am proud of it. I am more than just a color. And to classify me as just a color does not do me justice. That does not describe my race either. Color is just a physical trait. Do you understand?"

I was caught completely off guard. By living and growing up in DC (Washington), I usually talked with people who were like me. Black. There were never any other races represented in conversations that I had. So, the thought of classifying another's race by color, and only color, was just common practice. I never gave it a second thought. When I saw Tony (short for Pierantonios), I automatically classified him as white. As that summer I spent at Camp Rising Sun with Tony progressed, I learned many things, one being that he was Greek and that he was very proud of it, too.

I began to see that classifying people into a minute category, especially one such as color being the sole determinant in one's race, was wrong. It was wrong of me and an injustice to whomever I classified. By doing this, I quickly shortened a person's identity so that it was "convenient" for me. In that one conversation, Tony helped me to change my entire outlook on people. I came to the realization that you cannot look at someone and determine who, or what, they are, whether Greek, African-American, or any other race. I also understood that doing so was a disservice to that person.

I took this new outlook that I gained from Tony and our conversation back with me to DC. I took it to the family table. I took it to school and any other place where I could find someone to listen. This outlook developed as I returned to Camp Rising Sun for a second year. From it, I have gained a desire to participate in other programs where I am able to meet people of different ethnic backgrounds and engage them in conversation concerning issues such as race. Am I still learning about how people classify themselves? Yes, I am. The difference is that I now see people and not just color.

AMELIA P., UNIVERSITY OF CHICAGO

A neon installation by the artist Jeppe Hein in UChicago's Charles M. Harper Center asks this question for us: "Why are you here and not somewhere else?" (There are many potential values of "here," but we already know you're "here" to apply to the University of Chicago; pick any "here" besides that one).

— Inspired by Erin Hart, Class of 2016

I like to think of my life as a graph. Picture a blank coordinate plane. Focus on the horizontal axis dividing the plane in half. The lower half of this division is where the events outside my existence are graphed. The line that passes through these quadrants represents the events preceding and succeeding me. What fills the quadrants above the x axis, you ask? That is where my lifetime is plotted. Rising above the x axis at my birth and crossing the x axis upon my death. My "here" is defined by a set of coordinates. Each coordinate has a story embedded within its value. There comes a point where everyone must return to below the x axis. The plot of the graph past this point is defined by one's legacy. If the person continues to have a lasting impact on people's lives, their graph remains close to the line x axis, in other words, close to the graphs of those still plotting their own graphs. Alternatively, a person's graph can sink into oblivion.

Let's take a closer look at the section of the parabola leading up to the x axis. It is the section that represents the decisions of the world made before my birth. The slope of the line measures the benefits with which I would be born. The circumstances into which one is born can either be advantageous or deterring. Each coordinate is derived based on how the world's events will impact these circumstances.

Subsequently, my graph took a leap when my great-great grandmother passed through Ellis Island, entering America, the land of opportunity, leaving Poland behind. The graph sunk dramatically on Black Tuesday, when the Great Depression cast unemployment and hardship through society. Slowly, the graph crept back up as the rewards of hard work passed through the generations. My father's new job as a lawyer causes the graph to spike from his success. Another rise occurs when my parents met under the fireworks at the Esplanade on the Fourth of July sealing my fate. And, as one might say, the rest is history. I will change this cliché to state at this point it would be my turn to make history.

October 5, 1996. I cross the x axis and begin plotting my own graph. Each decision, however small it may seem, raises me up or down on a scale of achievement measured by the y- axis. If you don't use the resources given to you at birth, the slope of your graph levels off. On the other hand, taking advantage of your opportunities pushes the slope higher and steeper. Achievements are not limited to prestigious accolades. An achievement ranges from bringing a friend a milkshake the day she had her wisdom teeth removed to reading an extra article about a current neuroscience study. Achievement can be measured by how much one learns from the experience or the action combined with the benefits given to the community, friend, or recipient. The goal, over the course of your lifetime, is to not let the graph level off, for that would mean you have reached a limit.

At this moment, I am at a set of coordinates specific to the cumulative result of seventeen years of my life as well as the lifetimes of everyone who has lived before me. My coordinates are specific to me. They cannot be replaced with someone else's coordinates. Now, this graph cannot predict the future, but I can only hope that all my actions thus far have been achievements poising me to rise above any limit.

ANONYMOUS

"I don't know where the valve is, Howard," yelled Dom from the garage in the Sunoco service station.

"Well, you better find it or order another, 'cause she's comin' in this afternoon to pick up the car," replies Howard, the station's owner.

I work in this gas station two blocks from my house. I pump gas. I wash windshields and I check oil. I do all the odd jobs that the mechanics don't have time for. This job is dirty, the office smells, and the mechanics can't articulate a single sentence without cursing.

It's the greatest job in the world.

Now, my family is pretty well off financially, and realistically I don't have to work. I choose to work at the gas station because it gives me a sense of responsibility and the extra cash doesn't hurt. I have had other part-time jobs that, to put it mildly, I was indifferent toward. Compared to other jobs, though, the Sunoco has been a different, more meaningful experience for me.

First, let me introduce the cast of characters. There's the station owner, Howard, who hired me. Everyone in the community knows Howard; every little lady with a car problem has unending faith in him to remedy all their automotive ills. Not only is he a fair and understanding boss, but he is also a friend to his employees.

There's Dominic, the mechanic. Dom and I went to the same high school and Dom started working at the station when he was my age. He's now 23 years old, a husband and a father of two and he works at the station seven days a week. On the side, Dom manages to find time to volunteer as a fire fighter and paramedic.

Old Sam, 73 years old, works with me every Saturday morning. Sam has the art of the full service gasoline pump refined and perfected, from squeegee to tire gauge. He sits while chain smoking and sipping Budweiser each Saturday, and is very curious about what plans I have for my future. "Doctor like your father. None of this accountant, lawyer stuff," he commands every week. Between customers Sam hunches over sheets of handwritten numbers trying to decipher the mysterious code of the Lottery. Sometimes he wins a "Pick Four" or a "Big Three." Usually, he does not.

None of these men went to college, nor do they ever regret living the blue-collar life of the gas station. They are honest, extremely hard working and all have families to support, and most of all, they are happy. I believe they are happy because they are real, and they know they are real because every aspect of their lives confirms the truth of their existence through tangible, real situations. The satisfying sense of production and accomplishment after finishing a job completely; the bellowing laughter that fills the station following a crude joke; the wrenching pain in your back at the end of the day that fades away the moment your children run into your arms. I have witnessed all these things in these men. These essential pieces of life, these real, indispensable elements of existence, tell them in full stereo that they are real every day of their lives.

What I have learned working at the Sunoco? I have learned that looking a man in the eyes and having a firm handshake tell more in a first impression than any number of words. I have learned that the word "poor" is not a synonym for "unhappy." I have learned the value of a warm jacket and baseboard heat in the bathroom on a rainy November morning is greater than gold. I have seen the men that truly are the components that combine as a nation to create the American spirit is something that I should strive for, whether I end up as a mechanic, repairing carburetors and intake valves, or a surgeon replacing arteries and aortic valves.

EMARCHEZ R., UNIVERSITY OF VIRGINIA

PCP

May 3, 2010, was the last straw. I woke to the sounds of objects being thrown across the room and flung onto the floor, doors being opened only to be slammed shut again. However, I never flinched. I was so used to the nonsense that I refused to assist her with anything. No matter how many times she called for help, I vowed to myself that I will not let her get to me, until she decided that they were after us. She maintained she was under attack and decided to charge into my room and hurl everything, from my lamp light to my dresser. Unlike most nights where this toxic ritual would occur, this day I officially lost all hope—I felt I was in danger. Although she was my mother, I can tell that she was too far gone to even take into account the fear that she has instilled in her oldest daughter. That evening marked the day I decided that I had enough, and decided to flee my own home to get help. Never would I have thought that this day would come, the day I would finally have to turn on my own mother in order to keep my family safe.

Most would identify their motivations in life with someone who is important to them, or some would even go as far as to say that they are solely self-motivated. However, my motivation has been Phencyclidine. I have not been tempted to try it, let alone sell it, but this is my motivation because it has been a key component in my life ever since elementary school. My mother has an addiction to PCP. This dependency causes her to have living nightmares of people inflicting harm to us all, a side effect which usually results in violent reactions on her part. I never knew that this drug could turn my mother, the one person who I loved the most, into someone that would take me through so many trials and tribulations. Ultimately, these dangerous cycles could have led to exhaustion, if not my downfall, if I was not strong enough to overcome these struggles.

There were nights when I woke up out of my sleep from the loud noises and hallucinating side effects of phencyclidine. Nights such as this often left me suffering from fatigue on the days that I had to attend school. Being the only person in my household that was fully aware of the complications began to take a toll on me. I had to discipline my little brother and sister who would often laugh at my mother when she was on drugs and think that it was a good time to take advantage of her by asking her for things to which she would normally say "no". I would often find myself acting as their parent, encouraging them to act a little more mature about the situation or even sending them to their rooms until she was back to her normal state.

Many people would break under this type of pressure, not knowing what to do next or where to go. However, I continue to strive for the best because I want to make it in life. I always said that I wanted to be like my aunt, the one who went to college, who earned a degree and had property to call her own; never had the thought of growing up to be like my mom occurred to me. Although she has been ill, I know that without her help, I would not be where I am today. I believe that this was a test to see what I am really capable of doing. By seeing the mistakes that my mother made, I was able to become the type of person that wakes up every morning to go to school to get an education because I know that this is the only way out, the only thing separating me from potentially becoming like my mom.

ANONYMOUS

Walking through the hallways of the emergency room, I could visualize the struggles that each of the women and girls encountered trying to overcome their experiences of abuse. Each of the shirts hung represented one story, one person who now has a voice. As I walked further down the hallway, I became even more disheartened. Looking at the shirts that the girls and I made in the Girls' Club, my heart began to ache because these voices now had faces. Faces of young girls with bursting personalities, bright smiles, and dark secrets behind their beautiful brown eyes. Secrets that haunted some of them for the rest of their lives. My thoughts became heavier as I walked further down the hall. There was a familiarity in the voice I heard. It was that of my own. I, too, had a bright smile and a dark secret hidden behind my brown eyes. I, too, was witness to the abuse in my home. And I, too, kept the silence.

Confusion was the most memorable feeling of my childhood. Nights of unrest and endless crying for fear that I would not wake up with my mother by my side. Yet, although there were never bruises, my father's words were like poison that seemed to slowly kill my mother. And although he never directed it towards me, I always felt as if I was a child in my mother's womb. However, unlike some, my story was like that of a fairy tale. My mother grew stronger and no longer could his words weaken her. Their distance stopped the arguments, stopped the worry, and we became the family that I always dreamed of.

Yet the wounds were there, and instead of treating them, I allowed them to remind me of the battle and my position on the front line. And as soldiers have flashbacks that haunt their very existence, so did I. Speaking nothing of it, I disguised my pain with my bursting personality, bright smile and brown eyes, until the secret turned from a memory that was being pushed further into the back of my mind to a reality that I had to face.

The Clothesline Project and the Girls' Club forced me to speak, forced my voice to be heard. Its message—"Although you don't hit her, doesn't mean it's not abuse. And just because you don't direct it to me, doesn't mean I don't feel it, too"—is not only a means to help others break the silence but also became a way to help myself and to heal my own wounds. Therefore allowing me to be another girl with a bursting personality, bright smile, and beautiful brown eyes.

CHANCELLOR A., COLUMBIA UNIVERSITY

I vividly recall being in the second grade and my mom going against the advice of the teachers at the French Immersion school I attended—not to attempt to teach the student to read English. Unfortunately, things did not turn out the way Mom had anticipated. Instead, whenever presented with an English book, I inevitably broke into tears no matter how simple the text and complained that reading English was "too hard." Mom quickly gave up. In the meantime, because I loved reading, I read every French book and age-appropriate French periodical I could put my hands on.

At some point during my fourth-grade year, I recall picking up an English book in a series by British author, Enid Blyton. It was entitled Five on a Treasure Island. The protagonist was a girl who called herself "George" despite the fact that her name was really "Georgina." The other three children were siblings and George's cousins. The fifth member of the group was Timmy, the mongrel. The book was the first in a series in which the four children always happened upon strange incidents, ended up having adventures and solving mysteries. George's family owned an island not far away from Kirrin, where George lived and the others visited. The children often spent lazy days and nights on Kirrin Island, swimming, having picnics, exploring dungeons, and sleeping in the old castle. In this particular book, the children happened upon treasure on an old shipwreck while staying on the island, encountered crooks that wanted to purchase the island in order to get the treasure, and were eventually able to prove the reason for the men's interest in the island.

Without realizing it, I approached reading this book just as I had any other until those instances when I came across words that I was unable to fathom. I must have used contextual clues because, in each instance, after some pondering, I was able to figure out what the words were and comprehend the text. The book took me more than twice the amount of time it typically took me to read a book that size; however, because of the author's fast-paced writing and ability to fuel the reader's imagination, I struggled through the book until I completed it.

Five on a Treasure Island made an impact on me because completing it was a major accomplishment as I had read a language that I had never been taught to read or write. Throughout the process, I was challenged to find clues to understand unknown words. In addition, I was forced to use my imagination as Blyton did not provide details about the scenery or develop the characters. On the other hand, she paced the story in such a manner that one was unable to put down the book. Thus, it was both challenging and stimulating. It is memorable to me, not only because I read it independently, but also because this and subsequent novels by Enid Blyton and other British authors helped me to understand my grandmother. I no longer felt that she used strange words and phrases such as "tap" (faucet), "I'll box your ears," or "There are apartments to let." I also realized that she did not have strange taste in food, e.g., sardine sandwiches, ginger beer, and tea with milk. Rather, I began to develop an appreciation for British English, culture, and writing style.

CHRISTIAN C., UNIVERSITY OF MARYLAND, COLLEGE PARK

The detention center at my old high school is located in the basement, hidden behind a nondescript wall and a stack of milk crates. It's an old classroom, like any classroom, filled with chairs and desks, and even a clean chalkboard. The room is stained in black marker, and the clock has read 2:43 for a year now. You can hear the security transceiver of the guard outside, students are fighting again, there's a teacher here somewhere. The room is always full, with the same brown faces; we keep forgetting the same rules. You can see the word "slavery" carved into the ceiling above us.

I began attending Wilson midway through my junior year; I was miserable at my former school, a private institution located in the Maryland suburbs. I had a lot of friends there, probably most would talk highly of me, but I was tired of constantly being reminded that I was one of the few blacks. When I first started attending the school in the 6th grade, I was one of two blacks in my grade, people would call us "one-and-a-half" when we hung out (I am half black). Someone used the "N" word to the other kid's face, but most of it was never intentionally racist, more of a running joke. Most of them were my friends, but they couldn't understand how hurtful their words were. By my junior year I was tired of the joke and I decided to leave.

The first day I attended Wilson, my basketball shoes were stolen from my locker. I was lost for the entire first month, most of the time spent trying to adjust to the new atmosphere. I was shocked by the metal detectors, the force of security guards and the graffiti on the walls; who could believe that I had wanted to come there. It is a large inner city school, with kids from every part of the city, which resulted in a lot of conflict between students from different neighborhoods. To the students, Wilson was a place to see your friends, not to receive an education. Hard work and success in the classroom was looked down upon there; people would ridicule those who cared about grades. The teachers had given up long ago; most of them sat at the front of their rooms, talking to themselves. Everyone was holding each other down, and I fell into that mentality in my desire to assimilate, but I was happy.

In January of my senior year, I saw a student stabbed to death at the bus-stop in front of my school; I realized then that I was a slave, not held down in physical chains, but rather bonded by a cultural psychology. My classes weren't filled with black people; my friends were off skipping school and playing basketball. They used to laugh at me, tell me I didn't have to go to class, try and convince me to skip. Most of the time, I would go with them and inevitably end up in that same basement classroom, end up in "slavery." Every time, I saw the same faces and they were always black. No one ever saw "white" at Wilson, but when they saw "black" succeed, their "brothers" would grab hold of them.

It's been half a year since we graduated; my friends are still playing basketball, but I don't really know them. People say that I've changed; they tell their friends that I'm "faking," that I don't want to do anything. "Come and chill," they ask me. No, I'm tired of doing nothing. "He's different," they say. No, I'm just tired of being held down. I saw that same detention room last week, but it didn't bother me anymore because I am no longer a slave. Some are still down there, hidden away from everybody. It's always 2:43.

CHRISTINA H., BOSTON COLLEGE

"Our flight's canceled! We have to hurry!" My older brother, Michael, told my younger brother, Matthew, and me as he began running through the airport.

Every year, our connecting flight home from camp is inevitably canceled. It was no different this time. After dealing with every manager and supervisor working that day, we were given the dreaded red and white striped pin, which noted our new status of "Unaccompanied Minors." We waited patiently for three hours before we were put on a flight going to New York City. None of us cared that we would be landing at a different airport; we would let our parents worry about that. We were sprinting fast as we could to the gate so we would be able to get home as soon as humanly possible.

As I walked to my seat, which was separated from my brothers, I saw a grown man sitting in the aisle seat of my row. "Hello," he said cheerfully enough, but he failed to stand up so that I could more easily get to my seat. I mumbled to myself about his lack of manners, as I climbed over him. Soon after I sat down, he introduced himself and we began talking. In an attempt to seem interested, I asked him what his occupation was. When he told me that he was a motivational speaker and a wheelchair racer, I was shocked. His words enraptured me; I truly was interested in the conversation then.

My heart sank as he told me of the car accident that changed his life. The driver of the other car was drunk as he drove past the stop sign at over fifty miles per hour. He walked away from the accident with minor bruises, but his actions caused the paralysis of an innocent man. The man would never be able to walk again. I was disappointed in myself for judging his "poor manners," as we discussed the wheelchair races in which he had competed. We soon began talking about his experiences as a motivational speaker. He told me that he traveled often by plane to his various destinations around the country. I was stunned that he used an event that paralyzed him as a springboard to make himself more visible and mobile.

We were the last four people to get off the airplane when it landed in New York. My brothers and I walked around the waiting area, trying to find our parents. My new acquaintance stayed with us until they arrived. I reflected on the day during the two-hour drive home to Pennsylvania. I thought about how this man was trying to make the world better. I wanted to do my part, such as improve myself, for a start. But I hoped to help in more ways than being more patient or less judgmental.

As an active member in my school's SADD chapter, I also helped to start the club. When I was a sophomore, several of my friends and I worked tirelessly to get an active SADD group into our school. I had the man from the airplane on my mind constantly as the club was forming. I attended meetings and conferences outside of school to help the program run more efficiently. With each progression, I saw my hopes fulfilled. The thought of that man's accident kept me motivated.

In many ways—small and large—I have worked hard, trying to make life finer for those around me. I do not remember the man's name from the airplane, but I will always remember his message. I attempt every day to make the world a better place, just as he did from his wheelchair.

CONSTANCE L., DUKE UNIVERSITY

Summer, 1988. My cousins and I are swimming in a hotel pool in Spartanburg, South Carolina. My family is having a family reunion. We're splashing around in the pool, racing up and down. Uncle Walter, my grandmother's brother, is trying to teach us how to swim.

"Come on. You've got to cup your hand like this."

We all kind of follow the motion of his arm, but our attention span is short and so we go back to gallivanting in the blue green-chlorine water. Finally, we are all forced to get out of the pool by our parents after hours of fun. Everyone goes to their room to get ready for dinner. We all put our t-shirts on that say "Clowney Family Reunion" on the front and have a large block-lettered "eighty-eight" on the back. The shirts are blue and come in all sizes, which reflect the vast array of age groups that have come to celebrate our family history.

After dinner, everyone goes back to someone's room that is adjoined to another room connected by a door. The children file into one room, the adults go into the other. The door is slightly cracked. My cousins and I are piled onto the double beds that are in the room. After about two hours of raucous laughter, my mother sticks her head in the door.

"Grandpa is dead."

My older cousins Tracey, Rochelle, and Eddie began to cry. The younger ones looked sad and started to cry, but didn't quite know why they should be upset. I just sat on the bed as my mother explained what happened. There were tears in her eyes.

"One minute, we were all talking and laughing and the next, he was just quiet with his head tilted to the side. Grandma called his name, but he didn't respond. Uncle Bobbie and Uncle D tried to take him to the hospital, but by the time they got there, he was gone."

By the time she finished the story, she was beginning to crumble and left the room. We sat there, not knowing what to do. I sat so confused. I knew that I should be upset, but I didn't quite know why. I had not really ever talked to Grandpa. The last years of his life, which coincided with the beginning years of mine, he was in a wheelchair and suffered from diabetes.

We flew back home and the strain of the funeral proceedings was evident. My mother and her four siblings tried to comfort Grandma. Everyone who was at the family reunion came home with us to go to the funeral. A couple of days after the funeral, the excitement died down, Grandpa's obituary appeared in the Washington Post, "RENOWNED NIH RESEARCH CHEMIST DIES AT 72." When I read the obituary, I learned so much I didn't know about Grandpa. He served in the Army during World War II and was sent to Officer's school, which was highly unusual for a Black man during that time. After Grandpa's war service, he returned to college at Morehouse College in Atlanta and was in the same class as Martin Luther King, Jr.

Grandpa went on to become a chemist at NIH (The National Institute of Health), where he was one of few people of color. Because he was Black, he was underpaid and had to wait tables at a country club as a side job. He sent all five of his children to good schools. He worked hard to provide them with what they needed. After I learned these things about Grandpa, I developed a whole new respect for him. Because of him, my mother was able to achieve all she has accomplished in life. Grandpa indirectly enabled me to live the quality of life that I have. Every day, when I drive to my prestigious private school, I pass the country club where Grandpa humbled himself to wait tables. Every day, I am reminded of his dedication and perseverance, and I use his resolve to engender tenacity in myself.

EBONEE S., NORTH CAROLINA A & T STATE UNIVERSITY

As I sit here pondering what to say, my mind travels back to the time when a friend asked me, "If you could describe yourself as any shape what would you be and why?" I can recall being completely stumped, and I did not answer her question. But now, as I sit here contemplating my life and all that I have done, it finally hits me: a circle. A circle is what best describes me.

Many may wonder why I chose a circle. Well, one reason is because circles are round, and I am a well-rounded person. I can remember my very first day of high school. As I walked the halls to class and soaked in my surroundings, I began to wonder, Where is my place in the graduating class? Then, I immediately began answering my own question through hard work and determination in all that I did. In my quest to find my place, I found myself spending countless nights in front of the computer putting the finishing touches on an English paper. Every once in a while, I was calling up a friend to get help on challenging assignments. I found myself in tutoring and in ACT preparation classes to help me strive for perfection in order to be more like a perfect circle. I began dedicating my time to singing in the Glee Club and participating in an organization called Role Models, coaching, teaching, and guiding my peers. I had earned a spot on the Honor Roll for three years. I received recognition from organizations such as, the U.S.A. Achievement Academy and Who's Who Among American Students. I found myself on the National Honor Society at school and on an all-expenses paid trip to Washington DC to participate, as well as, represent my school in a program called Close Up. Most importantly, I realized that my place in the graduating class was in the Top Ten.

Another great factor about circles is that they have insides and outsides. The most important factor inside my circle is my family. Many students have it all academically, possess some of the best leadership skills and volunteer for every good cause outside of home, but they lack family values. Being with family and loved ones is what completes my circle. There is nothing like having a strong support system in my corner to help guide me along the way as I build the outside of my circle through academics, volunteering, clubs, and organizations.

Circles are also shapes that come in a variety of sizes. They can start out small but end up big. The great thing about them is that there is always room for expansion.

That is how I have lived my high school experience. I started off small by taking honors classes. Then, I expanded by taking AP classes and venturing outside of school to participate in programs such as Saturday Scholars and College Summit.

Though I have accomplished a great deal in my life, like a circle, I think of myself as a never-ending cycle. I have made my mark in elementary school as graduating valedictorian, found my place in high school as one of the top students, and now I am ready to advance onto the next level. I am ready to make college a part of my never-ending cycle and explore a bigger piece of the world and take on new challenges to add to the inside and outside of my circle.

ELIJAH I., ALLEGHENY COLLEGE

Writing is one of the most monumental accomplishments of mankind, but oftentimes, we take good writing for granted. There is something refreshing about reading a simple passage, poem, or essay that is brought to life by brilliant writing. It's almost like it quenches a thirst that we didn't even realize we had before reading! But what makes good writing good? For me, the quality that distinguishes good writing from average writing is a writer's ability to make the mundane seem extraordinary.

My friend and I had a long conversation about this the other day at school, and his opinion was the exact opposite of mine. "The thing that makes good writing so good is when a writer makes the most exciting things seem normal or even more exciting than they are in reality," he said in a matter-of-fact like manner. "But isn't that a lot easier to do than making regular things seem irregular or special?" I retorted. When I said that, I was thinking of The Scarlet Letter and Nathaniel Hawthorne's reverential descriptions of the simple letter "A" on Hester's chest. The crimson letter "A" is central to the progression of the story and many of the story's themes and plot points would be lost without it. The simplicity of the crimson letter "A" reminded me that authors and poets choose which details they include in their works very carefully. In that moment, my mind had returned to all of the wonderful poems and stories that have touched me over the years that were about everyday activities or objects that go unnoticed. I felt that it would be a great disrespect to the writers if I did not stand up for their approach to their craft. So, while I did agree that making the extraordinary seem normal is a part of what makes some good writing good, I couldn't just leave it at that. "The parts of stories that we enjoy most are usually the most intense or unexpected plot points," he continued. "But the impact of those moments would be lost without the vivid descriptions of the small details we usually gloss over in everyday life," I pointed out. "But the whole purpose of including those small details is to highlight something bigger," he asserted with traces of annoyance in his voice. "While that may be true, the beauty of those small details isn't completely lost without some goal," I insisted. But before I could continue, the first school bell of the day intervened with a "briiiiiing!"

almost as though it was mocking our petty argument. "I guess we'll have to agree to disagree," I said as we prepared to face the day.

I didn't realize it then, but we had come to an agreement. The quintessential quality of good writing is a kind of intercourse between a writer's approach to the ordinary and the extraordinary. Together, they bring a writer's full potential to fruition, but I probably wouldn't have reached that conclusion if I hadn't challenged my friends view on good writing. Sometimes, we get so absorbed in our own views that we forget that there is always room for us to improve our thinking, and an outside view might just be what helps us to do that. The beauty of having conversations like the one I had with my friend is having your view transformed while trying to get it across, so I will always listen to other people's opinions in the hopes that my opinion will either be changed or enhanced and I will be able to better understand them.

FRANK W., BATES COLLEGE

I had the wonderful opportunity to be a delegate representing the United States at the Children's International Summer Village (CISV) in Paris, France. CISV is an international exchange program that enables students to visit different countries to meet their contemporaries and learn about each other's culture. Although I felt a little nervous about being away from home and staying with a new family, I was at the same time excited and eager to meet new people and experience a different place. For me, Paris was new and mysterious and would help me gain a new perspective on life.

I lived with the best host family ever, but also learned that despite the beauty of the Eiffel Tower and the Louvre that not all places are as perfect as they seem. After being in Paris for two weeks, I went shopping with my fellow delegates, including my cousin Jasmin. A woman in the store was staring at us from a distance. She came closer and started yelling racist, belligerent words. She called us "dumb Americans" and then said, "Ugly black people, get out of the store and leave France." We immediately ran out of the store and told our counselor. Our counselor and the store owner called the police as the woman ran down the street. We learned from the store owner that the woman was unstable.

My host family was saddened and so apologetic about the woman's words. Their caring feelings and concerns made me appreciate that all people are not alike and to not judge others because of the actions of a few. The hateful words of the sick woman taught me an important lesson, too. She made me realize that people may see me as a stereotype and not who I actually am. There's nothing I can do about that except to make sure I do not stereotype others.

I am Frankie W., Jr. I am not a stereotype. I am a well-rounded student and person. I enjoy singing R&B and gospel music. I also love playing piano, and I enjoy playing basketball and golf. I hate to admit that I like writing poetry and seeing my emotions on a piece of paper. I believe in dedication and hard work. I am a young man who intends to continue to study hard so that I can achieve my dream of becoming an anesthesiologist. Medicine will allow me to make a difference in people's lives.

The CISV international experience taught me to be open to new experiences and to learn from them. I now know that there is much to be learned from the "school of life" through experiences outside the classroom.

JIDE O., BROWN UNIVERSITY

The alarm buzzes throughout the 600 sq.-ft. apartment as the brink of dawn awaits another strenuous yet productive day. After giving Daniel a hasty shower, waking Jennifer up from deep sleep, and warming up Eggo waffles while frying scrambled eggs for the three of us, we head out the door and towards the X2 bus stop. We stroll pass the raunchy smell of marijuana, red-bricked apartment buildings, and neighbor-hood crew posted on the corner of 21st and H St. I shake my head in disenchantment and recall the last time I sat in a classroom with the same guys who are now "slanging rock" for fast cash on the corner while I'm tugging this overweight backpack throughout D.C. The dis-enchantment transmutes to a degree of optimism as I hope that one day I will be able to help bring those in my community up with me once I reach the top because my success is not valuable until I have passed it on.

It takes two busses to arrive at Daniel's school. Daniel jerks away from my grip as soon as he sees his friends from afar. By the time Jennifer and I begin our journey back uptown to Banneker it's about 8 AM. I miss the luxury of being driven, but since the recent eviction transpired, I have had to carry more responsibility on my shoulders. Again, we take two buses and arrive at Banneker by 8:30.

Benjamin Banneker Academic High School is a school prestigious in name and family-oriented at heart. Aside from having to go through the metal detector, the school gives a vibe similar to liberal art schools. This college-prep institute acts as a second home. I get a feeling of ela-tion after wrapping my belt back around my waist and being greeted with a "Good morning, Mr. President" from Vice Principal Hilton along with Principal Berger's warm smile in front of the 6 ft.-long fish tank. School is where I thrive. While most the neighborhood crew gets high on weed, I get high on the adrenaline rush of taking timed exams, seeing the epiphany when my classmates understand concepts that I explain to them, and being praised by my teachers for a job well done. Through Banneker, I am establishing a network, connecting with life-changing students across the country, developing skills for my future career, adding substance to my college application, and making life worth living.

Guides like Principal Berger, Dr. Ezeze, Ms. Francis, Dr. Leighty and Mr. Goldfarb all play significant roles in my life academically and socially despite coming from extremely different backgrounds. Whenever I am stressed out or just need to express my concerns to someone, I am able to reach out them. I often like to play the independent role and hold accountability to the burden of mixing the academic, social, and financial struggles on my own, but there are times when I reach my limit and need a shoulder to lean on.

In order to remain productive outside of Banneker, I indulge myself in math and science equations at Phillips Academy during my summers, research at Howard University's Nanoscience facility, work at the public library, and volunteer with the Students Opposing Modern Slavery team. While I am deeply grateful for each of these forums for inspiring me to strive for excellence consistently, my most fortunate connection through Banneker is Phillips Academy. It is not easy to fathom the bond I have developed with those scholars over the course of three summers. Where else could I have had brothers and sisters who are all African, Latino, and Native American all at once? Where else could I shed tears, secrets, struggle, and laughs without shame? Where else could I have lived with people with similar struggles and aspirations yet all of different backgrounds? Where else could I experienced the time of my life and be willing to give up almost everything just to spend one more day with such amazing scholars?

So, after another strenuous yet productive day, Jennifer meets me at Daniel's school and we head back home. As soon as we enter, either Aunty has food in the oven to heat up or instructions for me. Dinner is served; homework is completed by 10:00 PM for everyone else and around 2:00 AM for me. I used to lay down complaining about the stress life gives, but I am 17 now, and age comes with responsibility. Aunty always told me to be fortunate as my burdens are always relative: "Jide, the man with no shoe, became fortunate when he saw the man with one leg. The man with one leg became fortunate when he saw the man with no legs. The man with no legs became fortunate when he saw the dead man." As I lie down and reminisce before I get my brief 4 hours of rest, I always remember to go to bed thankful for each breath that I take, knowing that something miraculous will soon be in store for me.

NNAMDI O., UNIVERSITY OF VIRGINIA

If your life story could be told with music, what would it be? Would it be an upbeat rap song that everyone could dance to? Would it be a slow country ballad that brought an audience to tears? Would the lyrics follow the melody, or would they be so profound that they carry their own weight?

First Movement

The music begins slowly. The melody only whispers because there is no one to hear.

Though bland, it somehow finds a way to capture your attention. You become intrigued by its sound. It tells the story of a stagnant young child who seems to not be going anywhere, but has his mind on everywhere else except where he is. Because of this tension, the music confuses you and, not surprisingly, it confuses him, too. He plays on, hoping to one day be rid of this blandness. As the songs draws to a close, his issue remains unresolved. He is still there, but only a little older. The world has only given him a room to stay the night, yet he wishes to one day own the entire house. He plays his last chord loudly and holds the keys until the sound is heard no more.

Second Movement

This movement is a bit different from the first: more cheerful and less melancholy.

The melody is syncopated, so much to the point that you feel the notes skip, hop, and jump. It seems this piece is a refined version of the first, taking its successes and making them standards and taking its failures and making them lessons. As the melody hops and skips, you can tell this child is now a little less stagnant than before, yet he still seems discontent. He still yearns for more. The music gets faster as we feel him reaching—to the point where he has overstepped his boundaries. With a descending scale at the end of the song, we learn he has fallen and quickly. It ends with his woes unnoticed.

Third Movement

It is fast, very fast. All blandness and stagnation are gone. He adores this pace, but struggles to keep afloat. The music is played swiftly not missing a note. It is what he has been waiting for. The chords roar and the melodies wail. He seems content. When the music is done, he realizes that something is still missing.

I hope I have performed an adequate job illustrating what my life would be like in sonata form. My reason for transferring comes from my desire to find out what is missing. See, most people want to transfer schools to be more challenged academically or to move to a school closer to home or even for financial reasons. I would not be telling the truth if I said that any of these reasons haven't influenced my decision to transfer. These reasons alone tell only half the story. As I noted in the Third Movement, the pace is fast and that there was also something missing. There's a reason for that.

There is a reason why my description of the Third Movement is shorter than the previous two. I truly enjoy having a fast-paced lifestyle and this pace has a purpose. I am in search of something, something that I have ultimately decided that my present institution cannot fulfill. This does beg the question as to why I think your school can help me find what I am looking for, and my response is that my desire to apply to your school is no random act. I won't leave you in the dark. I probably should tell you what the reason is. What I'm looking for is merely a direction. It sounds simple, but to me it feels like I'm juggling the stars all at once. I want to do so many things in such little time.

Life is all too short and my patience is even shorter. I feel as though your school can help me whittle my way down to reality. Apart from academic excellence and notable alumni, your school has the tools I need to learn more outside the classroom, which I value as highly as learning within the classroom. Movement, whether musically or literally, has been the story of my life. I thrive on it. Hopefully, if I am granted the chance to attend your institution, I can find a home.

NICOLE F., VANDERBILT UNIVERSITY

"Beep, beep, beep," sounds my alarm clock at 6:45 a.m. I want to go back to sleep, but then I remember that I have basketball practice at 7:45 a.m. "One week and two days until spring break," I say to myself over and over. Finally, when I'm ready to leave out for school, I realize that I have to pack my lunch, which will take another ten minutes.

At the end of the school day, when the dismissal bell rings, I watch all my classmates leave for home, but I cannot. "Oh, no, it's Monday, I have a student council meeting," I say disappointedly to my friend, Tsedal. Then, when that's all over at 4:10 p.m., I go to my private tennis lesson with Coach Larry S. On the way, I stop at my house to pick up an extra bottle of water, knowing that I'll be running after tennis balls for the next two hours. Of course, I grab fruit to eat in the car.

Finally, I return home to do my homework. "That will take about 3 1/2 to 4 hours including studying," I estimate. Once I finish that, the time is about 10:30 p.m., so I get ready for bed, knowing that I will have to repeat this process over again tomorrow.

Like most kids who attend school, I'm looking forward not to spring, but summer vacation. Currently, I'm overwhelmed with exams, quizzes, projects, and book reports. It seems like every day there is something big that I have to do. Especially being an athlete and scholar like a lot of my peers.

To solve this problem, I think it is necessary for everybody to use good time management. For example, not waiting until the night before to complete long-term assignments, which I find myself doing less frequently now. Students should just continue to work hard and do well at school and other activities. Eventually, everything will pay off.

NICOLE F., VANDERBILT UNIVERSITY

My interest in tennis grew slowly. I watched my older sister struggle to learn the game with little success and a lot of frustration. But, some encouragement from my family and the thrill of making my junior high school team caused me to reach higher. At the age of twelve, I entered my first tennis tournament. The world of junior tournament tennis, as I soon realized, was no place for the uncommitted.

I lost in the first round of nearly every tournament that year. Most of my opponents had dedicated several years to the game and in dress and manner seemed so professional to me. I'll never forget my feeling of inadequacy when I was told by the director of a tournament in Lawrence, Long Island, that the girl who just arrived carrying four rackets and wearing a FILA warm-up suit was ranked number 2 in the East and would be playing me. With my single racket under my arm and my school team jacket on my back, I began looking for a place to hide, but the tournament rules were clear—no hiding allowed.

I lost to Grace K. that day (she now plays on the pro circuit) and thereafter to a lot of other Grace K.s and found that losing hurt and I didn't enjoy it one bit. At some time during that year, I was forced to make the first real adult choice of my life: either quit tournaments and enjoy the social side of tennis or devote the time and hard work necessary to become a competitive player. I had no idea that, in choosing to go on, I would benefit in ways far beyond the ability to hit a spin second serve.

At thirteen, I began working in every way I could, at least three hours a day, month after month, making personal sacrifices and constantly fighting frustration and disappointment. I was still losing to some of those same girls, but I was staying on the court a little longer and starting to learn from my mistakes. Often, I thought of giving up, but I am not a quitter, and I guess, with each setback, I just became more determined to improve my game. I think the turning point was the Arthur Ashe Tournament in 1982 when I finally beat a "ranked" player. Looking back, now, at that moment of triumph, I realize that something far more significant happened. I was beginning to develop a new sense of self-worth and confidence that was spilling over into all my other activities. I also started feeling really good about myself. Not only did my grades improve, but I also began enjoying a broader range of people and activities. That is, I seemed to have the energy level to do pretty much everything I wanted.

My tennis skills continue to open doors of opportunity. I travel to tournaments out of state and in Europe and meet people with backgrounds very different from mine. Through these experiences and the tennis regimen of hard work and reward, I'm clearly more independent and mature than I would have been had I not chosen to be a serious player. My non-tennis playing friends often ask me whether the time and dedication I give to tennis is really worth it. My answer is an emphatic Yes. I love the game, I love the prestige of being one of the best tennis players in the Eastern United States, and I love the emotional strength that tennis has given me.

PABLO V., GEORGE WASHINGTON UNIVERSITY

As I descended from the plane and handed the soldier my passport, I realized things were different here. Sure, the soldier above the airport terminal pointing a rifle at us was a bit out of the ordinary, but there was something in the atmosphere that told me as said in the Wizard of Oz, that "I wasn't in Kansas anymore." We had touched down in Havana, Cuba, at about 5:30 p.m. on a dark day in late July of 1998. We went for two reasons: to meet my family and to bring them much needed supplies. While in Cuba, l discovered something else, something that was known to me only from history books and dinner table discussions at my family's house. This was the element that has been separating families, eliminating progress, and dismantling relations for forty years. What I found on the beautiful, yet decaying island were the effects of Communism.

The drive was long from Havana to my mother's childhood home of Santa Clara, a smaller and more tight-knit community in central Cuba. It was exciting to finally meet the aunts, uncles, and cousins I had never seen before. This was a special joy for us because, even though we'd never met, it felt like we had always known each other. I learned that even though the politics of Cuba have kept us apart, because of the unity our family is strong we found a way to finally come together.

My family, like most Cubans on the island, lives a very tough life. Although we send them clothes and canned goods from time to time, the Communist system frustrates even that progress. For example, the Cuban government limits the amount of food, medicine, and clothing that can be sent to the island. Also, the people have to exchange the Cuban currency (which has no national value) for American dollars so they can get by. This made me realize how many countless things I take for granted and how God has blessed me with all that I have. This experience has caused me to reflect on the fact that my mother left the island, and, as a result, I was born into freedom.

Cuba's current situation exists mainly because there is a lack of exposure to foreign influence. Communism thrives on this and keeps people brainwashed into thinking they live on constant alert. For example, people are very distrustful of others and everyone is under suspicion. While the revolution has brought security in the sense that the people feel safe from outsiders, it also brought internal insecurity within the island because the inhabitants have become distrustful of each other. I learned by observing the Cubans in their daily routine, that where democracy and justice do not exist, there is no peace, only survival.

My experiences in Cuba have taught me many things, especially about the evils and abuse of Communism because it leaves people hungry—hungry for food as well as knowledge. I learned about my cultural roots and the true importance of family. The trip has made me a more gracious and generous person. I recognized the privileged of living in a democratic society and the importance of being free to express ideas and to really grow as a human being.

This event has sparked an interest in me to pursue a major in International Politics. I believe one of the most important issues facing our nation today is achieving strong and lasting relations with other countries and global peacekeeping. I want to play an active role in promoting peace and goodwill in the world.

SARAH G., TUFTS UNIVERSITY

The End of Friends

It was Thursday night and I sat on the sofa crying with five of my closest friends. There were chips and dips and bottles of soda scattered on the table in front of us, all covered with crumpled tissues that we used to catch our tears. For us, this was it. We were saying goodbye to six people who had been there for us for the past ten years. It was the Friends series finale, the last episode, and we all thought our lives would never be the same again.

Nothing could prepare me for the reality of the next day when I was forced to say goodbye again. This time it was two of my real friends and classmates who had died in a tragic car accident. Again, I gathered with my closest friends and this time we cried uncontrollably, devastated by our loss. Kevin sat in the front of me in math class, always with the best grade, and David sat behind me in homeroom, always walking in casually after the bell. I never dreamed their seats would be empty when I returned on Monday.

I think my dad said it best one night when he was trying to console me. "You and your friends are forced to grow up and face the harsh realities of life at a time when you're not ready, and there is nothing more difficult than that." It was true. The following week was the hardest of my life. It was filled with memorial services, wakes, funerals, and receptions as we said goodbye. I spent that week hugging people I had never talked to, crying with my friends, and being supported by a small community that has seen more than its share of tragedy.

The island of Martha's Vineyard is seen as a tourist attraction by the rest of the world. It lures the rich and famous who come to relax and experience a glimpse of what has become our daily lives. However, the Vineyard's beautiful scenery and cute little towns are not our island's greatest assets. It's the people that make this piece of land special. The year-round population is not fancy or wealthy. They are down-to-earth, hard-working people, some whose families have lived here for generations. Somehow, being set apart from the rest of the world makes us closer and more dependent on each other. I have seen this entire island come together to cheer and celebrate football championships, and I have also seen the amazing outpouring of love and support after tragedies. Though my community has rallied together through difficult times, I have never quite experienced the magnitude of warmth and caring in the island's hearts as I did in the days following my friends' deaths.

It wasn't until a week later that I thought about Friends, when the clock struck eight on Thursday, and I remembered that the show I had been attached to for so long had ended the week before. For ten years, I had followed my weekly ritual, watching every single episode without fail, and now that it was over, it didn't matter. I thought about my life and how it had changed so drastically in just a few days. How foolish tears I cried over television characters had turned into real tears of loss and mourning. Friends would be a phase in my life, something that I loved but would soon forget. Not so with Kevin and David. They will always be with me. When I thought my life would never be the same after Friends ended, I had no idea how right I was.

SHAWNA' H.L., ELON UNIVERSITY

Maybe it was his plain clothes that caught my eye, maybe his handsome face and short haircut were the one source of normal that I could find. At the back of the narrow streets, in between the fly-coated candy stand and the people getting ready to head in the temple for prayer stood Karim. At that moment, I could have sworn I saw him before—maybe on the train or walking down the street in DC. Karim stood alone in the bazaar; he spoke near perfect English and bargained with a sense of life or death.

I wondered why he was standing in the middle of this stench selling bracelets at 3 in the afternoon on a 110-degree summer day. As he began to try to sell his merchandise, he answered the questions floating through my head. I saw a spark in his eyes when he began to talk about the reason for his current predicament. He described school as a great responsibility, but one he could not afford. Therefore, instead of spending the summer in a foreign country, learning about different cultures, and experiencing new adventures like I was, Karim had to stay home, take up a job, and be outside in the sun for hours on end just to be able to pay for school. I could not believe my ears: the one thing that in my mind was a given was not granted to everyone.

At that moment, I could not imagine my life without school. It was the one place that I thrived. It was my refuge when I could not handle the stresses of the real world and the place where, as a kid, the cursing and screaming in my home could not be heard. At that moment, in the corner of the Moroccan market next to Karim, I felt a deep pain in my heart. A pain not from the nauseating smell or the hazardous heat, but from knowing that Karim may never be able to share in the joys of education. He may never be able to write a paper on slavery in the modern era or make a PowerPoint on the different functions of the brain or enjoy the pleasure of going to school.

At that moment, my grades, club positions, or anything that I have accomplished meant nothing because of my foolish and blatant disregard for the bigger picture. I, along with many of the teenagers in my neighborhood, take for granted our free and easy access to education. As our tour guide rounded us up and the prayer bell began to ring, it all began to click: I needed to change my thinking. I started to notice things that I ignored before. Subtle things like the merchant holding his daughter's hand, the young woman finding her children for prayer, and Karim's eyes, which were filled with impatience of course, but also a desire to be someone, do better, dream bigger, and work even harder.

My chance encounter with the Moroccan boy at the bazaar woke me up to the realities of our human experiences, and I am now more aware that there are people like Karim, sitting in 110-degree weather, selling bracelets and other trinkets to get an education. So, from now on, instead of worrying about people who call me countless amounts of colorful names, because I like the idea of a cup of coffee and a good book on my Saturday nights or getting angry at the bus that was 30 minutes late, I think of Karim and his eyes that were filled with determination despite his circumstances. So, I gather up my nerves and turn on the next song on my playlist, pop open the ravioli, and sit back, determined to make what I have work despite all odds.

STEPHEN G., BOSTON COLLEGE

Dancing Across Worlds

I'm in Washington, DC, in ninety-degree weather for my cousin Lauren's wedding. It's been a long day. I've gone through breakfast, pictures, the wedding, more pictures, and now the reception. I'm sitting at a table with my brother and sister, overwhelmed with the feeling of embarrassment as we watch my dad perform his signature "running-man" dance. After what seems like an eternity, the music stops, and my dad, Mr. Saturday Night Fever, is forced to sit back down.

Two distinctly different looking men stand up and approach the microphone. One is the Rabbi and the other is the Imam, which I learned earlier, is a Muslim cleric. The Imam begins speaking and after a few minutes he says something that grabs my attention. "I wish that CNN could be here, because Lauren and Nasser's love for one another sets an example that the world should follow."

My cousin Lauren grew up in Connecticut in an upper-middle class Jewish family. She attended private school, followed by an Ivy League education and law school. Her new husband Nasser, however, had a different background. As a child from war-torn Eritrea, his parents, in desperation, sent him to live in the United States. He spent his teenage years moving back and forth between foster families. Once he was old enough to live on his own, he worked long hours to support himself and eventually put himself through college. I first met Nasser when I was six years old and instantly became comfortable with him. Through the years, he was always present whenever I visited Lauren, and he taught me many of the essentials in a young boy's life, like how to play pool and shoot a jump shot.

Although Lauren and Nasser had been together for eleven years, our family seemed oddly surprised when Lauren announced they were getting married. The Imam finishes speaking and hands the microphone over to the Rabbi. "It is my pleasure to introduce two dances; the first will be the traditional Jewish "Hora," followed by the Eritrean "African Money Dance." The bride and groom ask that all those who wish to join, do so."

I look over to my dad. His eyes light up with excitement because he knows he's getting back on the dance floor. If only my entire family was that excited when they learned Lauren and Nasser were getting married. Although my parents have always taught me and my siblings to be accepting of all people, I was surprised to discover that some of my other relatives, particularly the older ones, were not so open minded. As I heard some of their negative comments, I realized that for the first time in my life, I felt ashamed of my family. These were people I had thought of as fair minded, people who had themselves experienced prejudice first hand. It struck me how much easier it is for people to talk about being tolerant in the abstract than to actually live it, especially when it hits close to home.

As the dancing began, I realized how brave Lauren and Nasser were for following their hearts instead of society's norm. Their love and spirit seemed contagious as I witnessed everyone in the room, black, white, Jewish, Muslim, the willing and the reluctant, move seamlessly from one traditional dance to the other. For at least a moment, it seemed that all the foolish barriers that divide people simply melted away. What started out as just my cousin's wedding turned out to be one of the most powerful experiences of my life. If only the problems of the world could be solved by dancing "Hora" and "African Money Dance." CNN, where are you?

TANIQUE A., RIDER COLLEGE

I walk up to the brown-haired lady at the desk. She sits there typing on her computer; she is most likely scheduling appointments. I wait, hoping she will look up and see me standing there and she does. "May I help you?" "Yes, Mr. O. is expecting me. My name is Tanique." "Oh, yes, he will see you now. Please go right in." I thank her and walk towards Mr. O.'s door. As I approach, I'm slightly nervous because I am afraid I will somehow embarrass myself as I sometimes do. I walk in confidently, truly believing everything will go smoothly. "Ah, Tanique, come on in and sit down. How are you?" "I'm fine thank you. I'm here about my schedule. It has a few mistakes." "Oh, yes, I remember. I'm afraid there are no mistakes. You cannot switch into Honors English or Honors Anatomy and Physiology because your Co-Op class interferes. You will have to drop Co-Op if you want those classes."

My heart skips a beat. I can't move or speak right away. I recover quickly so that he doesn't catch my pause, but my voice is shaky. I am now faced with an extremely tough decision, the hardest one I have ever faced. "There is no other way that I can have those classes and still keep Co-Op?" "No, I'm afraid not. It's up to you. Why don't you go home and think about it, talk it over with your mother. Then, come see me tomorrow with your decision" "Ok, I will. Thank you," I say with a strain.

I walk around the rest of the day very upset while my friends attempt to make me feel better. I just keep thinking this can't be happening. But it is, and it is really hard to focus on the classes with this heavy weight on my mind. But I force myself to because I will make the best out of the classes I have. When I arrive to English, my last period of the day, I am depressed. I think to myself, This is unfair; I don't need to be here; I'm better than this; I'm an honor student. Last year, with the exception of math, all my classes were honors and I did really well in them, so, how can I be here? I know why, but it's still hard to digest. I promised myself that even though I'm a senior, I would still work hard and take challenging classes. Not because I needed to, but because I wanted to. If I can't get honors English, then life goes on, and if I do, it's all the better. But for now, this is my English class; I sit up straight and turn my attention to the teacher. I won't slack just because I'm unhappy; that is not me.

Unfortunately, I could not get into the other honors classes without dropping my Co-Op. I put up a big effort, and so did my mom, but we just had to accept the facts. I decided to keep Co-Op because I felt that it would be a great opportunity for me. This truly was one of the worst days of my life and most definitely my hardest decision. I was worried that not having those other honors classes would make me appear less competitive and, therefore, some colleges would not accept me. I don't regret my decision to keep Co-Op because it's something I really wanted to do and it turns out that I really enjoy Ms. M.'s English class. If a college does not feel that I have what it takes to be in their school because of my lower-level classes this year, then that is their decision. Hopefully, the college will empathize with my experience of picking my senior schedule.

Yes, I have taken challenging classes before and would have done this year had my schedule permitted. Not because it looks good on my transcript, but rather, because I love learning and the intellectual challenge that comes with demanding courses.

TYLER B., STANFORD UNIVERSITY

A Punitive Forgiveness

"TWC is saying that a storm is coming. I want you boys back at home by at least 5:00 so you don't get drenched." Dad has a way of saying things when there is a problem. He uses mediums like "bad storm" or "something isn't working" to communicate how he feels about a workday, stories on the news, and other happenings in Chicago that loomed ominously over its citizens. Dad is a person who is influenced by his environment, which is why he has to look deeper into cities for their inner beauty. In effect, every time we see the stories, the litter, and the "people," we frown upon it. I look to the sky often for hope, but now even clouds—the various shapes and shades of them that made me a carefree kid—do not make my world better like they once did. And one day in early May, the sky showed that it, too, was just as unhappy.

"If you feel that it will start to pour down, give me a call. I'll be in the area." l was taking the No. 87 down to Indiana Street when the tinted windows of the bus began fading gray to black. People continued to talk is if it had been a normal day in Chicago, but my eyes would not leave the glass. In front of my face, phantasmagoric, and they were rapidly picking up speed. Then a woman in a long blouse hit the STOP button on one of the standing poles, and the bus driver found the nearest sign to let her off, unaware of the fact that, outside, leaves rustled madly on their trees. In an instant, the bus's flimsy door flew open and her purse flew from her hands onto a weakening branch. My phone then rang.

"Tyler, where are you now? They're saying that strong gusts'll be going eastward—are you are close to 87th street?" I told him that I was nearing my stop and was going to be walking, so he told me to stay put. The bus rocked towards the concrete where the woman had left to chase her purse and the people fell silent. The kids stopped cursing, the adults dropped their books, and the driver sat immobilized. The bus rocked numerous times until a metallic whine came from the bottom of the bus, seeming to be the effect of all of the bus's weight shifting to one side. "Everyone move to the left half of the bus! If we don't, it'll fall over!" yelled a panicking passenger. Chaos ensued shortly after, but in due time, everyone had conformed. I sat my bags firmly between the window and the head of the seat, grabbed hold of something, and closed my eyes, praying that no glass is broken or the bus is flipped upside down.

"Push! Push!" yelled our bus's leader. My phone rang several times, but I didn't reach for it, fearing that if I focused my attention elsewhere, I or everyone else would be hurt. The gusts pushed and we pushed. It seemed almost as if nature and man were having a showdown on a spring afternoon. However, we were not without assistance with this could-be-dire situation; sirens and loud voices were traveling in a direction towards us; spinning chopper and flashing camera sounds followed. We were being rescued at the same time as we were becoming a story for tomorrow's news. My phone rang all throughout the save. I finally became able to answer it as the bus let off its distressed passengers. Exiting, I caught a glimpse of the broadcasting and interviewing, by-standing and gossiping, sobbing and speechlessness. I then came to, and Dad stood right there, taking me into his arms and letting his bold heartbeat soothe the throbbing pain of my head that rested on it.

"Are you ok?...Where's your stuff?...When did they hit?..." Dad asked many questions that came spontaneously and outran my answers. He and the rest of my family were worried sick. Flipping channels, talking furiously and loudly about the "what-ifs," and running up the phone lines, they jumbled their outrage and concern. I, however, quietly sat in the center of all of the noisy conversation when my attention shifted particularly to something else. For some strange reason, the sky had gone from an ominous black to a fluorescent white instantly. It held silently for a moment, and, suddenly, the silence was broken by sounds of pounding rainfall. Staring through the window, an illuminated feeling was transmitted to my spirit as I saw the rain that once fell from darkened skies now fall even harder from a glowing blanket sky. I heard a reporter say at some point, "Things always come without precedence, so, all you can do is do what you can and keep hope alive." It was funny to hear that, because, at the same time, nature said the exact same thing, and all Chicagoans heard it speak.

TYLER B., STANFORD UNIVERSITY

Standing ten feet away from him, dad and I folded our arms and gave a keen beam of interest from our eyes while he gave a speech. Dad was aware of the thousands of adult hecklers who verbally attacked the man like a dissatisfied mob, but what was particularly more interesting in my father's eyes was his manner of keeping control. Bill Cosby is not the kind of person that a normal citizen can regularly converse with, all due to the fact that he carries himself as a father, grandfather, and role model for rising teens and young adults. It did not surprise us that he would travel America to be Chicago's guest speaker for a "Men Only meeting" at the McCormick place on a Wednesday where all of us were in mid-week and attentively listening. And in it being a "Men Only" event, it did not surprise me that an epiphany about the definition of a man would be sparked through the wise words of men as sharp as Bill Cosby. I looked at my tie, my dad, and, finally, my year-old K-Swiss pairs at my feet because all of them were implying the detailed road I would walk–years from now–as an adult and as a man.

I remember wishing, years ago, that I could have big feet like Spyro the Dragon or Crash Bandicoot, as they were Sony Playstation®'s mascots for heroes. And though those fond figures recently faded to championed protagonists like Schindler, I retained the strong belief that a man could be defined by what he does–his profession. And then it hit me: if it called my name, I would venture off for various episodes of virtue, but the greatest of men master their fields and are then honored for that. My father will become Chicago's greatest construction worker and contractor and that will be so because he works non-stop for twelve hours.

In the respect of doing, thus, a man is a "man of action," though that is decided by the direction of the action. Statistics show that 50% of Chicagoan boys (as well as those all around the country) will not even graduate, which, in my eyes, eliminates 90% of the horizon. I've had my eyes set on MIT for the longest, mostly for the John Nash and Einstein-est of reasons; but as the "other half" has spent most time within the American gutters, I have had a shifted focus in which the reality associated with the filthiest of conditions overwhelms my fantasies of fusing spirit and technology for the better of the people. Sadly, though, I hardly know what some people want besides a break.

Then, man becomes defined by however much he can become a blessing for someone else; some males have defied the rules of adolescent boys and have assimilated into the culture of expression or expressive language. Half of me is headed in that direction while the other half is headed in a direction of research and deep thought (of which many black males have never even heard spoken of for more than two seconds). Others will believe that the only way of blessing is through entertainment, like sacrificing morals as a celebrity or focusing all energy on physical activity. The last of us will believe that the only way to help is through reputation, usually equating to suicide or conducting and following through with the activities of a criminal. In those extremes, I feel like I'll either have to shape into one name on a page; help one person, or help everyone.

But that would be filling about six-and-a-half billion shoes when all I have is thirteen. Michael Jackson created number-ones for the gist of his life, traveled worldwide, and, because of allegations, almost brought an end to his career (as well as sanity). Bob Marley and Jimi Hendrix were gods of music and avid members of the 1960s and 1970s revolutions but died before they could even live to tell about it. I am choosing not to live the tragic life of an artist or genius, but I will require much resistance, boldness, and stamina if I want to achieve that notable kind of brilliance. My dad will keep telling me, "You don't have to go through hell to get to heaven," and I will listen attentively though I do not even know where the greatest of men have gone after life.

THE INTERVIEW

In the Glossary, there is a detailed definition of the word "interview." I wanted you to think more creatively about the word so that you would not assume that the only way to think about the interview was the traditional way. However, in this section, think about the more traditional, formal interview where you will be sitting face-to-face with either an alumnus or admissions officer who will be asking you questions.

Interviews are usually structured into three sections: icebreaking, information sharing, and closing.

Icebreaking: The first few minutes of the interview are usually devoted to such pleasantries as the weather, your trip to the campus, or comments about the campus tour. This time gives you an opportunity to calm down and relax. The key is to be yourself. Also, you are a consumer, and, as such, you want to check out the people who are connected to the school. If you think of it that way, you are also interviewing the admissions officer. If you can get yourself in that frame of mind, you will feel more relaxed.

Information Sharing: Here is where the admissions officer addresses the serious questions of the interview. They expect you to do most of the talking. Your responses should be concise but not too concise. It is also important to avoid rambling. Most interviewers consider the interview a success if the interviewee has talked about 75 percent of the time. You don't have to wait until the end of the interview to ask your question if it seems natural during information sharing. If you are talking about track and the admissions officer says casually that when they were in high school, they ran the same event that you run, you might take the spotlight off of you and ask them about their experience with track. After the admissions officer responds, you could lead into a statement about your desire to contribute to the track team in their college if admitted.

Closing: The interviewer will bring the interview to a close by asking you if you have any questions. It is a good idea to have two or three questions prepared. Also, during the information sharing section, something might have prompted a question, but for whatever reason, you decided not to ask the question at that moment. You can use this time to ask the question if you choose. The bottom line is, you will be expected to have some questions, and these questions should not be ones that you should already know from the information the college has sent you. For example, you should not ask a question about what the average SAT score is because you should know that. But you could ask, "If my SAT score is somewhat lower than the average compared to those of admitted students, would that decrease my chances from being a serious applicant?"

The interview usually lasts about twenty to thirty minutes. If it goes over that time, that is a good sign; if it only lasts ten minutes, that is not a good sign. Regardless of the length of the interview, follow up with a thank-you note. (See Appendix D for a sample letter.)

One way to prepare for the interview is to simulate one with a friend, teacher, or counselor. In preparation for that exercise, consider some typical questions that have been used during the interview process. A good strategy would be for you to write out your responses to these questions so that if and when you are asked to respond to any of them, you would have already thought about some ideas to use in your responses.

Sample Questions

- What do you enjoy doing in your spare time and why?
- Have you faced any personal challenges in your life and how have you overcome them?
- What is your favorite book and why?

- What is your favorite movie and why?

- How do you enjoy spending your free time?

- If your friend were to describe you, what would he or she say?

- What is your favorite subject in school and why?

- What is your least favorite subject in school and why?

- Who is your favorite teacher and why?

- What are three things you value most in life?

- What do you see yourself doing ten years from now?

- What kind of qualities do you look for in a friend?

- What do you feel about a female running for President?

- What do you feel about global warming? (A current event topic)

- What inspired you to choose your major?

- If you were rich and did not have to work, what would you do?

- Do you have any questions?

TIPS FOR YOUR TEEN: THE INTERVIEW

- Acquaint yourself with the school beforehand.

- Arrive a little early.

- Shake the interviewer's hand firmly.

- Be sure to make eye contact.

- Be prepared to ask questions.

- Exhibit positive body language. Do not slouch, but try not to be stiff either. Think comfortable and you will look comfortable.

- Answer questions directly, but don't be afraid to elaborate.

- Be yourself.

- Be enthusiastic.

- Be honest.

- Do not interrupt the interviewer.

- Listen, take your time, and reflect. It is better to say something thoughtfully rather than impetuously.

- Remember, the interview is only an additional acquainting process, one meant to give the school information about you that cannot be seen on your written application. It is not an inquisition.

- Make note of your interviewer's name and promptly write a thank-you note after you return home (Appendix D).

TIPS ABOUT INTERVIEW ATTIRE

Dress appropriately for the occasion. If you were going for a job interview, you probably would not wear jeans and sneakers; you should regard the college interview the same way. For a young woman, a skirt or slacks with a simple blouse is appropriate. A young woman need not wear heels; flats will do; but if she opts to wear heels, I would recommend that they not be too high as she does not want to trip or have an accident. A gentleman can wear dress slacks and a dress shirt. A tie and jacket would be welcomed but are not necessary. Loafers or dress shoes would be essential for a gentleman. You need to and should want to make a good initial impression. The first image that an admissions counselor will see is how you are attired; let this image be positive or simply neutral, as you most likely do not want what you were wearing to be what the interviewer most remembers about the meeting.

SECTION III
SPECIAL CATEGORIES

WHEN PLANNING FOR AND APPLYING to college, there are a number of special categories of students that come to mind. This guide includes several such individual chapters, e.g., students with learning disabilities and the high school athlete. This section aims to address considerations for students involved in the visual and/or performing arts. It is important to note that all students follow, for the most part, the same procedures but that students who fall under "Special Categories" have additional tasks to which they must pay particular attention.

THE VISUAL AND PERFORMING ARTS STUDENT

There are two major types of students in this category. Some students want to attend a regular university that offers the option to take courses in the visual and/or performing arts areas, while other students want to attend schools or conservatories that only offer visual or performing arts. There are some cases where a student may elect to enroll in a conservatory at a university. The University of Indiana at Bloomington is a good example. It is a major university with many schools offering a number of majors. It also has the School of Music, which is one of the most competitive music conservatories in the country.

Whether or not the student chooses one type of college setting over the other, she or he may be asked to present a portfolio in the case of the visual art student or a tape or video in the case of the performing arts student. Also, there are many colleges that require auditions for students who are interested in the performing arts.

Visual Arts Students

- When your teen researches her schools, she must find out if any of the schools requires a portfolio. If any does, your teen should ask for guidelines on developing a portfolio. Your teen should ask her high school art teacher to help her. In many cases, she is taking art classes at her school and may already have a portfolio.

- Your teen should attend the NACAC College Fair in her area for students interested in the visual arts. Information on these fairs is available at www.nacacnet.org.

- If her high school doesn't have a strong art program and your teen doesn't feel that she can adequately put together a portfolio, she can find good art programs that don't require portfolios as part of their admissions process.

- When a school does require the portfolio, your teen will have to ask if the school has what is called a Portfolio Review Day when your teen brings her portfolio to the college to be reviewed by professors from the art department who then make a recommendation to the admissions committee.

- While your teen will be expected to submit grades and test scores as all students must do, at schools that require the portfolio, a high rating on Portfolio Day may trump average grades and average scores. Of course, this will vary from school to school.

- Make sure your teen inquires about scholarship opportunities for visual arts students.

Performing Art Students

- When your teen researches her schools, she needs to ask if tapes, videos and/or auditions are required.

- Your teen needs to schedule her audition dates and, as with the college interview, if she has more than one audition, try to schedule the first audition at the least favorite school and schedule the last audition at the favorite school.

● Your teen should ask her music, dance, or theater teacher/private coach to assist her with this process. She might even ask a friend or family member to tape the audition so that the teacher/private coach and she can evaluate her performance.

● Your teen should attend the NACAC College Fair for students interested in the Performing Arts. Information on these fairs is available at www.nacacnet.org.

● If your teen doesn't have formal training in the performing arts, she may want to apply to a school that does not require an audition.

● For those students who will have an audition, keep in mind that they will also have to submit grades and test scores but that an outstanding audition could offset average grades and average test scores.

● Make sure that your teenager inquires if the college has scholarships for performing arts students.

As you can see, there is a lot of detail to which a student must pay close attention in what I call the mechanical process of applying to college. Throughout this process, parents must pay close attention to the student's level of engagement. After all, if she cannot handle what is expected of her at this stage, I would question whether she will be able to navigate the many responsibilities of college once enrolled. Give her guidance, support, encouragement, and within reason, some assistance; but, in the final analysis, you want to be confident that she has done most of the work and not you.

● ● ● ●

We were very involved in all aspects of the college application process. Shayla applied to nine colleges. Due to the sheer volume of applications, she needed as much assistance as possible to keep up with all the deadlines and various requirements. Because of her major, she had to prepare for auditions as well as to create a CD portfolio of original music productions for one university. This submission required some level of studio recording, mixing, etc. Shayla had twice the amount of work to do through the process because she had to submit a general college application, which included essays, plus complete applications for the School of Music that had its own set of requirements.

Shayla was blessed with the opportunity, initiated by an independent counselor whom my wife and I hired, to participate in a summer enrichment program at Carnegie-Mellon University during the summer preceding her senior year which prepared her for the vocal auditions required for some of the colleges. At Carnegie-Mellon, Shayla was exposed to singing classical music, which she needed to audition at several colleges. During her senior year, she took voice training in preparation for all the vocal auditions. Even though Shayla's interest was not in vocal or instrumental performance, the Audio/Sound Engineering major falls under the School of Music for the majority of colleges, and thus, she had to show that she was competent in music.

—Steve and Andrea Hines

GLOSSARY

Alumni Interview: An off-campus interview with an alumnus from the college who usually lives in the student's city or town.

Application Fee Waivers: A service provided by the College Board for eligible students. Under this program, a student will receive four college application fee waivers. Students should see their school counselor to determine if they are eligible.

College Search: A list of colleges to which a student will apply based on a number of characteristics informed by his or her interests.

Common Application: Allows students to apply to several schools by completing one application. The student should check with each college to determine if additional essays and materials are required.

Early Action: EA. The application is due by November 1 with a notification date of December, usually before Christmas. EA is not binding, so, if admitted, the student does not have to attend.

Early Decision: ED. The application is generally due by November 1 with a notification date in December, usually before Christmas. ED is binding, thus, if the student is admitted to the college, he or she is required to attend.

Essay: The College Essay, sometimes referred to as the Personal Statement, is a written document that the student will submit to the college, which provides some sense of who he or she is beyond his or her class rank, GPA, and test scores.

Deferred Admission: This term refers to the scenario in which Admissions decides to postpone judging a candidate's application for re-evaluation with the Regular Admissions pool.

Deferred Admission Student: A student is admitted but decides to defer enrollment for one year.

GED: A General Education Development test that measures a student's proficiency in reading, literature, social studies, science, and math. Students who pass the test receive a general high school equivalency diploma.

High School Profile: A form that describes the demographics, programs of study, and unique features of a particular high school. This profile is used by college admissions officers so that they can understand an applicant within the context of his or her school setting.

Interview: Any contact a student has with a college representative. Whether the student is visiting a college for a formal interview, or speaking to an admissions officer at a College Fair, or simply speaking with a college representative who is visiting his or her high school, he or she should view all of these experiences as an interview.

Notification Deadline: The date that students have to inform the colleges of their decision to attend. The standard notification deadline date is May 1.

Open Admission: A policy that allows all students to be admitted as long as they have graduated from high school or have earned a GED.

Online Application: The process by which a student can submit his or her application. Today, most colleges would prefer that students submit their applications electronically.

Recommendation: A narrative written by a teacher and/or counselor and required by many colleges. Most selective colleges require academic recommendations from two teachers and one character recommendation from the school counselor.

Rolling Admission: The process by which an institution reviews applications as they are received and offers decisions to students as applications are reviewed, usually within three to four weeks.

Regular Admission: Applications are generally due by January 1 or February 1, with students notified by April 1.

Reach School: A very competitive school to which the student has a small chance of being admitted.

Safe School: A school to which a student will definitely be admitted.

School Report: The School Report, sometimes called Secondary School Report Form, is the part of the college application that students give to their college advisor or guidance counselor. This is a recommendation form that is also used to provide academic information about the student. Usually, the counselor will send the transcript and the School Report to the college in the same mailing.

Teacher Report: A form, part of many college applications, that is given to a teacher so that he or she can provide an academic assessment of a particular student. Often this form is accompanied by a recommendation.

Wait List: A list of students not initially accepted at an institution who may be admitted at a later date, usually in June.

RESOURCES

Antonoff, S. (2008). *The college finder: Choosing the school that's right for you.* Westford, MA: Wintergreen Orchard House.

Barron's Educational Series College Division. (1998). *Barron's compact guide to college,* 11th edition. Hauppaugge, NY: Barron's.

College Board. (2015). *Book of majors,* 10th edition. New York: The College Board.

College Board. (2016). *The college handbook,* 54th edition. New York: College Board.

Fiske, E. B. (2015). *The Fiske guide to colleges,* 32nd edition. Naperville, IL: Sourcebooks.

Gelband, S. and C. Kubale (1992). *Your college application.* New York: The College Board.

Mamlet, R. and VanDeVelde, C. (2011). *College admission: From application acceptance, step by step.* New York: Three River's Press.

Mayher, B. (1998). *The college admissions mystique.* New York: Farrar, Strauss, and Giroux.

McCloskey, W. and S Davidson (1996). Peterson's. *Writing a winning college application essay.* Lincoln, NE: Peterson's.

Pope, L. and H.M. Oswald (2012). *Colleges that change lives: 40 schools that will change the way you think about college,* 4th edition. New York: Penguin.

Ruggs, F.E. (2009). Rugg's Recommendations. *Rugg's recommendations on the colleges,* 27th edition. Fallbrook, CA: Rugg's Recommend.

Schneider, Z. D. (2012). *Campus visits and college interviews,* 3rd edition. New York: College Board.

Steinberg, J. (2003). *The gatekeepers: Inside the admissions process of a premier college.* New York: Penguin.

Tanabe, G. and K. Tanabe (2016). *Get into any college: Secrets of Harvard students,* 10th edition. Belmont, CA: SuperCollege.

Utterback, A. S. (1989). *College admissions face to face: Make the most of campus visits and interviews.* Newport Beach, CA: Seven Locks Press.

Yale Daily News Staff (2014). *The insider's guide to the colleges: Students on campus tell you what you really want to know,* 41st edition. Boston: St. Martin's Griffin.

CHAPTER III

FOR STUDENTS WITH DISABILITIES

My English Teaching Fellow returned my first paper to me with a C- and I was anxious to get his feedback. I had never received a grade lower than B throughout my high school years, but now I was in college and things would be different. Before I could speak, the tutor surprised me by apologizing. I was taken off guard and I thought to myself, Why is he apologizing? Maybe the paper deserves a higher grade and now he is going to tell me he made a mistake. I was wrong—he was not apologizing because of the grade; he was apologizing because he felt bad for having to upset me because of my physical disability. In a word, he felt sorry for me and he did not want to cause me any pain. I was able to assert myself and inform him that I did not want nor need sympathy. What I needed was to learn how to write and I thanked him for taking the time to give me the detailed feedback. It was the first time in my life I had been told that my academic skills in writing needed much improvement. In many ways, having this frank and honest discussion with my tutor made me feel more human and served me well throughout my college years.

—Joshua Williams

STUDENTS WITH DISABILITIES ARE SOMETIMES thought to be extraordinary for their accomplishments, or they are characterized as fragile and helpless. While their disabilities may present more challenges for them than the average person, they are no less human, and as such, should be treated with respect. At the same time, they should be expected to achieve to the best of their abilities like any other human being. In Joshua's case, he did improve his writing. His major in Journalism and subsequent job in that profession are a testament to his abilities.

73

Whether you are or are not a parent with a disability yourself, you know the challenges your child who has one can face. Unfortunately for students with disabilities, they live in a culture that is designed for and by those who do not have disabilities. The good news, however, is that individuals with disabilities are protected by laws, and those laws are designed to inform a student's education in positive ways.

The purpose of this chapter is to briefly discuss how families can use these laws to support their teen as he is planning for, applying to, and getting through college. Like all parents, they tend to advocate for their child during the pre-college years, but once their child is in college, it is expected that he will begin to advocate for himself. For the student with a disability, being able to become more independent in college is imperative since it can be a marker for his success as an independent person in life. Preparing for and choosing the right college is essential in this journey for the student with disabilities.

DEFINING DISABILITY

According to the American Disabilities Act (1990), a civil rights law that prohibits discrimination against people with disabilities, a disabled person is defined as an individual with a physical or mental impairment that limits one or more of the major life activities: performing basic personal care, walking, seeing, hearing, learning, and working. Some of these disabilities are more apparent than others, particularly those of a physical nature, such as muscular dystrophy, and some are less apparent, such as dyscalculia, which is defined as difficulty with calculations or the rapid processing of math facts.

Whether your teen has a visible or invisible disability, current assessments of his strengths and weaknesses are imperative. To make this diagnosis, a school psychologist will provide a battery of tests at no expense to you. Many of these tests will include at least the Woodcock Johnson III Tests of Cognitive Abilities and the WAIS-III–The Wechsler Adult Intelligence Scale (WAIS) intelligence quotient (IQ) tests–the primary clinical instruments used to measure adult and adolescent intelligence. The Wechsler Intelligence Scale, 4th edition (WISC-IV), is used for students from ages six to sixteen. To consider and assess both emotional and neuropsychological factors, more projective measurements are necessary, for example, the Thematic Apperception Test (TAT) and/or the Rorschach for older teens and adults. For younger teens, the Roberts Apperception Scale, 2nd edition, is commonly used. Finally, the Tell-Me-A-Story is a projective measurement for African and Hispanic American students up to age sixteen. The results of these tests will indicate if your teen has a learning disability, what the nature of it is, and what, if any, services and/or special accommodations are needed in the classroom setting. This document is generally referred to as an IEP, Individualized Educational Plan, and should be updated and sent to colleges at the appropriate time.

For those with physical disabilities, such as hearing or visual impairment, other issues are paramount. You and your teen will have to evaluate the infrastructure and make sure that it is designed to accommodate your teen's physical impairment. For example, is the terrain hilly or flat? Are campus buildings user-friendly for students with mobility-related disabilities? Are public bathrooms wheelchair-accessible? Is the campus shuttle accessible to students with disabilities throughout the regularly scheduled class and meal times?

Part of your teen's IEP that is sent to the college should address the unique academic as well as the physical needs of your teenager.

THE HIGH SCHOOL YEARS

CLASSES

While all college-bound students should begin their high school career with a well-defined plan to direct them towards college, for some, unfortunately, this is not the case. Rather, they go through their high school years meeting the minimum standards for a high school diploma with little deliberate thought on a plan to position them to and through college.

This is not the case with students who have a learning disability. In high school or before, the learning disabled student will be evaluated through assessments of some or all of the aforementioned tests. Teachers, counselors, and physicians are usually asked to present evaluations that will be shared in the formal meeting with the student and his parents. In this meeting, usually led by a school psychologist, the guidance counselor and teachers will also be present. After each person presents the results of his evaluation, the student and parents are allowed to ask questions after which the IEP is presented, outlining the individual educational plan for the student. More importantly, since everyone is at the table, everyone knows what is expected of each other, parent, student, and school staff alike.

Like all students, those who have a disability who are college-bound need to think about laying a foundation to reach that goal. That means, with the appropriate support services, they should be expected to take college preparatory courses and, when possible, stretch themselves by taking some of the Advance Placement and/or honor classes as well. Some students who have a learning disability will have an IEP, which will inform what classroom accommodations are needed. Students with

physical disabilities may be attending schools for the blind, or other examples are students who are limited to wheelchairs but who may attend
regular school. Independent of what category your teen is in, he should
make the most of high school and know that he, too, can go to and succeed in college.

TESTING

All students will be expected to take either the SAT or the ACT; some
students who have a learning disability will be required to take these exams under standard conditions while others may not. Students who need
accommodations for the SAT and ACT must request these accommodations from either Educational Testing Service (ETS) in Princeton, New
Jersey, or from American College Testing (ACT) in Iowa City, Iowa.
Speak to your teen's guidance counselor early in the school year to make
sure that the paperwork is processed on time. It usually takes four weeks
before the regular registration deadline to process the paperwork, and
parents will need a copy of the student's IEP, which in most cases should
also be in the guidance office at the teen's school.

In addition to the standardized college entrance testing, parents
should also be aware that their teen may qualify for special accommodations in his classes at school, as well. For example, he may need extended
time on tests and exams, or he may need to be moved to a room that is
very quiet with no distractions so that he can focus. He may be allowed to
use a computer for an essay test to help him to organize his thoughts and
handle issues around spelling; or, he may need a teacher to re-explain
written instructions. It is up to you to advocate for your teen since the
teacher may not always know that he qualifies for these services.

EXTRACURRICULAR ACTIVITIES

Encourage your teen to get involved with in- and out-of-school activities. He may be able to participate in sports and clubs with students in
general and/or he may want to join a club for students who have disabilities. Some students who have physical challenges elect the latter though
there is no reason why a student who is confined to a wheelchair cannot
join the chess club at his school if that is his interest. Similarly, there is
no excuse for a blind student being discouraged from attending his high
school's football game. Hopefully, with family and community support,
the student with disabilities, too, can benefit from what life outside class
in high school can offer.

APPLYING TO COLLEGE

As your teen begins the research for college, keep in mind that you want the college to know about your teenager and your teen wants to learn something about the college. While learning about the college, keep in mind three basic requirements: the admissions requirements for each school; the general graduation requirements for the particular college; and, if your teen has decided on a major, the graduation requirements for that particular major. These are central questions that should be answered before your teen decides if a school is right for him. For example, your teen may not have the qualifications to get into a school of his choice, or a school that he thought would be good for him, or the school may not offer his major. But, once your teen has found some schools that meet his basic requirements and whose requirements he meets, he is ready to advance to the next level.

If your teen's disability is not obvious when applying to college, he will have to self-disclose. Self-disclosing will not work against him. In fact, it can help him ultimately by guaranteeing that he has chosen a place that is right for him.

While searching for a college can be filled with an equal set of rewards and challenges for most, it is particularly challenging for students who have disabilities because they have so many more factors to consider when researching schools. They also have the added burden of struggling to become more independent while still having to be dependent in ways that other students do not.

When sitting down with your teen and helping him assess his strengths, weaknesses, and needs, try to let him come to the answers to those questions on his own. Let him take control over defining who he is and what he wants and needs. It is a good transition stage as he moves away from letting you advocate for him and moves towards advocating for himself.

Make sure that your teen has an up-to-date Psycho-Educational Test with the most current IEP. He will need to submit this document to colleges when he applies. Also, before conducting his college search, he should read the test reports and the IEP. In most cases, the jargon will be easy to understand and interpret. Hopefully, this will not be the first time that the student has had an opportunity to discuss the results of these tests with you and the school counselor.

One of the best resource guides for students with learning disabilities is The *K&W Guide to Colleges for Students with Learning Disabilities* by Marybeth Kravets and Imy Wax. This does not mean that your teen should not reference other guides mentioned in this book, but for the student who has a learning disability, this one is a must. Please know that there are hundreds of schools in the country that have wonderful services and programs on their campuses to assist your teen with his journey to become independent and well-educated. It is your responsibility, along with your teen's, to do the homework and find that right school. Knowing your teenager and what his needs are is the first step. By now, you have already achieved that first step; you are ready to search the web, read through the guidebooks, make some phone calls, and eventually get on the road and visit some of the schools.

While I value the knowledge one can gain from talking with friends, reading, and surfing the Internet, there is nothing like a face-to-face visit to a campus. In that way, your teen can test out some of the services first-hand. While on campus, make certain that your teen visits the Office for Students with Disabilities and be honest about what your teen's strengths and weaknesses are. It would also be advisable to bring the IEP with you when you visit the school in case you have to reference it or in case an academic advisor or counselor requests to see it. These offices will vary in the kind and quality of services they provide, but most should offer support in academic advising, vocational counseling, personal counseling, diagnostic assessment, and remedial skill development, to name a few.

In addition to the characteristics that shape many students' college searches, students with disabilities sometimes have to consider other factors, for example, if the school offers a learning environment that will accommodate their learning style. Some students prefer small schools because the way they learn requires a smaller classroom setting, while others may not want to be as visible and may prefer a larger school. Still others who have a physical disability may want a campus that is more flat or at least one that has wheelchair accessibility within buildings and shuttle service to and from buildings. In a larger school, navigating one-self across campus could consume too much energy and, thus, a smaller campus could be more appealing. Still other students prefer to live at home and commute to school. At home, they have resources and know what they can expect, whereas while at college, they will have to depend on the unknown and, in some cases, it may not work. On the other hand, staying at home could stifle growth and limit one's independence. For other students, distance learning is an option, but this, too, has its limitations since one does not have the opportunity to interact with fellow classmates and benefit from the undergraduate experience that living on campus offers.

Your research and subsequent visits should help your teen narrow down his college search which should consist of at least nine or ten schools, with at least three that they definitely can get into, generally referred to as "safeties" or "safe schools."

FINANCIAL AID

In addition to applying for the Pell Grant and Federal Supplemental Educational Opportunity Grant, your teen should also check with his college to find out what scholarships are available for students with disabilities. The Nordstrom Corporation annually awards competitive scholarships to students with disabilities, and the National Federation for the Blind offers scholarships for outstanding students. Of course, students with disabilities should be encouraged to compete for scholarships that are open to all students, particularly those earmarked for students with competitive GPAs.

GETTING THROUGH COLLEGE

Hopefully, your teen has chosen a school that will accommodate his needs and provide you as a parent with the comfort level so that you will not have to worry about your teenager living independently and being his own advocate. You and your teen are aware of the support services at the college, and you both are aware of how and when they should be accessed. Your teen is now off to navigate this new landscape as an independent agent. Trust that you have provided the wisdom, knowledge, and common sense for exercising sound judgment. Know that you have taught your child how to stand up and be counted—to do so even under the worst of conditions and to do so in a dignified manner. While it was true for high school that successes or failures were a reflection on you as the parent, in college they are more a reflection of your teen. Let him make his mistakes. He is human and entitled to do so. But know that it is the end result that counts and, in four years, armed with your emotional support and love, your teen will be okay.

● ● ● ●

My daughter had to defer entry into college for a year due to orthopedic complications from kidney disease. She took a year off in order to heal from double hip replacement surgery.

As a third-generation graduate from a historically black college, I was delighted by the prospect of Etienne becoming a fourth member to attend my alma mater. Her first semester went well, she was able to live in the dormitory, and she performed well academically. Then, at the end of the semester, she had a serious medical relapse and that is when the bottom fell out in terms of support services from the university. Although Etienne followed university protocol, registering as a medically compromised student, and provided all the documentation from our doctor, the university failed to meet her physical and educational needs. The list of egregious slights, incidents, and errors is too numerous to mention.

We transferred to a predominantly white institution not far from our home, hoping that we would not have to face the same challenges experienced at the previous school. Unfortunately, basically the same scenario came to pass there as well. Each situation, though slightly different, had the same effect. It demoralized and depressed my daughter, and she eventually expressed a desire to quit school. My response to her was, I could lower the bar because of her circumstances, and I would extend the finish line.

I am proud to say that her spirit has not been broken entirely by these obstacles. She has enrolled in a local community college that is meeting all of her needs and doing so in a timely and professional manner. Two and four-year colleges should review the policies and practices from this community college on how to respond to students with physical disabilities.

Etienne eventually found out that a live donor was prepared to give her a kidney in the middle of second semester at the community college. Despite the fact that her recovery would take five to eight weeks, she did not withdraw from classes. With the help of positive support from her instructors, she is back in class and did not miss a beat.

I strongly recommend to parents that, whether their child has a physical or a learning disability, they thoroughly evaluate the university's policies and practices and challenge the protocol if they feel it is not responding to the needs of their child. Take them to task if they fail to live up to their promises and transfer your student if you must. They already suffer enough confronting the medical and physical challenges.

—**Carol Cromer**

RESOURCES

ABLEDATA. 103 West Broad Street, Suite 300, Falls Church, VA 22046. Phone: 800-227-0216 Website: www.abledata.com

ACT. 500 ACT Drive, PO Box 168, Iowa City, IA 52243-0168 Phone: 319-337-1000 Website: www.act.org

American Association for the Advancement of Science. 1200 New York Avenue, NW, Washington, DC 20005 Phone: 202-326-6400 Website: www.aaas.org

Association on Higher Education and Disability. 107 Commerce Centre Drive, Suite 204, Huntersville, NC 28078 Phone: 704-948-7779 Website: www.ahead.org

Council for Exceptional Children. 2900 Crystal Drive, Suite 1000, Arlington, VA 22202-3557 Phone: 800-232-7733 Website: www.cec.sped.org

Disability Rights Education and Defense Fund. 3075 Adeline Street, Suite 210, Berkeley, CA 94703 Phone: 510-644-2555 Website: www.dredf.org

Distance Education Accrediting Council. 1101 17th Street, Suite 808, NW, Washington, DC 20036 Phone: 202.234.5100 Website: www.deac.org

Educational Testing Service. SAT-Special Services for Students with Disabilities, 660 Rosedale Road, Princeton, NJ 08541-6226 Phone: 609-921-9000 Website: www.ets.org

Heath Resource Center. 2134 G Street, NW, Washington, DC 20052-0001 Phone: 202-454-1220 Website: heath.gwu.edu

Kravets, M. and Wax, I. F. (2014). *The K&W guide to colleges for students with learning differences*, 12th edition: 350 schools with programs or services for students with ADHD or learning disabilities. Princeton, NJ: Princeton Review.

Sandler, M. (2008). *College confidence with ADD: The ultimate success manual for ADD students, from applying to academics, preparation to social success and everything else you need to know.* Naperville, IL: Sourcebooks.

CHAPTER IV

THE COLLEGE ATHLETE

I played quarterback at Woodson High School in Washington, DC, which has the reputation of producing some excellent athletes. I was an excellent student as well, because I was expected to be, and if I was not, my family would not allow me to play football. Because I had good grades and was a strong athlete, I was a strong prospect for numerous college coaches; Fordham was one of them.

My high school coach was very engaged in the process, by making sure that I complied with NCAA Clearinghouse Guidelines with respect to my high school roster, and he also made sure that I prepared for and took the SAT by my junior year in high school. By doing so, when recruiters came, he would have all my stats available as well as tapes to share with the college coaches. Once the college coaches saw my tapes and they were sufficiently impressed, then they would want to know my GPA and SAT score to see if I would make the cut. In the case of the Fordham coach, I did, and the Assistant Coach came to my home, and then the Head Coach came and eventually I was invited, along with one family member, to visit the college with all expenses paid.

Lots of guys have the talent, but they do not have the stats. If I had one piece of advice for future high school athletes who want to play ball in a DI or DII program, they should go online and access NCAA Clearinghouse Guidelines their first year of high school as well as have their parents send them to football camps in the summer where they can test their athletic skills on a national circuit and also learn from college coaches what the academic expectations are in high school. Then, they will know what they need to do and all that is left is to get busy.

—Derric Daniels, Fordham University graduate

STUDENTS AND PARENTS ALIKE SOMETIMES have an unrealistic sense of their teen's athletic ability. However, if your daughter or son has expressed an interest in participating in sports at the college level, you will need to stay front and center and be vigilant about the stages involved. This includes the planning, recruiting, and marketing process as well as a thorough understanding of any signed agreements once your teen has committed to playing sports at a particular college.

Early on, families need to develop an understanding of the athlete's responsibilities throughout high school as well as during the entire recruitment process. Parents must be familiar with the NCAA Initial Eligibility Rules and ensure that a successful academic experience is the overriding consideration for the college decision. After all, the probability of competing in athletics beyond the high school level is doubtful for most. The statistics below are not to discourage students but rather to illustrate this point. If, however, after absorbing the statistics presented here, your teen is still committed to participating in sports at the college level, then this chapter is for you.

Men's Basketball

- 1 in 35 high school senior boys will go on to play basketball at the college level.
- Approximately 1 in 13,000 high school players will be drafted by an NBA team.

Women's Basketball

- 3.3 percent of high school players will go on to play in college.
- 0.02 percent of high school players will play professionally.

Football

- About 5.8 percent of all high school senior boys will go on to play in college.
- 0.08 percent of all high school players will make the NFL roster.

Baseball

- Only 6.1 percent of high school players will play in college.

Men's Hockey

- Only 11 out 100 high school senior boys will play hockey in college.

Source: NCAA

The level of college athletics at which students compete will depend on their talent and the commitment they are willing to make to that sport. As you read further in this chapter, remember that tracking the educational planning and college placement process of an athlete is a team responsibility: that of the student, parent, school counselor, and coach.

What follows is an overview of the various stages with which families must be familiar as they guide their college-bound athlete toward fulfilling her or his goal of participating in sports at the college level.

HOW SPORTS ARE ORGANIZED AT THE COLLEGE LEVEL

If your teen is an athlete and he wants to participate in a competitive sport program at the college level, there are several divisions. For those who choose to participate in sports but choose not to do so competitively, they can participate through intramural sports which can be just as much fun without the pressure.

NCAA Division I, commonly referred to as "DI," is the highest level of intercollegiate athletics and includes many of the universities that you see competing on television. Colleges that field football teams are further classified as Football Bowl Subdivision, formerly Division IA, and Football Championship Subdivision, formerly Division IAA. The difference between these levels is the quality and depth of talented athletes and the philosophical and financial commitment a university makes to its athletic program. Whether a DIA or DIAA athlete, they all face an enormous time commitment; there is no off season. Athletes sometimes feel like playing their sport is a job and often feel pressured to perform.

NCAA Division II or "D2" includes small-sized schools with lesser-known athletic reputations. The teams usually feature a number of local or in-state student-athletes, with most paying for school with some combination of scholarship money, grants, student loans, and employment earnings. Even in "D2" programs, students still face a substantial time commitment to the sport.

NCAA Division III or "D3" is the largest within the NCAA. However, "D3" athletes receive no financial aid related to their athletic ability. Emphasis here is on the participant rather than on the spectators. Generally, athletes compete because they love their sport. They are highly skilled and competitive, and in some cases they have as much talent as their peers at "DI" and "DII" programs, but the time commitment is not as huge as at Divisions I and II. Some athletes at DIII schools maintain that while they love playing sports, playing at a DIII school also allows them the opportunity to have a more normal undergraduate experience.

Some colleges maintain concurrent memberships in two different divisions, so, for example, a school may have a men's ice hockey team playing at the Division I level and play at the Division III level in all other sports.

NCAA ELIGIBILITY RULES

Prospective student-athletes must meet established standards to practice, compete, and receive athletically-related financial aid. In Divisions I and II, students must be certified by the NCAA Eligibility Center. In Division III, eligibility for admission, financial aid, practice, and competition is determined by institutional regulations.

Sometimes, the rules for NCAA eligibility can change; so it is important to make sure that one is clear that the rules that are informing the decisions of students, parents, and coaches are the most current. Generally speaking, students must graduate from high school with a minimum number of core courses. They also must have minimum core course grade-point average, and, finally, they need a qualifying score on the SAT or ACT.

With respect to the grade-point average, it is important to emphasize that the grade-point average has to be calculated among the required core courses. Each high school has its own list of NCAA-approved core courses. Only courses that appear on this list can be used in calculating a student's core grade-point average. A student may have an overall grade-point average of 2.8 out of 4.0, but when one deletes the non-core courses, the grade-point average could go down and thus jeopardize the student's eligibility. If you want to find your high school's list, go to www.ncaaclearinghouse.net and select High School Administration. Then, you should click on List of Approved Core Courses and follow the prompts. It is vital that your high school's list of approved core courses is current. Review your list at least once each year to avoid eligibility issues.

It is also important to note that when I am speaking of grade-point average and qualifying test scores, I am doing so for only eligibility with the NCAA specifically. This does not mean the student has necessarily satisfied the requirements for a particular college. When students are conducting their research, they should contact the coaches and/or admissions officers at the colleges in which they have an interest to determine what specific requirements are necessary for college athletes. Requirements for college-bound athletes at some colleges do vary from those required of college-bound non-athletes, but at other colleges they are the same. This is particularly the case at many of the competitive colleges. See the GPA and Test Score Sliding Scale on the NCAA student website at www.ncaastudent.org.

ACADEMIC PLANNING IN HIGH SCHOOL FOR THE COLLEGE-BOUND ATHLETE

Before discussing the specific core curriculum that a college-bound athlete would follow in high school, it is important to note that there are specific high school courses that the NCAA Eligibility Center will accept. Spanish I or Algebra II, if it is placed on the high school transcript with a grade and a credit and it is on the high school's list of approved core courses, are two examples.

If your teen is aspiring to participate in sports at a Division I college, he must earn a minimum GPA of 2.3 in the core courses (see below), a combined SAT score of 910, or a sum ACT score of 76. Listed below are the following core courses:

- 4 years of English

- 3 years of math in Algebra I or higher

- 2 years of natural science and one must be with a lab, for example, biology

- 1 year of an additional English, math, or science class

- 2 years of social studies

- 4 years of additional courses in any area above or foreign language, non-doctrinal religion, or philosophy.

The prospective student-athlete must complete the core curriculum by the graduation date of his class based on entry into grade nine. If the prospective student-athlete graduates on time, one additional core course may be used for initial eligibility purposes, may be completed at any high school, must be completed within one year of graduation, and can be used to improve the core-course grade-point average.

If your teen is aspiring to participate in sports at a Division II college, he must earn a minimum GPA of 2.0 in the core courses (see below), a combined SAT score of 820, or a sum ACT score of 68. Listed below are the following core courses:

- 3 years of English

- 2 years of math (Algebra I or higher)

- 2 years of natural or physical science (including one year of lab science if offered)

- 2 years of additional English, math, or science

- 2 years of social science

- 4 additional courses in any of the above areas, English, math, natural or physical science, social science, foreign language, or comparative religion or philosophy.

The prospective student-athlete must complete the core curriculum before initial full-time collegiate enrollment.

The grade-point average and test requirements for Division I prospective student-athletes correspond to the sixteen-course rule and can be found on the Initial-Eligibility Index Sliding Scale (see www.eligibility-center.org). For Division II prospective student-athletes, there is a minimum core grade-point average of 2.0 and a minimum SAT score of 820 or an ACT sum score of 68. For Division II prospects, there is no sliding scale.

Whether a DI or DII prospect, all tests must be taken on a national test date under standard test conditions unless you are a student who has been classified with a learning disability and has a documented Individualized Educational Plan (IEP) that allows you to take the test administration under different conditions. In all cases, test scores must be reported directly to the NCAA Eligibility Center by the testing agency. Test scores on transcripts were deemed unacceptable as official documentation as of August 1, 2007.

WORKING WITH YOUR HIGH SCHOOL COUNSELOR AND COACH

If you are fortunate, your teen attends a school where the high school counselor and coach are working in chorus to assist you and your teen in the planning and application process. While it is important that the staff at your teen's school work constructively on his behalf, they also are developing and sustaining relationships with appropriate professionals at the various colleges and universities nationwide. More specifically, the school counselor has a strong network across colleges with the various admissions counselors, and the coach has also established a working relationship with several coaches at a number of colleges. In this way, the counselor and coach can use their leverage to support you and your family.

Earlier on in this chapter, I discussed the importance of families, counselors, and coaches working as a team, and I want to re-emphasize this here again since I judge this to be vitally important. Of course, this same principle applies to the non-student athlete as well, but since the focus in this chapter is on the prospective college athlete, I am addressing them as a specific group. With that in mind, I would recommend that you as parents think about your counselor as a resource who can also work in chorus with the coach in the best interest of your teen in several ways.

Counselors and coaches first will know, or at least should know, the eligibility requirements. With this knowledge, they will be in a better position to coach your teen appropriately. They can also work together in shaping a high school program that speaks to the requirements established by the NCAA Clearinghouse, and they will be able to do so in a timely manner so that by the time your teen is a junior or senior, he is well on his way to satisfying these requirements. If for some reason he hasn't yet, there should be time in the junior and senior year to compensate for what he did not achieve in the earlier years of high school.

Not only should the counselors think about the courses, but they also should design a testing schedule that prepares the student for the SAT and the ACT earlier in high school by exposing the student to the PSAT and the PLAN. Furthermore, if the student has the resources—either in school or through a private firm outside of school—he or she should enroll in an SAT and/or ACT preparation class. These classes, when taken seriously, have been able to improve a student's test score significantly. If enrollment in a test preparation program is not an option, minimally, the student is encouraged to review the SAT and ACT preparation booklets that can found in the school's guidance office. Having access to one or all of these aforementioned resources can increase the student's ability for success when taking these tests. Finally, it is always advisable to take the SAT and ACT at least twice since colleges will super score, i.e., take the highest sub-score from each test administration.

Once the student has accomplished the desired GPA and SAT or ACT score, he is able to position himself more competitively for the college team of his choice. Before the student can determine if he has the desired GPA, he will need guidance on how to calculate it, and here again is where the counselor can be of value. Parents should encourage counselors to sit with the student and family to discuss the GPA of the student at the end of each academic year. The student should be advised that it is imperative to start off with a strong GPA because, if not, he will be under pressure to bring up a low GPA throughout his high school years. Once the student knows how to calculate his GPA, he can do so independently. A counselor will emphasize the importance of academic performance at every step of his or her high school career (and ninth grade counts). Poor grades and test scores can result in future eligibility problems and decreased interest from college recruiters.

Parents who have a student with learning disabilities should expect that his school counselor will understand the policy and practices specific to LD students. For example, the counselor may work very closely with the Special Needs department because the student may have been given an Independent Educational Plan. The student may qualify for extended time on the SAT. If this were the case, the counselor would coach the family on how to register for the test under these circumstances. One thing to keep in mind, if your teen fits this category, is the timing factor. To register a student who qualifies for specific accommodations for the SAT, one has to do so much earlier than for those students without special accommodations who are registering for the SAT. For more on students who have learning disabilities, please refer to Chapter III.

All counselors will create an efficient system for processing clearinghouse applications, including submission of the final transcript. Generally, a counselor will arrange a meeting with the parent, student, and, ideally, the coach, if he can attend the meeting, to evaluate the past performance of the student and to make recommendations for the final years of high school. This assumes, of course, that this meeting is occurring at some point in the junior year, separately from an earlier meeting that should have taken place in the freshmen year and/or in the sophomore year.

Parents can also expect that the counselor will arrange a meeting about conducting a college search. Depending on the counselor's caseload, this meeting would be combined with the aforementioned one, where the counselor evaluates the student's past performance and makes recommendations, for example, for the senior year, and can then move to a discussion about the college search.

Too often, college-bound athletes approach this process re-actively, when in the ideal world, all students should approach this process proactively. Athletes, on the other hand, are always being told what to do, as opposed to being encouraged to think for themselves. For example, it is not uncommon for talented athletes to receive letters of interest from a number of colleges. Upon receipt of these letters, some students focus their college search exclusively toward these colleges that have reached out to them. What is important to note is that these letters are not a commitment and that they are sent to hundreds of other high school athletes nationwide. That being said, students should be advised to approach these letters of interest with a cautious optimism. If a college is seriously interested in a student, he will receive more outreach communication through the high school coaches and/or league coach. He may even receive a phone call from a college coach.

Rather than depend entirely on those schools reaching out to athletes, athletes should think pro-actively and come up with the schools in which they have an interest based on their individual needs. This is where meeting with a school counselor can help.

That having been said, when choosing a school, ask the counselor to help the student identify colleges that fit his criteria, for example, size, location, campus setting, availability of academic programs, and, of course, level of athletic competition. A question that I would also recommend that families consider is: Would my teen still attend this college even if he were injured and could never again compete? If the answer is yes, then that sounds like the school would be a good match; but if the answer is no, the student might want to think about whether he should seriously consider the school since there is no guarantee that he will be able to play all four years.

Much of what has been said up to this point has placed much of the responsibility in the hands of the counselors, and, from my position, that is as it should be. Counselors work with a wide range of students, and as part of their caseload, they will have some athletes assigned to them. However, earlier I spoke to the importance of team effort, and thus it is incumbent on the counselor to reach out to the high school's athletic department to identify potential college-bound students. The counselors and coaches could meet to develop a guide for the college-bound athlete that includes academic and athletic tasks for each year. As part of the high school athletic program, the high school coach can invite college coaches to meet with college-bound athletes and their parents, in addition to appropriate school staff, e.g., other high school coaches and guidance counselors. In some high schools, there is one counselor who works with all of the athletes, but in most schools, one counselor has a more general caseload and thus is working with the non-athlete as well as the athlete.

For all students, planning for and choosing a college is not a static process. One day, a teen may be interested in playing sports at Duke, and two weeks later, Duke could be off the radar, and the University of North Carolina is now being seriously considered. Whatever the process, the student's parents and coaches must stay involved. Remember, this is a team effort.

MARKETING YOUR TEEN

Earlier, I spoke about the importance of team effort with respect to planning for college, but there are students who do not have a good working relationship with either their counselor or their coach. This is not to say that the student is a problem; in fact, he could be a very good student academically, a well-respected member of the school community, but have the misfortune of having a counselor and/or coach who is inundated with multiple problems and tasks. In this case, the student may not receive the attention that he deserves and needs. If a student fits into this category, parents have to be more deliberate about marketing their teen.

Marketing your teen comprises a three-step process: as parents you need to honestly assess your teen's academic and athletic abilities, identify appropriate colleges based on that assessment, and communicate with the college coaches.

In assessing your teen's athletic ability, you have to be very objective and rely heavily on the coach. Whether or not the coach is directly involved, he should give your son and you an honest evaluation to prevent an inflated sense of your child's athletic skill sets.

If your child does not have a good relationship with the high school counselor, hopefully, he will have a good relationship with his league coach who can sometimes serve as a resource for the parents and the student. In very few cases, the student may have to identify colleges independently. The final list should be based primarily on the quality of the academic program, not just athletic interest.

Once you and your teen have developed the college list, he can begin reaching out to the coaches at these schools. It's important to:

- Identify the names of the head coaches.

- Send an email to the coaches expressing interest in that college of interest.

- Create an athletic resume that summarizes their academic and athletic accomplishments.

- Promptly return a coach's request for information and always be truthful.

- Be seen at summer camps, recruiting showcase events, travel teams, summer leagues, etc.

- If possible, earn the recommendation of the high school coach that the college recruiter may contact.

- Do not depend on coaches to make a DVD: develop your own and make sufficient copies in the event that, during the recruitment process, a college may ask for one to be sent to the recruitment office.

THE RECRUITMENT PROCESS

If your teen has prepared for college, both from an academic and athletic perspective, he is going to make a very marketable candidate, and when coaches begin their recruitment cycle, your teen is going to stand out. College coaches evaluate recruits in three areas: athletic ability, academic achievement, and quality of character.

Early in the recruitment process, college coaches have to identify prospective athletes, and they can do so in several ways:

- Evaluations from high school and club coaches
- Varsity competition, sports camps, showcase events, summer leagues, and tournaments in which athletes play
- Newspaper clippings
- Recommendations from current student-athletes, alumni, or community leaders
- Reputable recruiting services
- Student-athletes marketing themselves and introducing themselves to the coach

Once the coach has been made aware of who is potentially a prospect, he can now be more deliberate about reaching out to your teen. There are several ways that college coaches indicate their interest in a prospective college athlete:

- Letters that are sent directly to the home of the student
- Personal handwritten correspondence sent to the home
- Students may receive questionnaires, brochures, or media guides
- Talking with the high school, summer league, or club team coach
- Phone calls to the home
- Watching games and/or practices at the student's high school
- A school visit where the high school coach may show some tapes of the student's performance on the field, court, etc.
- A home visit where the coach would speak with the student and the family
- Invite the prospective student to campus for an official visit

Students and parents should be able to gauge the recruiter's level of interest by the quality and quantity of the contacts from the coach. I would not be too aggressive. If you find that the coach is not responding to your calls and/or emails, she is probably not interested. However, I also would not give up. If you qualify for admission to the college, independent of your athletic abilities, you will have the opportunity to make an appointment and visit the coach to discuss the possibility of being considered as a walk-on.

RECRUITING SCOUTING SERVICES

If you have the means to hire a professional recruiting scouting counselor, please know that like most counseling services, some are reputable and some are not. Since your teen is your most precious resource, I would recommend that you do your homework and gather as much information as possible about the recruitment scouting service before you sign on. I certainly feel that asking for two or three references is in order. You also want to compare fees, as sometimes fees can be quite hefty for a private consulting service. In addition to references, I would also suggest that you determine if the counselor is a member of any professional organizations. For example, the Independent Educational Consulting Association sometimes has members who provide private educational consulting services for the college-bound athlete. A final thought is to contact the colleges in which your teen has an interest and inquire if any of the coaches are familiar with the recruiting scouting services. In the ideal world, the counselors from the private company should be working jointly with your teen's school counselor, but in other cases, families may hire a private counselor because they lack the confidence that the school counselor and/or school coach can adequately represent their teen. Since I have worked both as a school-based counselor and an independent counselor, I recognize that in both one can find a reputable advocate for you and your teen.

CERTIFICATION AND NON-CERTIFICATION DECISIONS (DIVISION I)

By the end of the recruitment process, you want to know that your teen is certified, which means that he has met all of the requirements, is able to practice with the team, compete, receive aid, and eligible to do all of the above for four years.

If the student is designated as a non-qualifier, he has not met all of the requirements, e.g., lacks core courses, has not graduated, and does not meet sliding scale requirements. Since he does not satisfy the aforementioned, he cannot practice, may not compete, and may not receive financial aid.

CERTIFICATION DECISIONS AND NON-CERTIFICATION DECISIONS (DIVISION II)

As in Division I, the "Qualifier" meets all requirements, may practice, compete, and receive aid for four seasons of competition. But unlike Division I, Division II has "Partial Qualifier" status as long as the student has graduated from high school, has satisfied the minimum test score requirement, and has a GPA of 2.0 on a 4.0 grading scale. If the student satisfies these requirements, he may practice and receive aid and compete for four seasons.

The non-qualifier does not meet the requirements for the qualifier or partial qualifier because he lacks the core courses, the GPA, and the test score requirement and has not graduated from high school. Therefore, he may not practice, compete, nor receive aid any of the four seasons of competition.

EARLY CERTIFICATION (DIVISION I)

When thinking about athlete certification status, he may want to position himself for Early Certification. This means that he can certify as early as his junior year. A student must earn a GPA of 3.0 in thirteen core courses and have a combined SAT score of 900 or a sum score of 75 on the ACT. The thirteen core courses must include three courses in English, two in math, two in natural or physical science, and six additional courses in any NCAA core area.

EARLY CERTIFICATION (DIVISION II)

An athlete for a DII program will need a minimum combined SAT score of 900 or a minimum ACT sum score of 75 and a core-course GPA of 3.0 on a 4.0 scale in a minimum of twelve core courses upon completion of six semesters or the equivalent. The thirteen courses must include three in English, two in math at the level of Algebra I or higher, two in natural science, including at least one laboratory course if offered at your high school, and six additional core courses in any NCAA core area.

IMPORTANT POINTS TO REMEMBER REGARDING SCHOLARSHIPS

All athletic scholarships awarded by NCAA institutions are limited to one year and are renewable annually. A four-year award does not exist in the athletic world. Athletic scholarships may be renewed annually for a maximum of five years within a six-year period of continuous college attendance. Athletics aid may also be canceled or reduced at the end of each year for any reason the coach deems necessary.

Finally, please note that athletic awards vary widely, ranging from full scholarships—including tuition, room, board, fees, and books—to very small scholarships and books only. Your Letter of Intent, which is your contract with the college athletic program, will spell out the details of your scholarship. As with any other contract, make sure that you read and understand the contents before you and your teen sign.

● ● ● ●

The best recommendation for a parent who has an athlete applying to college is to make sure that your son or daughter has a backup plan in case of injury, getting cut, or simply losing interest in the sport. The backup should be a good, solid education. So few college athletes ever make it to the pros; so, life after sports has to be addressed.

There are rewards and challenges of being a student athlete. The difficulty is not only the time and commitment entailed in most sports programs, but also the loss of being a part of the social fabric of a school.

The rewards are that, from day one, an athlete has an instant group of friends/teammates and can avoid the inevitable awkwardness of being a freshman in a new setting having to make new friends.

And because there is little time for an athlete to find time to party between practices, games, and academic classes, he or she often has more focus and discipline, especially during the months the sport is being played. Often that structured environment transfers into better grades, especially if the sport has coaches that oversee study hours and tutors to make sure the athletes are not falling behind.

—DD Eisenberg

GLOSSARY

Blue Chip Athlete: A highly skilled, accomplished, visible athlete who is known to college coaches at a relatively early age. Most people in the school and community are familiar with this athlete.

Intramural: Sport programs developed within the confines of a particular college or university where students can compete with their fellow classmates.

NAIA: The National Association of Intercollegiate Athletics is the governing body for a group of smaller colleges.

NCAA: The National Collegiate Athletic Association is a governing board for most sports at the college level. Intramural sports do not fall under the aegis of the NCAA.

NJCAA: The National Junior College Athletic Association is the governing body of two-year college athletes. NCJAA members compete at the Division I, II, or III level depending on the institution's commitment to athletics.

National Letter of Intent: The NLI is a voluntary program administered by the NCAA Eligibility Center. By signing the NLI, a student agrees to attend the institution for one academic year. In exchange, the academic institution must provide athletic financial aid for one academic year.

Official Visit: An official visit is any visit to a college campus by a student and his parents paid for by the college. The college may pay for the following expenses: roundtrip transportation, room and board, and reasonable entertainment expenses, including complimentary tickets to a home game. For Division I students, before a college may invite a student on an official visit, the student will have to provide the college with a copy of his official high school transcript and SAT, ACT, or PLAN scores and register with the NCAA Eligibility Center.

Redshirting: In college sports, a term referring to delaying a college athlete's participation in order to lengthen his eligibility.

Unofficial Visit: Any visit by a student and his parents to a college campus paid for by the student or by his parents. The only expense a student may receive from the college is two or three complimentary tickets to a home athletic game. A student may make as many unofficial visits as he would like and may make those visits at any time. The only time a student cannot talk with a coach is during a dead period, which is a planned period, often in August, during which there is no involvement or contact by the school or coach with students in order to limit the time coaches can coach their athletes.

Verbal Commitment: A verbal commitment describes a college-bound athlete's commitment before he signs or is able to sign a National Letter of Intent. A college-bound athlete may announce a verbal commitment at any time. While verbal commitments have become very popular for both athletes and coaches, this commitment is not binding on either the athlete or the school. Only the National Letter of Intent, accompanied by a financial aid agreement, is binding by both parties.

Walk-on: A student who is not formally recruited by the school but who becomes an official team member. An outside party may have brought the student to the coach's attention; sometimes, the athlete was of interest to the coach at the time of his candidacy for admission but not courted by the school because of budget limitations. While a walk-on may receive financial aid, the student is not supported by an athletic scholarship.

Yellow Chip Athlete: Skilled athletes who can continue their athletic careers beyond high school but are less visible to college recruiters. There are differing opinions on the college level at which these athletes can compete.

RESOURCES

Brown, S. (2016). *The student athlete's guide to getting recruited: How to win scholarships, attract colleges, and excel as an athlete*, 4th edition. Belmont, CA: SuperCollege.

Wheeler, D. (2009). *The sports scholarships insider's guide: Getting money for college at any division*, 2nd edition. Naperville, IL: Sourcebooks.

ESPECIALLY FOR STUDENTS OF COLOR

While studying at Swarthmore, I worked in the Music Library. I recall working on one occasion and listening to music at the library's circulation desk, which was a fairly common experience among student library workers. This particular day sticks out for me because I was asked to lower my music by the librarian. This would not have been an unreasonable request even though the volume of my music was relatively low. What the librarian said to me was shocking and disheartening. He added to his request for the lowering of my music that the student, the only student in the library at the time, a white woman, was entitled to study un-molested because she paid full tuition. Though it was never made clear whether or not she had paid full tuition, the insinuation was clear: I was a second-class citizen in the librarian's eyes. She was entitled to all that the college had to offer, and I wasn't. According to him, I was less worthy to reap its bounty by virtue of my presumed economic status and, as quiet as it was kept, my race.

It was a sobering moment for me. I realized that for many at Swarthmore, my presence was merely tolerated and not entirely welcomed. I'm grateful, however, that I had the tenacity to know that my self worth and right to be at Swarthmore was not predicated on my economic status or my race but simply on my ability and desire to learn and to develop myself holistically. So, in response to the librarian's classism and racism and to all who felt that I was only at Swarthmore by quota and/or government mandate, I simply graduated…along with the "legitimate" students.

—**Allen Pinkney**

WHILE THE COLLEGE ADMISSIONS PROCESS bestows rewards and obstacles for all students, it can be especially challenging for students of color who want to attend one of the nation's highly selective, predominantly white institutions of higher education or one of a number of the country's increasingly competitive historically black colleges. Although the decline in the popularity of affirmative action has undermined race-based scholarships at some public institutions, there are other colleges, particularly the private schools that are not dependent on state funding, that still provide scholarships for students of color. Do not let recent headlines frighten you. When researching schools, ask about these scholarships, and keep in mind that if your teenager is viewed as someone who can add value to a college community, schools will want him. That means when putting together the financial aid package, they will offer the student more grant money and fewer loans as an incentive to attend. The more selective schools often have a larger endowment and can consequently offer better financial aid packages. For this reason, it is important for your teen to perform well academically so that he can qualify for the institutions that are more selective and thus offer applicants greater funding.

AFFIRMATIVE ACTION AND YOU

While some students of color relied on affirmative action admissions decisions to gain acceptance into highly competitive white schools in the past, that option can no longer be taken for granted today. Recent changes in affirmative action have forced colleges to rethink the way they handle race-based admissions and scholarships. For example, a court case involving the University of Maryland College Park and Daniel Poderesky (1990) became a litmus test for scholarships based on ethnicity. Poderesky, who is of Hispanic and Jewish extraction, claimed ethnic minority status in applying for a scholarship earmarked for African-Americans and was rejected for the scholarship on the grounds of racial ineligibility. He applied for the Benjamin Banneker Scholarship Program for African-Americans, a program devised by university officials to attract minority students. Claiming that he was racially eligible, he initiated Poderesky v. Kiwan and eventually obtained a court ruling in his favor. The university took the case to the appellate level where it was denied. Some of these earmarked scholarships have been made available to all students, regardless of race, and a few schools that offer them have been told by their state's Attorney General that they can no longer offer raced-based scholarships even if the scholarship comes from a private source.

This change of heart toward affirmative action has already produced significant results. After a ban on affirmative action by the University of California, the law schools at the University of California at Berkeley and at the University of California Los Angeles reported a drop in African-American applications of about eighty percent. These decisions have influenced admissions policies at the undergraduate level, as well. In the year 2000 at the University of California at Berkley, race was not used as a factor in admissions decisions; the much-publicized result was the number of African-Americans accepted that year fell dramatically from the previous year's figure, and the number of Latino students also dropped.

Is affirmative action still an issue today? I would say, "Yes." Should it still be an issue today? Some would say no, and I would say yes. For a current case addressing race as one consideration in the admissions process, I would refer the readers to www.theatlantic.com/politics/archive/2015/when-can-race-be-a-college-admissions-factor/419808. For the second time, the Justices of the Supreme Court are struggling with Fisher v. Texas—and the divisive questions it raises.

In 1997, a student who graduated from a Texas public high school submitted an application to the flagship campus of the University of Texas at Austin where she was denied admission. She sued, arguing that the use of race in any part of the admissions process violated her rights, hence Fisher v. Texas.

THE MYSTERY OF ADMISSIONS COMMITTEES

These issues may or may not play a role in a college's decision to admit your teen. One thing you can count on, though, is that some admissions committees view students of color differently; this is particularly the case for those who are first-generation college-bound. Here, we are taking into consideration race and class. Your best source of advice on how to prepare your teen is his guidance counselor. If he has a reasonably good relationship with the admissions staff at a particular college, your teenager may get an idea of what that school's admissions policies are for students of color. For example, if a student of color misses a deadline date and the college really wants and needs your teen, it may make an exception. Similarly, if a white student who is first in his family to attend college misses the deadline, the college may overlook that fact and consider his application. Here, the assumption is that it needs more students who are first-generation college-bound to round off the entering class. Some schools will take students of color with a slightly lower than average SAT score if the student has an exceptional GPA and is willing to participate in a summer enrichment program at the college preceding his freshmen year. Others will look more seriously at leadership qualities and place less importance on the SAT or ACT.

Whether your teen is a student of color from a privileged background or from an economically disadvantaged background, if he has problems with standardized tests, he is encouraged to take the most rigorous academic program his school can offer. And, once your teen has positioned himself in those challenging classes, make sure that he studies four to five hours a night to obtain good grades. In that way, your teen can lever-age his academic record if his scores are average or below average. This advice is especially useful for students who are first in their families to attend college, and who, generally, attend economically poor schools. In schools where resources are low, students tend to score poorly on stan-dardized testing. This is not to say that good test coaching cannot help them improve their scores, nor is it to imply that they are unintelligent. On the contrary, it is just simply to say that kids who score better on standardized testing tend to attend the more selective high schools that are in the more high-income areas, and, thus, they have a competitive advantage over poor students. Most colleges recognize this factor and try to make amends for it when reviewing these students' applications.

Students of color, especially those from economically under-resourced schools, can receive fee waivers for not only their SAT but also for appli-cations to most colleges. This is not usually the case for historically black colleges. Most of them do not offer fee waivers. Meanwhile, many of the selective predominantly white colleges offer fly-in programs for students of color as part of their recruitment process. Here you will be offered an invitation to visit a college for usually two days, which includes your transportation, housing, and meals.

Since your teen can never be certain how any particular admissions committee views students of color, it is imperative to make a strong case for admittance. This chapter will explain his options in detail and advise you on how to make the most of his educational opportunities.

SCHOLASTIC CHOICES AND PERFORMANCE IN HIGH SCHOOL

You have undoubtedly heard of high school athletes competing rigorous-ly to receive the nod from certain college teams. That's just how competi-tive your teen must be during his high school academic career if he wants to increase the chances of getting into the college of his choice. There are many variables in the admissions process, and your teen will not have full control over many of them—admissions policies and the quality of your school system; even SAT and ACT scores have an element of chance. But, your teen does have more control over his GPA, and he has a much better chance of getting into a selective college of his choice with a strong GPA and a low SAT score than someone who has low grades and high SAT scores. Now, there are many exceptions to this rule. In fact, many state schools and second-tier schools would welcome a student with an above-average SAT score, even with low grades, because that high SAT score can bring up the average score for the incoming freshmen class at that particular institution. While that may help the college, it will not nec-essarily be good for your teen when he is admitted and does not perform well because of poor study skills. At the end of the day, nothing can take the place of demanding classes and good grades.

Your teen is given four years of high school to take the appropriate classes. Encourage her or him to use those years to absorb English, math, science, history, and foreign languages. Don't just allow him to take the minimum academic requirements—he should go all out and stretch and challenge himself. If you live in a community that does not offer challenging academic programs, do not worry. Your teen will not be penalized for what the school does not offer; your teen will be penalized for not taking advantage of what the school does offer.

If your teen is fortunate to attend a school that offers Advanced Placement classes—college level classes offered in high school—then he should be strongly advised to take some of them throughout his high school years. Most teens take them in the junior and senior year, but, sometimes, one can find students taking AP European History as sophomores. Your teen should not hesitate to take the challenging courses if you judge, based on your knowledge of his work ethic and abilities, that he can handle the rigor.

Unfortunately, students of color are not often enrolled in the AP classes. In some schools, still today, they are neither encouraged nor expected to do so. In other cases they are encouraged to do so but they choose not to take advantage of the opportunity. This underutilization is most disheartening because it speaks to a larger societal issue. Historically, for example, we as people of color were denied access to certain opportunities, but today, when we have access to these opportunities, we forgo them. It is important for you as parents to remind your teen about our history and let them know that an opportunity denied is no different than the opportunity forgone. At the end of the day, your teen is still left behind and eventually losing the race.

For students of color who want to be enrolled in AP classes in school districts where such classes are either minimally offered or not offered at all, some school districts have formed partnerships with local colleges and universities. The more industrious students, who in many cases have exhausted all of the academic offerings at school, are being allowed to dual enroll in high school and in a local college to take college classes for credit. Make it your business as a parent to explore all of the available school and community-based academic programs that are available to accelerate your teen's intellectual growth. As always, I recommend that you start with your teen's school counselor, but do not depend on only one person as a resource. Ask people in your community, on your job, and in your church about academic enrichment programs. More often than not, someone in your personal or professional circle can give you some information that will advantage your teen.

ACHIEVING COMPETITIVE SCORES ON THE SAT AND ACT

The courses your teen takes in high school and the grades he receives are far more important than a single SAT or ACT score. Now, having said that, please know that standardized test scores are still part of the formula for gaining admittance for most colleges. A solid SAT score can tip the scales in your favor for getting into your number-one school of choice and/or obtaining a private scholarship. Preparation for taking the SAT should begin with the experience of preparing for and taking the PSAT.

While most students take the PSAT in their junior year, consider having your teen take the test as early as sophomore year. This is not uncommon at many schools. In fact, some students are exposed to the PSAT as early as their freshmen year. Here, as a parent, you have to be careful to make sure that your teen has the appropriate course content to handle the test subject matter. For example, while many students from affluent areas and some from middle-class and lower-income communities may have already taken Algebra I in the eighth grade, other students will not be taking Algebra I until the ninth grade. Students will be introduced to Algebra on the PSAT, and if they have never seen the subject, they can be discouraged and turned off indefinitely with respect to standardized testing. In all cases, students will have been exposed to Algebra I by the tenth grade and, if not, certainly by the eleventh, which is when all juniors are expected to take the test.

Taking the test in the sophomore year increases your teen's chances of obtaining a higher score in his junior year, when the test really counts. High scorers who are Hispanic can be nominated for the National Hispanic Scholars Recognition Programs. The National Achievement Scholarship Program for Black Students was dismantled recently, and it is still unclear as to why. All students who take the PSAT in their junior year, of course, can be considered for the National Merit Scholarship program. If they make the semi-finalist cut, they will be informed in the spring of their junior year. In the senior year, the student and their counselor will be asked to submit additional information, and the student will find out if he was a finalist at a later date in the senior year. During the 2015-16 academic year the College Board introduced the PSAT 8/9. See Chapter I for more detailed information on this test.

DON'T FORGET ABOUT TEST PREP FOR YOUR TEEN

Students of color who attend school systems with limited resources are often not prepared for the ACT and SAT, putting them at a disadvantage.

If they are not aware of the existence of test preparation courses such as Kaplan and The Princeton Review, to mention just two, they are at a second disadvantage. If they cannot afford the course, they are at a third disadvantage. If they don't know that they can sometimes obtain scholarships to pay for the courses, they are yet at another disadvantage. And if they believe that they can't do well on the test, they are at the worst disadvantage of all.

Test prep courses are definitely helpful, and they are more accessible than you might think. I would invite you as a parent to call the test preparation centers in your community and ask about financial aid and other special programs. Your teen may qualify for a scholarship, or perhaps, she or he may be able to take advantage of a prep course offered by an increasing number of community-based organizations that have partnered with national test prep centers like Kaplan and the Princeton Review. Two smaller test preparation programs that also offer tutoring services are Summit Educational Group and Huntington Learning Center.

Many students of color I have counseled report that the ACT is an easier test than the SAT. The ACT is more content-based, so it measures what a student knows in specific subject areas. While I have not witnessed any particular data that shows that, on average, students of color who take the ACT score higher than they do on the SAT, my intuition suggests that students who score well on one tend to score well on the other, and students who have challenges with one standardized test, i.e., the SAT, will have challenges on the ACT. However, if the culture of your teen's communities is promoting the ACT as an easier test, when your teen takes the test, they probably would have less anxiety and perhaps more confidence, thereby increasing the chances of better performance.

Since most colleges today accept scores from both exams, it is a good idea to recommend that your teen prepare for and take both. Presenting scores from two different tests gives the admissions counselors more information about your teen, allowing them to make more informed decisions. However, please note that your teen can determine what score he wants to send; thus, if the ACT score is indeed higher, then he should only send the ACT.

PARENTS, BE CAREFUL NOT TO ACCEPT JUST ANY PREP COURSE

While I applaud test prep companies that are trying to bridge the gap between those parents who can afford to send their teens to schools with unlimited resources and those parents who cannot, I also caution parents to be aware of a crash course or poor quality prep classes. Too often, what I see being offered to students of color from poor schools is a watered-down version of the SAT or ACT prep course. On the contrary, what they really need is a program that is more comprehensive and one that is tailored to their skill sets. A thirteen-hour crash course most likely will not be able to add value for a teen coming from a poor high school with limited resources.

A class that meets twice a week for 1.5 hours each week and spans a half year in high school is one in which the student might see some change. This also assumes that the student is doing his part in class and at home.

Finally, students, parents, and educators should be expected to set reasonable goals. For example, if your teen has a 280 on his EBRW section of the SAT, it is unreasonable, in most case, for to you to expect his score to jump to 580. A more reasonable score increase might be 400. That will not get him into an Ivy League school necessarily, but with a solid GPA (3.5) and a combined SAT score of 950, EBRW 400 and Math 550, it could open a few more doors to some second- and third-tier schools.

STANDARDIZED TESTING AND STUDENTS OF COLOR

There is nothing new today about the perceptions that people in general have about standardized testing and students of color. Research has shown year after year that students of color tend not to score as high on standardized testing when compared to their white counterparts. These discussions started over thirty years ago and still exist today. Why is this?

To begin, I think the question needs to be addressed across class lines. Having worked with a variety of students across different classes, I have witnessed that my students who come from economically advantaged backgrounds score, on average, higher on the SAT than those from lower-income backgrounds. Whether I am working with an Italian from East Boston or an Irish from South Boston (before gentrification), or a black from Washington, DC, when these students came from working-class families, they all tended to score below their peers who came from more affluent communities. In the case of my Italian student from East Boston, his counterpart may live in Lexington, Massachusetts, and attend the affluent high school in that community where, on average, SAT scores place their students above the seventy-fifth percentile, or, in the case of my Irish students who lived in South Boston and whose counterpart could live in Wellesley, where the average SAT score for the Irish American in that community is higher than the average in Lexington. In Washington, students—whether black or white—attending the exam schools such as Benjamin Banneker High School or one of the private schools such as the National Cathedral School always score higher on their SAT exams compared to students from lower-income families who attend one of several local public or charter schools. The charter schools nationwide report that they are making progress in increasing poor students' test scores, but, with very few exceptions, the empirical evidence is inconclusive.

As an educator, what concerns me is not the obvious discrepancy in scores but the perceptions that people have about students who receive low scores on these tests, and more importantly, the perceptions that students hold of themselves when they receive low scores. Why? Because those perceptions impact their self-esteem, which often contributes to lower academic performance.

For the parent of color who comes from an economically advantaged background, I urge you to encourage your teen to read more and to take advantage of all of the resources available so that he can increase his scores. Many students of color who are second- and third-generation college-bound already have good scores but could do better. I have worked with them, and some have received near to perfect scores but, in general, they have not received the scores that I would have expected them to achieve, given the relatively economically privileged backgrounds from which they come.

For the parent of color who comes from an economically disadvantaged background, know that your teen can get into college with low SAT scores. Some schools do not require them—commonly referred to as Test Optional Schools— realizing that students from high-income communities are advantaged in this area, and they want to even the playing field. However, as mentioned earlier, there are programs to help your teen improve his or her scores, within reason. Earlier, I spoke to what others were doing to help you, your teen, and your family. What I want to address next here is what you can do for your teen and, by extension, what he can do for himself.

WHAT YOU CAN DO

Students who do well on the SAT READ everything all the time. Of course, they watch television and play video games, after all they are teens, and we expect them to do that, but television, computers, video games, and texting have to be limited. Your teen needs to read every day. That does not mean that he has to read a book a day, but he should be expected to read one or two articles in the newspaper or a magazine article. Hopefully your teen is one of the fortunate ones who is given homework daily that necessitates that he read two or three hours each night. Should your teen finish his homework, or if he does not have homework, you should stipulate that he complete your required reading homework. This works well with younger students, since, if the expectation of reading is not established early in their lives, it is more challenging to incorporate at later stages.

You should also take your teen to museums and art galleries. Through these experiences, he can absorb a great amount of information and vocabulary, which introduces him to new words, a great exercise for preteens. And your most powerful tool is his seeing you reading something every day. Books, newspapers, and magazines should be in the house, in the living room, bedrooms, and bathrooms. If your teen sees you reading, he is more likely to read. You can't expect your teen to read if you are not reading.

If you cannot find an SAT prep class or you cannot afford to purchase one of the SAT prep books or online programs, you do have access to the practice test booklets that your teen can obtain from his guidance counselor. Those are wonderful resources if utilized. I encourage your teen to use the test prep booklet and to do so at least fifteen minutes a day. In that way, he is becoming familiar with the test structure and with the test items that will appear on the actual exam. But you have to be deliberate about encouraging all of the above, or else your teen will not experience long-term rewards.

FEE WAIVERS

Students of color who attend under-resourced schools have the opportunity to receive not only test fee waivers but also college application fee waivers. To find out more detailed information about these services, ask your teen's school counselor or contact the College Board in New York City at (212) 713-8000 or (212) 520-8570.

EXTRACURRICULAR ACTIVITIES AND COMMUNITY INVOLVEMENT

It is probably fair to say that students will have a good chance of being admitted to the college of their choice if they can convince the college that they have the skill sets to handle the academic work and that they would be an asset to their college community. What would make them an asset?

First, they must earn good grades and make the time to prepare for and take the appropriate college entrance tests. Then, they must add another dimension to their application by demonstrating that they are a well-rounded individual. They can do that by taking advantage of extra-curricular activities, community service projects, and summer opportunities.

Most high schools offer a number of extra-curricular activities. If the high school doesn't have a club that addresses an interest of theirs, students can create one that would then show leadership skills. They should broaden their horizons by exploring the various clubs and teams at their school. Outside of the classroom, there are many organizations designed to help students prepare for college while at the same time providing them with the opportunities for internships, tutoring, mentoring, and summer enrichment experiences. Through churches, mosques, community organizations, and schools, students can find a wealth of information to help them chart their path as they prepare for college.

As your teen begins to explore and identify these various programs that might be a good fit for him, ask him to sometimes think outside of the box, step outside his comfort zone, and try something new. You may also want your teen to defy the stereotype. It is not uncommon to find students of color, particularly males, participating in basketball and football, but how often do you hear about black or Latino students participating in golf, soccer, or skiing? Think strategically when pursuing your interest. Creating a unique profile for your teen as a person of color will capture the attention of the admissions committee.

SPORTS

If your teen is talented in sports, encourage him to go ahead and participate—but don't forget to advise him to develop other extracurricular interests outside of sports since an injury can end his career abruptly and permanently. Also, remember that students of color are often expected to play sports but not necessarily expected to cultivate other interests, and you want your teen to stand out.

If your teen is thinking about participating in sports at the college level, please make sure that the family does its homework. Take a look at the academic support programs that are available for your teen at the particular colleges that are interested in your teen, and in which, hopefully, he, too, is interested. More specifically, as a parent, you should be looking at the graduation rates, especially for those of students of color. If the school offers special programs for athletes, speak to athletes of color to assess the quality of those services.

PART-TIME JOBS

Students of color from poor families, as with all students from similar backgrounds, often work part-time during high school and throughout college to either purchase items that they need or, in other cases, items that they want. There are also occasions where students work to help out their family with household expenses. While working is a respectful endeavor and serves as an extra-curricular activity, it can also be a deterrent. Working long hours can impact the GPA both in high school and in college since it takes away from study time. Students who do not have to work either in high school or in college have a great advantage over those who do. What I would recommend that you encourage your teen to do is to count the dollars and not the pennies. By working fifteen hours a week at McDonald's throughout high school, a student cannot earn enough money to pay for one year's education at most schools. However, if the student focuses on his studies, he could earn a full scholarship worth $200,000 over a four-year period. This would free up your teen from having to work during college and, in so doing, increase his chances of doing well academically. Remember to encourage your teen to count the dollars and not the pennies.

THE APPLICATION PROCESS/FINDING SCHOLARSHIPS

For many people reading this book, their teen will come from families with average incomes, and they should know that, typically, high-income families tend to pay more for their teen's education and families with modest means or low income will qualify for financial aid. Our higher educational system tries to make it possible for all to attend college if they so wish.

Still, as is true for all students, students of color need to be proactive when it comes to searching for scholarships. *The Black Student's Guide to Scholarships*, by Barry Beckham, is a good resource. The Hispanic Scholarship Fund (HSF) is the nation's leading Hispanic scholarship organization; see http://www.hsf.net. Students of color primarily interested in one of the historically black colleges may be eligible for United Negro College Fund (UNCF) merit-based scholarships. Many historically black colleges, by way of attracting the best and the brightest students of color from predominantly white institutions, are offering merit-based scholarships to students who earn high scores on the SAT and ACT. One of these schools, Howard University, even offers scholarships to National Merit Finalists. Many predominantly white colleges still offer some scholarships earmarked for students of color. Some of the best-known scholarships of this type are the Ralph Bunche Scholarship given to an African, Asian, Hispanic, or Native American student at Colby College; the Walter N. Ridley Scholarships to support African-American students at the University of Virginia (UVA); the John B. Ervin Scholars Programs for African-American Students at Washington University; and the Presidential Diversity Scholarships for all students of color at Saint Lawrence University.

Keep in mind as a student of color that you have some leverage at predominantly white schools if the institutions are deliberately trying to increase their diversity across race. Thus, if you are fortunate enough to receive a scholarship but that scholarship does not quite cover the cost and you and your family require more funds, you can call the financial aid office at that college and try to negotiate your financial aid package. You might be surprised. If the college really wants you and really needs you because of what you can bring to the class because of your racial diversity, it may be willing to offer you a better financial aid package. If you don't ask, you know what the answer will be.

PRIVATE SCHOLARSHIPS AND YOUR FINANCIAL AID PACKAGE

Many students receive monies from both the college and from private sources outside of the college. If you are a student who has done your homework, you have identified many of these private sources, submitted applications to those for which you were eligible, and if you were one of the lucky ones, you received a few of them.

Let's assume that your full year's cost of attending college is $55,000 at a private institution and that you have received the following financial aid package at that school:

Pell Grant	$3,000
SEOG	$1,000
Institutional Grant	$35,000
Stafford Loan	$2,000
Perkins Loan	$4,000
Work Study	$1,000
Parent Contribution	$9,000
Total	**$55,000**

You received a $5,000 dollar scholarship from the Coca Cola Foundation, and you received an additional scholarship of $3,000 from your local church. In most cases, these private monies will be sent directly to the school. Some colleges will say that you no longer need a $35,000 dollar grant from them since you have $8,000 in private scholarships. As a consumer of education, you are not trying to make the college rich, but you are trying to reduce your out-of-pocket cost for your education. So, what you want to do is to use those funds to either offset the parent contribution, the student loan, or both. Can you do this? Well, it depends. Some schools will let you use the funds to your advantage while other schools will not. You may also be willing to negotiate with the college whereby they may allow you to use a percentage of the funds to reduce your loan, and they will take a percentage to reduce your scholarship. Here again, if they see you as an asset as a student of color in adding diversity to their campus, you may have some leverage.

THE ADMISSIONS ESSAY

In Chapter II, you were provided with some useful hints for writing an essay that will set you apart from others. (Examples of successful college essays appear in that chapter.) The issue for some students of color is the choice of topic: some feel obligated to write about a race-related subject while others do not. If you feel that your experiences as a person of color have contributed to your personal development in some unique way and that such a topic will make for a compelling essay, then, by all means, write about a race-based topic. For example, one of my recent students, who is bi-racial, discussed the challenges he faced in growing up with a white mother and a black father. He went to a predominantly white independent school where he and his best friend, who is black, were the only persons of color in the class. Some of the white students dubbed them "one-and-a-half" because his best friend was black and he was half black. That was how their peers greeted them throughout their high school years. My client spoke of the pain he endured while in high school and how it has taken him some years to come to terms with his racial identity. His essay was honest, compelling, and quite human, and it worked.

On the other hand, I have been associated with summer enrichment programs where staff have encouraged students to write about a racial issue, and, in my mind, that was not appropriate. It is your narrative: you decide what part of it you want to share and how you want it to be shared.

Finally, if the college gives you a choice to write or not to write an essay, it is in your best interest to go ahead and write an essay. It has been said that many males of color do not like to write. That is clearly a stereotype, as I know many who love to write. But also, I have noticed that some students of color, particularly in many of the urban schools for which I consult, do not apply for scholarships or do not apply to a certain college because they are required to write an essay. If you have a choice or if it is recommended, write the essay. If there are two applicants with similar GPAs and you write an essay that arrests the attention of the admissions committee, you are in and the other applicant is not. This is an opportunity for you to tell your story. Don't forego that opportunity.

THE APPLICATION: CHECKING THE BOX

Most school applications offer you the opportunity to identify the ethnic or racial category to which you belong. Whether or not you should place a check mark in the appropriate category is a personal choice. However, if you are uncertain as to whether you can be considered a student of color from the college's point of view, as in the case where one parent is black and the other is white, you should let the admissions officer know that you are a person of color. If the school is committed to diversity—and most schools are, this could increase your chances of being admitted.

There are some black, Hispanic, and bi-racial students who have protested and refused to check the box. In my opinion, this is not to their advantage since the question is not intended for the purposes of exclusion, but rather for inclusion. Therefore, you should not take offense if asked to check a box identifying your ethnic or racial identification.

On the other hand, once enrolled in college, if you find that the institution and its environs are confining you to a box in terms of what it expects from you, then that could be a problem since it limits who you are and may not be compatible with how you view yourself. Also, be careful about putting yourself in a box and thus limiting yourself. I have known some students who put themselves in a box and that, too, can often limit the nature and the quality of your undergraduate experience.

CHOOSING THE RIGHT COLLEGE FOR YOU

Many students of color are the first in their families to attend college, while many other families have established a legacy at various institutions. Whether you fall into one of those categories or exist someplace in between, the college selection process can be intimidating, but it does not have to be.

A logical place to begin your research in finding the right college is the student guides to colleges, available at bookstores, libraries, and your counselor's office. Do not be limited to the guides specifically aimed at students of color or to the general guides since both can be useful. Viewbooks and websites showcasing colleges can be another good resource, and you might be attentive to how students of color are positioned in these visuals. Are they only seen on the athletic field, or do they appear to be integrated throughout, in photos emphasizing academics as well? Sometimes, you may see only one or two students of color in a sea of white students, and if you feel comfortable being the lone minority, then it might be a consideration if the school offers an academic program and other characteristics in which you have an interest. Only you can define what diversity means to you and how much diversity— if any—you need. Remember, choosing the right college is one of the most important decisions of your life, and you need to equip yourself with as much information as possible.

THE CAMPUS VISIT: SEEING IS BELIEVING

After your teen has perused the college guides and picked several schools that he thinks offer what he is looking for, I would suggest that the family schedule on-campus visits. Don't despair if you feel that the travel expenses are prohibitive. Many colleges have visitation programs earmarked for families with limited financial means. Some colleges schedule visits to their campus for prospective students before the application process, while others invite prospective students upon acceptance. Students should contact the admissions office of the schools in which they have an interest to find out about these visitation programs, generally referred to as Fly-Ins. If the college doesn't have one, it may put you in touch with one of its students of color from your area, or even your teen's school can serve as a resource and may invite your teen as its guest for a visit. Another option for you is to contact the alumni association and to ask for names of individuals who live in your community. These contacts can also serve as helpful resources for you and your teen.

Campus visits are extremely important, especially when there is a stark contrast between your home surroundings and the college setting.

Consider the following scenarios:

- Is your teen a black student from a white upscale suburban neighborhood, attending a predominantly white public high school and planning on attending a historically black college in an urban area?

- Is your teen a Hispanic student from the South Bronx, attending a predominantly white boarding school in New England, and considering a competitive Midwestern university on the south side of Chicago in an upper-middle-class black neighborhood?

- Is your teen a black student from an urban black East Coast community, attending a predominantly black high school, considering a predominantly white college in a suburban community on the West Coast?

Do you think your teen can identify with any of the aforementioned students? If not, it might be a good exercise for you and your teen to sit and think about how he would identify himself in relationship to the types of colleges he is considering. There are a host of questions on which your teen needs to reflect. These are some examples:

- As a student of color at a predominantly white university, would you be prepared to have your intellectual competency challenged?

- Are you willing to be expected not to know much about Physics but to be expected to know everything about African-American history?

● Is it important for you to see yourself reflected in the faculty, administration, and student body?

● Some students report that they will feel comfortable with ten percent minority students, while others are indifferent and feel that they can be successful independent of the numbers of minorities. Others want more representation of students of color and a diverse faculty. What would make you feel comfortable?

● With respect to the curriculum, is it important for you to see the intellectual voices of people of color represented across the curriculum, or is it sufficient for you to have them represented only within the confines of the African Studies or Latino Studies Department? At institutions where students of color feel more comfortable, the contributions of people of color are taught throughout many disciplines and, at certain colleges, some of these contributions are not simply accessible to all but required by all of the students.

While your teen is visiting these campuses, he needs to find out about the attrition rates for students in general. He should then ask what the attrition rate is for students of color. That provides some indication of how successful students of color are at that particular institution.

Statistics at all schools, black colleges and predominantly white ones, can be misleading. A predominantly white college could have a high retention rate for students of color, but that does not necessarily mean that the students are happy with that college. Dig deeper because looks can be deceiving. Some students will remain at an institution for the wrong reasons: a boyfriend or girlfriend wants them to stay, or parents who are overly impressed with an Ivy League school may want their teen to stay because they want to say that their child graduated from an Ivy. This mismatch can be a problem, especially if the student is unhappy. A four-year stint in an unpleasant environment could translate into other problems such as alcoholism and drug abuse resulting from depression or feelings of powerlessness because of an overbearing parent. Make sure that you are not this kind of parent.

Encourage your teen to engage random students in unfiltered conversation so that he can learn more about the experiences of students who are not the work study students working for the Admissions Office. These students can provide more objective feedback and offer a viewpoint beyond statistics in a guidebook.

Also, seek out organizations such as the school's black or Hispanic alumni association. Groups like these can yield a wealth of information about how students of color feel about their campus life. You will find that students report that these Black Houses or Latino Houses provide them with a sense of community while also offering them a safe space to which they can retreat when necessary. From the perspective of the college's graduates, if a student has had a positive experience at his institution, he generally is going to be an active alumnus. Students of color who are active in the alumni associations are a good marker for the quality of their undergraduate experience at their alma matter. If they had a good experience, they will want to stay connected and contribute so that future generations of students will have the same, if not a better, experience.

On-campus conversations should also include a discussion about the school's financial aid policies and procedures. Pay attention to the details of the financial aid process, and, most importantly, make sure that you meet all of the deadlines. If the forms are completed correctly but sent late, your teen will be put at a disadvantage. If the forms are sent in on time but completed incorrectly, they will be returned for correction. Hence, you lose time. The bottom line: financial aid is very time sensitive. The forms must be completed accurately, on time, the first time.

Many students of color and their families are reluctant to take out loans for their education. Don't be reluctant to encourage your teen to finance his education with loans because this is a major investment in his future. I would recommend that you opt for the subsidized loans, where the federal government pays for the interest while the student is in college. The student will not have to begin repaying the loan until six months after she or he graduates. If a student decides to go to graduate school, he can defer the loan payments. If he is in the field of education and chooses to work in an economically disadvantaged community, he will be exempt from some, if not all, of the loan debt. In any case, the student will have ten years to pay off the loan, and the average income of a college graduate will be sufficient enough to meet that obligation if she or he budgets well.

If, as a parent, you are not pleased with the financial aid package awarded by the school, let the school know and try to negotiate a better package. Remember, your family has a voice in this process. It is not bad etiquette to negotiate a better financial aid package for your family. If your teen is not satisfied with all of the arrangements of the package, go to the office prepared to argue your position. You may also need to bring supporting documentation, but be willing to negotiate. You may not get all that you want, but you may end up with something closer to what you desired. I cannot say this enough. If you don't ask, you know what the answer is going to be.

THE ADMISSIONS INTERVIEW

Students who present themselves with confidence and poise are most likely to succeed in interviews. Some students worry about being asked about their ethnicity or race in the admissions interview, but this should not be a cause of concern. Usually, they will not be asked such a question unless there is something unique about their background. For example, an applicant's father could be African-American and his mother may be Japanese, and he may have lived the first seven years of his life in Japan. Moreover, his parents made certain that he was fluent in Japanese as well. If asked about his background, in this case, he should respond with confidence and let the admissions officer know that he is proud of his background and that the culmination of who he is has enabled him to identify with a broader range of people. If the interviewer does not raise the topic of your bi-racial status, your teen might consider doing so if it seems appropriate within the context of the conversation.

In general, though, issues of race and ethnicity would be more appropriate to discuss with other people on campus. Admissions officers are there to sell the school. So, bringing up potentially uncomfortable issues might backfire. Students, faculty, and administrators of color would be more likely to talk about these issues more candidly. Discussing race-based issues with white students, in addition, can also provide you with an interesting perspective.

HISTORICALLY BLACK COLLEGES AND UNIVERSITIES (HBCUS)

The decision to attend a Historically Black College or University—these schools are often referred to as HBCUs—is highly personal. These schools are naturally very attractive for black students who want to experience their education within a community with which they can most identify with the environs and the environment. They are sometimes very attractive for Hispanic students or bi-racial students who identify with black culture. And more and more, I am finding that white students are attending black colleges on the undergraduate level. They have historically attended their professional schools, i.e., Schools of Medicine, Law, and Dentistry.

Even if your teen is sure that he can excel at a predominantly white college, he might be better served at an HBCU if he feels that he does not have a strong sense of his racial identity. Or, he may have attended an all-white high school in a wealthy suburb and come from a family where the parents introduced him to knowledge to develop and enhance his racial identity, but the student may elect to go to a black college simply because he wanted to experience something new. On the other hand, as in the above examples, for a student who also has a strong racial identity but attended a poor school with limited resources and thus has a weak educational foundation, a less selective HBCU might be better choice, assuming that the student wants to attend a four-year college rather than a two-year community college. Since many historically black colleges have always had a mission to serve the under-served, their admissions standards are not as competitive as some white colleges, meaning the student would have a better chance of being admitted. And because many HBCUs market themselves as small and nurturing, the students could be better served academically.

If a student has problems with self-esteem and is not a strong student academically, an HBCU is definitely a good option. Here, he can improve his academic skills and enhance his feelings of self-worth and pride.

BLACK STUDENTS AT WHITE SCHOOLS: A BIT OF HISTORY

The black student on the white campus is a byproduct of the revolution that erupted in the 1960s. Prior to the sixties, on campuses such as at Penn, Bates, Cornell, MIT, and Dartmouth, one could see a few black faces, but they tended to be superstars. Amherst took a few blacks from the most prestigious families in the country as did schools such as Williams, Hamilton, Carleton, and Franklin Marshall, and a few others saw to it that a black presence continued in earnest.

However, something historical happened in February in 1960. Four students from North Carolina A&T University in Greensboro staged their historical sit-in at the Woolworth's food counter. The outcome was the dismantling of the legal basis for discrimination in public accommodations. Their actions and those of Rosa Parks—she refused to sit at the back of a bus—in Montgomery, Alabama, stand as two decisive events that changed America. Their actions emboldened the black educated classes and spearheaded a national movement that came to be called the Civil Rights Movement. It was natural, then, that the revolution of the sixties would eventually settle the role of the university and access in education.

Two very decisive events motivated administrators at white colleges to open their doors more earnestly to the presence of black students: the assassination of Martin Luther King, Jr., on April 4, 1968, and, three months later in June, the assassination of Robert F. Kennedy. As a consequence, one finds in the late sixties through the mid-seventies an increased presence of students of color in predominantly white colleges and universities. When they arrived in larger numbers, however, the administration, faculty, and student body did not always welcome them alike. In some cases, they were resented, feared, and avoided. It could be argued that they were misunderstood. In fact, it wasn't long after they arrived in larger numbers that the white administrators felt compelled to recruit black faculty and administrators from HBCUs to help them manage the presence of black students on white campuses. Of course, I could share with you many horror stories, but suffice it to say that the situation today for students is much improved when compared to that of the late sixties and early seventies.

Unfortunately, one still finds racial tension on many of the predominantly white college campuses today, and thus the lessons of history have not yielded much in terms of progress.

However, it would be unfair to say that no progress has been made. We witnessed Tim Wolfe's resignation as President of the University of Missouri's system. He resigned on November 9, 2014, after a series of campus demonstrations protesting his lack of appropriate actions regarding incidents of racism on the campus of the University of Missouri at Columbia. That historical moment not only emboldened black students at the University of Missouri, it did so for many black students on white college campuses nationwide.

And while race matters, some schools are improving, but not too much has changed at many. On November 29, 2015 a black student at Lewis and Clark College in Portland, Oregon, says he was beaten by white students yelling racial slurs. I, Too, Am Harvard revealed that black students at Harvard felt routinely mis-recognized and subjected to micro-aggressions that sometimes characterized them as having lower intelligence. These are simply a few examples of how race matters persist today.

CHOOSING A PREDOMINANTLY WHITE SCHOOL

Of course, there are many circumstances where a predominantly white school may be a logical choice for your teen, when, for example, her or his major course of study is found there. This is perfectly fine if your teen has the academic foundation to do well at these schools and if the school is open to the presence of students of color. Measuring that openness, however, can be difficult.

Here are some questions to investigate when considering a predominantly white school:

- Are faculty of color represented across all academic disciplines, or are they limited to those in the areas of ethnic studies?

- Are persons of color represented across all levels of the administration, or are they relegated to lower-level administrative and staff positions?

- Are students of color generally happy there?

- Are students of color participating in all levels of the undergraduate experience?

- Does the university have a strong African-American and Hispanic-American alumni association?

- Does the university address issues of race matters openly and fairly?

- Does the university discuss proactively issues of race, e.g., during freshmen orientation, or does it simply react to racial issues when they emerge?

- Does the university provide diversity training for faculty, staff, and students?

- What are the graduation rates of students of color in relationship to white students?

- Does the university offer any special incentives for students of color during the recruitment process?

- How do attrition and graduation rates compare between students of color and white students?

- Does the school offer raced-based scholarships? Are students of color generally pleased with their financial aid packages?

- What is the quality of life for students of color on campus?

- Is there an office to address the needs of multi-cultural students? What is its staffing and funding allocation? Where is it physically positioned, and how much influence does it have?

- How many tenured faculty of color does the university have?

- How are athletes of color treated in the academic setting? Do they feel respected? Are they assumed to be intellectually incompetent simply because they are athletes of color?

To answer these questions, your teen should speak to faculty, administrators, and students from all racial backgrounds, and when speaking to students, make sure your teen asks questions of both first-year and upper-class students.

THE ADVANTAGES AND DISADVANTAGES OF HBCU'S

Advantages

- They provide another option, just as women's colleges provide another option for females.

- They have a dedicated faculty who have the credentials to teach anywhere in the world, but they have elected to work at a college where they can make a difference in many black students' lives. While some work at Morehouse, Spelman, and Howard, to name a few of the most competitive black schools, others want to work at some of the lesser-known black schools that admit students who are faced with academic challenges and thus require more from this committed faculty once enrolled in higher education.

- Students can see themselves reflected throughout the institution. This can make them feel more comfortable, and, thus, they will be more likely to take advantage of the opportunities available to them, making for a more complete undergraduate experience.

- They provide academically marginal students access into a higher educational opportunity.

- When recruiters are looking for students of color, they tend to go to colleges where they exist in larger numbers, i.e., HBCUs.

- There tends to more diversity among the faculty: this is particularly the case at the larger schools, e.g., Howard University.

- They tend not to cost as much, and, sometimes, they do offer good financial aid packages.

- The social life on campus is informed by black cultural traditions of black culture, and one does not have to compete with white organizations for visibility since it is an all-black school.

- Students are more likely to be exposed to mentors who come from a similar background and who have had the same experience since many faculty and administrators working at HBCUs themselves went to HBCUs.

- Students can more often see themselves reflected in the faculty, and the faculty can more often see themselves reflected in the students.

Disadvantages

- They can be more conservative, particularly socially. For example, some black schools are not as open to gay and lesbian student organizations.

- Many of the dorms are still segregated across gender.

- Some black colleges still have curfews.

- They sometimes do not offer strong financial aid packages.

- The student body is more homogeneous, i.e., most of the students are all black or at the Hispanic-serving institutions, mostly Hispanic.

- They sometimes don't offer the elaborate facilities of many white colleges.

As your teen is thinking about whether a white, black, or Hispanic-serving institution is best for him, remember that our American higher education system offers a mosaic of opportunities ranging from black to white colleges, as well as women's to Jewish colleges, and it is okay to attend a school that is all black or predominantly Hispanic. Your teen should not be forced to go to one or the other, but rather to the one where he feels he will be most comfortable. Parents, respect your teen's decision and, as a consumer, advise him not to be pigeonholed into attending a black school because someone in your family swears by it, or into attending a white school because someone in your family has been ill-informed about the quality of an education at a black school versus one at a white one. Unfortunately, still today, black schools are informed by a historical legacy that they are all inferior. Furthermore, whenever one has a problem, that problem is generalized to all of them unfairly. Like white schools, black colleges represent the same range of competence and incompetence as institutions at large. All have their value for the right student.

As an informed consumer, then, your goal is to know everything about the product that your teen will ultimately choose. I am sure that your teen has had the experience of buying an electronic gadget such as an iPod, digital camera, or a Smart Phone. He may have even read consumer magazines and talked to his friends about the experiences they had with the brands and the models they choose. Perhaps he even compared the warranties and service plans offered by different stores and surfed the Internet to get more detailed information. Essentially, choosing a college involves the same process; though, this time the product is a four-year college education. Your family wants to gather as much information as possible about schools so that your teen can make informed decisions about where to apply and eventually where to enroll.

When senior year rolls around, your teen will be inundated with college applications and other materials from the schools that he has judged as possible matches. Hopefully, as parents, you will not have to exercise your veto power because the schools that are being considered are ones that you feel are also a good fit, knowing what you know about your teen.

Whether your teen is choosing a predominantly white school or a school where he will be in the majority, in the final analysis, he must have clarity of purpose about what he expects to gain from a college education. While parents have to be appropriately engaged, so, too, do counselors and teachers. Students should have their counselors and/or teachers look over their applications and essays. By this stage, preferably, your teen has visited the campuses of the colleges to which he is applying—or at least talked with a representative of the school about campus life. While I know applying to college can be overwhelming, it can also be fun. Try to enjoy the ride. Millions of other students have gone through the process and have not only survived but prospered. You can, too.

● ● ● ●

As a minority college student who attends (and who has always attended) a predominately Caucasian institution, I would say that one of the most difficult things for me has been coping with the notion that the very system I yearn to place my faith in harbors some deeply rooted biases. It is not so much the blatant acts of racism as it is the faint undercurrent of prejudice that seems to haunt this country's social structures and which is echoed by disparities across various demographics. I sometimes wonder if I am just imagining it. Most of the time, I can happily ignore racial differences between others and myself and immerse myself in my studies. Still, occasionally, there are times when I am harshly reminded of them. One minor incident (which I do not consider overt racism) that comes to mind is when I was taking my seat before a math lecture and overheard a white student criticizing the university's initiatives to support minority involvement in the Engineering program (and did all I could to remain seated without turning around and firing up a debate with a complete stranger). And, of course, every now and again, one of my white friends describes to me the tasteless remarks blurted out by another white student under the mistaken assumption that openly racist remarks will not elicit scorn so long as no people of color are present to hear them.

The unfortunate truth is that even in a supposedly progressive environment such as a college campus, these things are certainly bound to happen, and it would be naive to assume otherwise. Incidents such as these suggest to me that there remain some very large gaps in understanding between whites and minorities; namely, that different situations will often be interpreted very differently according to the race of the observer. The scary part about that is the possibility that these sorts of misunderstandings are irreconcilable. For example, judging from my own experience and understanding how the early social environment can have a significant influence on a person's success, I can appreciate the necessity for efforts to involve minorities in various academic fields in which they are underrepresented.

But, by no means can I expect that those who lack my experience and perspective as a minority will share my understanding, particularly since we Americans are all raised to believe that we all single-handedly pave our own roads to success. I as much as anyone would like to believe that each of us has a more or less equal shot, and I approach everything that I do with this conviction. However, when events such as those I described are more or less commonplace, and when it is ordinary for me to walk through the halls of the Physics building and not see more than one or two Black students on any given day of the week, I cannot help but wonder if, somehow, the cards are still stacked against us in ways that are not easily articulated.

—Patrick Jefferson

RESOURCES

Beckham, B. (1996). *The black student's guide to scholarships, revised edition: 600+ private money sources for black and minority students.* Lanham, MD: Madison Books.

Black, I. (2000). *African American student's college guide: Your one-stop resource for choosing the right college, getting in, and paying the bill.* Hoboken, NJ: Wiley.

Hispanic Scholarship Fund: http://www.hsf.net

Lee, D. (2007). *The 2007-2009 African American scholarship guide for students & parents.* Phoenix, AZ: Amber Books.

Walker, S. (2007). *The black girl's guide to college success: What no one really tells you about college that you must know.* Bloomington, IN: AuthorHouse.

THE FIRST-GENERATION COLLEGE-BOUND STUDENT

We all looked alike, but we were not all alike. More often, I was able to pretend to be something I wasn't. I was the invisible minority. Of course, I was ashamed of this deception, but I wanted to affiliate with students from affluent backgrounds, and to the extent that I could, I did. I can recall one specific occasion when I was unable to join my friends on a visit to the Caribbean during spring break, where they would spend more money in a week than my father earned in three months. Frankly, I could not afford to go. I told them that my mother was ill and that I would be going home. This duplicity, denial, and shame lived with me throughout my years at college where, because I was white and at a selective school, I was presumed to be at least middle class. The reality was, I was poor and ashamed of who I was, and it was not until years after I graduated from college that I was able to measure my success through my own eyes and not through the eyes of those friends who came from different places, places that positioned them as third- and fourth-generation college students.

—Anonymous

THIS IS THE VOICE OF an Italian-American female who went to an all-women's college and was the first in her family to attend college. Having graduated in 1989 at the top of her class from an urban high school in a working-class community, she was admitted to Wellesley College, a prestigious college in New England established historically for women who came from privileged backgrounds and whose families wanted them to receive a first-class education. In the late sixties and early seventies, like many of the selective institutions of its kind, Wellesley began in earnest to diversify its student body, thereby including not only more students of color but also more students of economically disadvantaged communities.

Throughout my years in education, I have had the opportunity and the honor of working with hundreds of students who were first in their families to attend and graduate from college. Their experience is at once similar and different from those of others. In fact, I was inspired to include this chapter as part of the book because of the similarities but mostly because of the differences.

First-generation college-bound students are likely to attend high schools that lack adequate resources. They also tend to come from families that are economically disadvantaged. These families rarely have individuals who can assist the student with the transition to, through, or beyond college. Moreover, these students tend to lack the resources in their communities to assist them as they enter graduate or professional school or the workplace. The world from home to the world of college and these other places is often quite different, but in these new places—college and beyond—all students are expected to adapt and excel. Learning how to negotiate these new environments presents significant and sometimes debilitating challenges, especially when there are no mentors or peers to guide them.

"First" students are not just different from those with a legacy of college graduates; their experiences are also different from other first-generation college-bound students. Some have difficulty negotiating class identity issues, while others have difficulty negotiating class and race identity. Others have problems when they return home and try to relate to members of their family and/or community. Some may even face hostility and jealousy from members of their community and from the friends they once knew. Then, there are those who choose for sometimes the right and sometimes the wrong reasons not to be identified with their community even though they are welcomed at home. Finally, there are those who face additional challenges because English is their second language. These are just a few examples of the many obstacles facing the first-generation college-bound.

It is my hope that parents whose children will be first in the family to attend college, as well as others who work with these families, will be better advised on how to assist these young people through the process of preparing for, applying to, and getting through college. Clearly, the entire book aspires to achieve that goal, but many families who are reading this book will not be first generation. They will come from backgrounds where they are empowered and thus can manage this process with more self-confidence. Too often, families who are first generation are managed by other peoples, policies, programs, and goals. What they will be able to do after reading this chapter and, hopefully, the whole book is to manage this process with greater confidence and determination.

A MESSAGE TO THE FIRST-GENERATION COLLEGE-BOUND STUDENT

You can do it. Do not let anyone tell you that you can't. This chapter will let your parents and support team know how. As you probably already know, a college degree is a basic instrument on the road to career success and achievement. Obtaining that degree has become increasingly competitive and expensive. You don't have to worry too much about cost, but you do have to concern yourself with academic performance in college-preparatory classes. If you perform well, you will be rewarded both financially and academically. Colleges will give you money if you qualify, and most first-generation college-bound students do.

An advantage of a college education is that it can enhance the quality of your life. You will meet friends who will remain your friends for a lifetime. You may even meet your future partner. You may find your first job as a result of a recommendation from a professor or a referral from your college's career placement center. I hope I have convinced you of many of the challenges you will face in college while also articulating some of the rewards. What follows in this section are some topic areas that you and your family should address to make all of you more empowered throughout the process.

There are many courses to think about, tests to take, applications to complete, and deadlines to meet before gaining admissions into those (what some call) "hallowed halls of academia." The application process alone can be an overwhelming experience if you are "first," and that is why you have to plan.

Your performance prior to high school will determine the courses you can take in high school and how you will perform in those courses. How you perform in high school will inform what colleges you will be able to attend, the money you will receive, and how you will excel once enrolled in college. If you have not performed as well as you might have, do not be discouraged, as you have the option of attending a community college for two years and then transferring to a four-year college.

If you are a parent or guardian and have never been to college, I would encourage you to consider the following: planning, picking, packaging, presenting, paying, persisting, and profiting. These seven words are very important in planning for, applying to, and getting through college. That they have come up in different formats throughout the book is not by error. It has been deliberate because of their importance, but, here, they take on special significance because first-generation college-bound youth and their parents do not have a history to rely on with respect to this mission.

PLANNING

From the moment that teenagers enter high school, they should think of themselves as an asset, and they should develop a plan to make that asset more desirable (See "College Applicant Profile," Appendix B). The way they do so is by taking advantage of all that the school has to offer. Do not worry if the school has limited resources and thus cannot offer much, but take advantage of what it does offer. When applying to college, a student will not be held accountable for what a school does not offer, but she will be at a disadvantage if she is perceived as a student who does not take advantage of opportunities.

With respect to courses, students should think about taking at least five academic classes times four years: four years of English, Math, Science, History, and Foreign Language. Those are the five solid academic areas in which colleges have an interest. Colleges also like to see students challenge themselves, and if the student is in a high school that offers Honors and Advanced Placement classes, she should be encouraged to embrace the challenge. This will only strengthen her academic foundation and make her more marketable once she applies to college. Whether taking regular college preparatory or advanced courses, if she is in the appropriate classes all four years and does well, she will be viewed as an asset to any college and will be rewarded in many ways.

As part of the plan, the student will be expected to sit for several test administrations: the PSAT, the practice test for the SAT; and the PLAN, which is the practice test for the ACT. Colleges do not require the PSAT or the PLAN. They do require that students submit either the SAT or the ACT.

Families that have the economic means will hire a private academic coach to help students prepare for these tests. Too often, first-generation college-bound students come from homes that do not have the resources for these services. Here is a case where families can contact the companies directly and inquire about financial aid options. Parents can also speak to the school counselor to determine if the counselor might know of some private funding.

What is encouraging is that some schools do not require test scores, or they make them optional. Other schools will use them but will also rely on other areas of a student's application to determine if the student would be successful at a college. Whether the scores are required or not, it is in the best interest of the student to do well in those college-preparatory classes. The tests show what the high school student can accomplish in three-and-a-half hours, while the grades are an indication of what they have achieved over four years. Scores alone are not a true marker of success in college; having a solid grade-point average (3.0+ over a 4.0 scale) in a challenging curriculum alone can be a better indication of college success.

Your teen should take the lead over areas where she has more control. She has more control over the grade-point average than over the SAT or ACT score. This is not to say that your teen should not do what she can to prepare for and do well on the test. On the contrary, she should prepare for it and take it seriously. However, I do not want parents or their teens to feel discouraged if their children have challenges with the SAT and ACT. It does not mean that they cannot go to college. Nor does it mean, if they score below average when compared to the scores at the college they plan to attend, that they will not excel. There simply may be other factors in their application that suggest they could excel, and most often, those other factors have to do with the strength of their academic record.

SUPPORT FROM HOME FOR ACADEMICS

If you want your teen to be seen as an asset by colleges, as a parent you have to lay the groundwork at home for that to happen. That can be done in several ways, but, in general, you have to provide your love and support constantly by being there for him or her. By setting a routine and a safe place to study at home, parents are encouraging academic engagement at home.

Students need a quiet place to study, and they should be expected to work on school-related assignments every night before a school day. If a student does not have homework, she should be expected to read ahead and/or to review past assignments in preparation for future tests. This is called studying. Too often, teens do not know the difference between homework and study. Once the assignment has been completed, then the review of the material begins. Three hours a night, combining homework and study, is not unreasonable for teens today. Some teens who attend competitive high schools have five hours a night of academic work.

If you expect your teen to excel academically, you have to monitor homework/study, and you have to be engaged in the school on a regular basis. In that way, you are not just telling her that education is important; you are showing her, while at the same time, helping her become an asset.

NON-ACADEMIC FACTORS

As you continue to think about how your teen can become an asset in high school and subsequently to a college, encourage her to become involved in extra-curricular activities both in and out of school. You can support those interests, in some cases financially. It is important to note, however, that your tax dollars pay for your child's public school education, and some of those funds provide resources for after-school activities. Money aside, as parents you know that the real support does not come in the form of dollars but, rather, in the form of emotional support. You can show that by simply showing up. If you are going to encourage your teen to play sports or to participate in a school play, it is important for you to attend the sport events and/or the performances.

COMMUNITY-BASED ORGANIZATIONS

More and more today, community-based organizations are also providing college access programs to assist parents and their college-bound teens. These programs are not new; there are just more of them. In fact, Upward Bound Programs, which were spearheaded by the Lyndon B. Johnson Administration in 1963, still exist today to prepare first-generation college-bound students from rural and urban areas to gain access to higher education. Upward Bound and similar programs are a good resource for parents and students if they find that the resources at the high schools are limited. The quality of these programs varies, so, parents should do their homework by speaking with other parents whose teens may currently or formerly have been in the program. A good litmus test would be the longevity of the program, its funding stream, and its placement rates of students in selective schools. Also, parents must make sure, when possible, that the counselors in the college access programs outside of the formal school setting are working in collaboration with the teen's guidance or school counselor. Everyone should be on the same page. Working at cross-purposes can put your teen at a disadvantage.

COUNT THE DOLLARS, NOT THE PENNIES

First-generation college-bound students tend to work not only in high school but also during their college years, and this sometimes puts them at yet another disadvantage. I recognize that some parents encourage their teens to work because they either need the financial help or they need their teens to not have to depend on the parents as much. Working is good for all the obvious reasons, but too much work can detract from a student's education.

From a planning perspective, your teen should be focusing on her education so that she can save you and the family some dollars in the long run. If your teen is working 20 hours a week or more and her GPA drops from a 3.5 to a 2.8, she is not going to be able to position herself for a selective college that could offer her a full scholarship. Twenty hours a week at $7 an hour equals $560 a month before taxes. In a year, your teen can earn $6,720 gross, and in four years, she will have earned $26,880. Even if she saved all of the money, and of course she won't, she would still not have enough money to cover the average cost of a four-year college education at a public school, $80,000, or at many private colleges, $240,000. However, if you encouraged your teen to study more and to work less, she could graduate with a GPA that could guarantee admission to a selective school which would offer her a need-based financial aid package as much as $240,000 or more, and at some schools, it could be a free ride.

SUMMER ENRICHMENT

For students who are first in their families to go to college, attending a summer program, particularly on a college campus, can be rewarding in so many ways. Apart from being away from home alone perhaps for the first time and developing some independence before actually enrolling in college, it may be the first time that these students will face what is called academic rigor. Having these kinds of experiences prior to college enrollment is vital. It allows them to experience academic rigor that provides insight into what they can expect from college. It also allows them to develop some independence. Finally, because of the work ethic developed in the summer program, students excel at a higher standard than they did prior to the summer enrichment experience.

Ideally, students are better served if they participate in a summer program earlier rather than later in high school. These programs not only provide leverage for the students once they return to high school, but these programs also increase their chances of excelling once enrolled in college. Parents can learn about these programs through school counselors or by contacting an administrator at the program directly. Also, some boarding schools, high schools where students live throughout the school year, offer summer enrichment programs for high school kids.

EARLY FINANCIAL AID RESEARCH

As a parent, you should not wait until the last minute to think about how your child's education will be paid for. In this case, the last minute is definitely too late. As a parent whose teen is first-generation, you probably don't have a great deal of disposable income, and if this is the case, I would advise that you meet with your teen's counselor early in high school to determine what private scholarships are available. In that way, not only will you know what is available, but you will also know what your teen has to achieve to compete for those scholarships before she is a senior.

PICKING

Picking, commonly known as the "college search" in the circles of guidance counselors and college advisors, is one of the most important assignments of your teen's young career, and as such, it should not be taken lightly. Up until now, you facilitated your teen's learning by laying a foundation which has provided her with the skill sets and resources necessary to engage the college application process. The first part of that process is researching a list of schools that inform by their academic profile what an applicant should bring to the table combined with the characteristics a student is looking for in a college.

In most cases, you can either depend on the school counselor or the college access provider outside of the school; and if you are fortunate, you can use both as a resource. But, let's assume that you are one of the rare parents who does not have access to either one. Then, your best resource is to contact your local college directly. More and more colleges are reaching out into communities, helping families prepare their teens for college and also making the application process more transparent. In short, many college admissions officers would welcome your visit or would come to your teen's school and answer any of your questions about the process. As a parent, you have the right to this information. So, pick up the phone or go visit your local college.

Before calling or visiting one college or several colleges, you and your teen may want to sit down and focus your college search by asking two important questions: what do I bring to a college and what do I want in a college? Teenagers can answer the first question by reviewing their transcript, test scores, involvement in their in- and/or out-of-school activities, leadership, and summer programs. The second question takes into consideration factors like majors offered, if they have decided on one (they do not have to declare a major until the end of the second year of college), location, and size of school. Some students prefer urban over rural settings, while others have no preference. Religious-affiliated schools are a plus for some while a turn-off for others. As a parent, hopefully, you will not have to veto your teen's decision though you may know her better than she knows herself. Ideally, you should let your teen make the choice of what type of schools to which she chooses to apply and ultimately where she decides to enroll.

PACKAGING AND PRESENTING

In the fall of the senior year, students will be inundated with the college application and financial aid process. They will have to attend college fairs, complete applications, write essays, go for interviews, submit recommendations from teachers and sometimes counselors, prepare for and go for auditions (for performing art students), present portfolios (for visual art students), and register for the NCAA Clearing House (for athletes applying to DI, DIAA, or DII programs).

When completing the application, students should pay attention to the presentation of the application, i.e., it should be well organized and void of grammar or spelling errors. Whether interviewing or auditioning, presenting a portfolio or an athletic tape, students have to be very deliberate about the way the contents are packaged and be mindful of their presentation. Also, they must be aware of how they present themselves not only in formal interviews but also in informal ones as well; for example, at college fairs when they are speaking with admissions officers or at their schools when admissions representatives come to visit. Students should know that they are giving an impression in these situations, and they should present themselves in the best light. Certainly, at a college fair they do not have to be in a suit and tie, but they should be dressed appropriately. Jeans and sneakers are okay at a fair, but a dress shirt and slacks and shoes are more appropriate for a formal interview.

PAYING: FINANCIAL AID

The financial aid process can be daunting for many parents, and not just for those who have teens who are first-generation college-bound. But the key here is for parents to pay their taxes, to do so on time, and to use the resources available to them.

Much of the information on the parents' tax forms will be similar and, in some cases, is the same as the information that is asked of the parent/s and the teen on the standard financial aid form that all schools require. This form is called the Free Application for Federal Student Aid (FAFSA). (See Chapter 7, "Financial Aid," for more details on the FAFSA.)

It is important to keep in mind that financial aid is very time sensitive. Students and their parents must complete the form on time and make sure that it is completed correctly the first time. Counselors at schools, college access providers, and college information centers in libraries in some of the urban centers in this country will be resources for families. Families can also call the financial aid office at one of the colleges to which the teen is applying and they can assist by answering questions about the form.

Beyond understanding the mechanics of completing the form and finding the right resource to help facilitate that goal, parents of first-generation college-bound students tend to have problems in three vital areas that hinder this process. Sometimes, they are unaware of how to navigate the system. They do not know that they can and should negotiate the financial aid package if the college does not provide enough funds. They may also not know that they can reduce the cost of college if their teen becomes an asset to the college and can then obtain a Resident Advisors position (upper classmen live in one of the freshmen dorms and serve as advisors to first-year students and sometimes second-years, too), which could provide them with free room or board or both. Other schools offer stipends in lieu of free room and board while some offer all three. Knowing about these resources can help students reduce the cost of their education. However, they first have to know that these resources exist and, secondly, how to navigate the system so that they can access these services or at least be in a marketable position to be considered.

Some parents do not trust the system because they are being asked a number of personal questions about their finances when the correct answers to these questions can only benefit their teen in the long run. Most parents who do not have a college education are not making a great deal of money; therefore, they will qualify for need-based financial aid. They have to trust that the system can and does work in their favor. In fact, if their teen is an asset and the family is poor, in this case, the family could end up paying less than a thousand dollars a year for a college with a price tag of $70,000 a year.

A third concern is the problem with loans. These parents often are afraid to take out loans and, by extension, their teens do not want to take out loans. On the other hand, some of these families have no problem with taking out a loan for a new car. The cost of a four-year education is more important than the cost of a car, which in almost all cases will begin to depreciate as soon as it is driven off the lot. The investment in a college education can only appreciate in its value over a lifetime.

PERSISTING ONCE IN COLLEGE

Parents know that simply getting into college for some teens is achieving a major milestone. The teen may have even been the first in her family to graduate from high school and now she is about to go off to college. While getting in is achieving one milestone, getting through is achieving another. This is particularly the case for first-generation college-bound students since they have few people, if anyone, to turn to assist them with this next important phase of their lives. The good news is that, unlike in some high schools, resources on most college campuses abound. What is important to know is how to access those resources and how to leverage them to assure success.

It is also important to note that some colleges have parent resource offices where parents can call to advocate on behalf of their teens. All colleges have student resource centers for a variety of issues, and some may even have offices that address the needs of first-generation college students specifically. Parents need to learn quickly what the resources are and how their teen can access them before a problem occurs; in other words, the accent should be on proactive and not reactive strategies. For example, if your teen has a roommate problem, and you don't have the resources to move her off campus, then what are the options on campus? Or, your teen could be depressed around the holiday season or spring break because you do not have the money to bring her home. Parents need to determine what college resources are available to assist students who may not be able to come home for all holidays throughout the year.

WORKING IN COLLEGE

It has already been noted that, in high school, first-generation college-bound students tend to have to or want to work. Unfortunately, the same phenomenon exists at the college level. While teenagers may be offered work-study as part of their financial aid package for the first year, I would advise that they not accept it. It is better for them to focus on their academics so that they can start out with a strong GPA. As they become familiar with college and accomplish success in their transition year, it may be more appropriate to consider a work-study job. On-campus work-study jobs may pay less than off-campus jobs, but on-campus ones are more accessible and more flexible since the employer respects the fact that the employee is a student first.

Paid internships are also recommended during the upper-class years of college since they could lead to a summer job and/or a full-time job in the student's major after college. However, keep in mind to advise your teen to be deliberate about time management and not to lose focus on the real reason why she is in college. Hopefully, your teen is one of those students who received a financial aid package that allows her the time and freedom to focus exclusively on her studies; but if your teen is not, urge her to work two jobs during the summer and save as much as she can so that she won't have to depend on working so many hours upon returning to college.

It is also important to note that these students sometimes can have a limited social life on campus because they are working so much. Thus, not only can the academic life of first-generation college students be affected. Their social life can be impacted as well, thus, for too many, rendering their entire undergraduate school years compromised because they are economically disadvantaged.

PROFITING

In an ideal world, I would want first-generation college students to have the same experience in college as their second-, third-, and fourth-generation college counterparts. However, we do not live in an ideal world, so my advice to parents has to be couched in reality. With the right long-term planning, your teen will be at an advantage and at least will not have to be preoccupied with money while in college. Does that mean that the playing field has been equalized? No, it does not; but, it does make life easier when one does not have to worry about money, and that would be the same for your teen going through college.

If money is not an obstacle and the student has the time to engage in undergraduate experiences more earnestly, then she should do so. It would be sinful to do otherwise since an opportunity denied is no different than one forgone, and we all know that there was a time in history when many poor families' children could not attend college.

You will find when you visit colleges that there are many students who persist. In other words, they finish college within a four- or five-year period and leave with a degree. However, many of these same students have failed to profit from all that the undergraduate experience had to offer: they have not been involved in the college community, they have not participated in any educational or cultural programs in foreign countries, they have not established relationships with any professors, and thus they could not obtain a recommendation for a job or graduate or professional school if they needed one. While they have a degree, they have not developed a strong network of friends on campus, which means that if they needed assistance from a friend's parent finding a job, they would not have that option.

Remember: education is not just what happens in the classroom. In fact, much of what a student learns in college will take place outside of the formal classroom setting from their peers. Your teen should be encouraged to profit from her college experiences in ways that will yield the greatest return on the investment that everyone has made, including you as the parent. While you may not have provided most of the dollars for the education, you have provided other resources in the form of emotional support, time, and guidance, and you, too, deserve a return on your investment.

AFTER COLLEGE

First-generation college graduates return home with a mixed set of emotions, circumstances, challenges, and rewards. In some cases, social class and economic mobility can compromise an otherwise stable family if one or more members of the family are threatened by this new social standing of the college graduate. In other cases, the graduate may attach feelings of guilt due to her shift in values. In other cases, again, family members may embrace your teen as well as her success, but the graduate may feel uncomfortable, questioning why she made it and a brother or cousin in the family did not. Still other graduates have parents who celebrate their success, but they do not feel worthy of the celebration because they feel they are not as successful as their fellow classmates.

They have continued feelings of being behind: they were behind when they arrived at college because of inferior schooling; they were behind once in college because of a poor educational foundation; or, if their education was solid, they still had to navigate a foreign and sometimes foreboding social and cultural environment. Now that they are home, they cannot make the kind of money or obtain the kind of job that their fellow classmates have. On top of that, some of them have loans to repay, hence they still feel left behind and not worthy of the celebration and pride felt by their parents and families. Of course, all of this is in their own minds and, in most cases, unreasonable as they should not define success so narrowly and should not measure their success through the eyes of students who come from advantaged backgrounds.

SUBGROUP TRENDS ACROSS FIRST-GENERATION COLLEGE STUDENTS

There are a number of trends that I have witnessed in working with different subgroups over the years. As it is unwise to use a broad brush in defining patterns of behaviors for other identifiable groups, i.e., women, blacks, and Hispanic-Americans, it is equally problematic to do the same when discussing issues relevant to first-generation college students. Of course, there are some generalizations that are legitimate, and much of those informed my earlier discussion about this important group of young people; when there were differences, particularly in the discussion of returning home, I did offer some variation.

What follows is a brief overview of some of the specific characteristics associated with the different subgroups. These observations are merely the ones I have observed and are not representative of a scientific study. They cannot thus be generalized across all students within each subgroup. Nonetheless, I think as parents you will find them interesting.

The freshman and senior year can be equally problematic. In the first year, they are told that they are special, but then they recognize the differences between economically advantaged and economically disadvantaged students that can make some feel insecure. These differences are more startling at the more selective schools, which tend to have a greater percentage of students from more affluent households. If they receive poor grades, this can make them feel more inadequate even though they have not had the same preparation as their peers. Further, they have to work once in college, which means there is a high likelihood that they are multi-tasking and therefore can't do any one job one hundred percent. As seniors, if they don't receive the first job paying lots of money or they have not been admitted to a graduate or professional school, they may feel inadequate if they judge their successes narrowly or through someone else's eyes.

White students who are first generation can mix in more since they do not have to reveal that they are economically disadvantaged. They are often described as the invisible minority, a label some light-skinned Hispanics share. Hispanics can also be invisible unless they have an accent; then their cover is revealed since the negative assumptions made by some about Hispanics in general can now be attributed to them. Being invisible does not necessarily make it easier. It might be better to be obviously needy because, in that way, they can get some help from what the college has to offer students who are first generation. Poor white students at rich white schools are marginalized. People don't want to talk about it because white folks don't like to admit that whites are poor, too. Nevertheless, on elite college campuses, class can raise its ugly head, and first-generation college students who are white can feel it.

Hispanic parents have difficulty letting their daughters go away to college. This can also apply to the males, but, generally, it is a female issue. On the other hand, black families generally encourage their teens to become independent, which means most do not have a problem with either gender leaving home.

Asians who are first in their families to go to college tend not to ask for help if they have a problem in class because they feel ashamed since they are supposed to know. It is assumed that they are smart. Once they realize that this is how they are stereotyped, they don't want it to appear as if they do not know how to do something. Some Asian students, particularly my Korean and Japanese students, are more prone to depression if they receive poor grades because shame often is associated with not doing well academically. This self-loathing is not confined to first-generation students, but is definitely a characteristic of those who are first.

African-Americans and Hispanic-Americans sometimes don't ask questions because it is assumed that they do not know, and they don't want to appear to be unintelligent in their asking or answering; therefore, they tend not to ask questions. White, Asian, and Hispanic-Americans tend to work in study groups. Black students tend to think that they have to do everything on their own. They assume that there is no one on whom they can rely. If they do not have a support system at home, the problem is further aggravated. This puts them at a disadvantage and impacts their GPA negatively.

White students measure their success by the people they have come to know in college and in the white world. People of color measure their success through the eyes of their immediate family members. Blacks may not have someone in their family pushing them through college, but they may have someone in the church who acts as an advocate. People of color in general may feel compelled to help out their families while in college and thus they may be giving them some of the scholarship and financial aid money.

As you can see, just through these few slices across these different groups, the experiences can be daunting for students who are first in their families to attend college. Yet, you can look at the glass half full and not half empty. It is indeed quite an honor to be the first in one's family to attend and graduate from college. It can also be a big responsibility, but one that is not necessarily bad if the student comes home to a welcoming family.

When your teen comes home, she will not be the same as when she left. This is particularly true of first-generation college graduates. If you are a wise parent, you will not expect her to be the same, and you will welcome and embrace her newfound wisdom. In fact, if the family is clever, it will leverage this new knowledge to help advance the family.

On the other hand, when your child comes home, she should not assume that she knows it all. The college student owes a lot to her parents for the support that helped her manage the years in college. And while I recognize that not all college students have support from home, most do. On this note, I believe that the values that shaped who the first-generation student was able to become is largely informed by the wisdom of his or her parents/guardians. For that reason, parents, too, should celebrate. I would hope that when a student returns home, there will be mutual respect on all sides. Parents may have something new to learn from their teen, and students will still have lots to learn from and share with their parents. After all, that is how it should be—families helping each other move forward.

QUESTIONS TO ASK

Please take advantage of the following questions at the appropriate times. They will help increase your college knowledge and empower you as a parent as you are assisting your teen through the various processes of preparing for, applying to, and getting through college.

Planning in High School: Questions for the School Counselor, Principal, Church Minister, and College Access Provider in Your Community

- How do I prepare my teen for college?
- What courses should he or she be taking in high school?
- What is a standardized test?
- Does the school offer fee waivers for these exams?
- What is a college entrance exam?
- How does my teen prepare for them?
- What resources are in the library or in the community to assist my teen?
- What summer programs are available, and is there money available to defray their cost?
- Does your high school or community offer any tutoring programs for teens?
- How can I get involved in my teen's school one or two hours a week?
- How much homework can I expect my teen to have each night?

The College Application Process: Questions for School Counselors, College Access Providers, and College Admissions Officers

- Does your college offer application fee waivers?
- What is the fee waiver policy?
- Does the high school have college application fee waivers?
- Does the college offer fly-in programs for students and parents?
- Does the college offer an orientation program for parents?
- When are college applications generally due?

- When should a student expect to hear from a college?
- What is Early Decision and Early Action?
- What is Regular versus Rolling Admission?
- Does your college offer pre-college programs for first-generation college-bound students?
- What kind of programming is available for first-generation students once they are enrolled?
- Does your school have a resource center for students who have learning disabilities?
- Does your school have an organization serving the needs of students of color?

The Financial Aid Process: Questions for School Counselors, College Access Providers, and Financial Aid Officers at College

- Where and when can I receive assistance completing the financial aid forms?
- What scholarship opportunities are available?
- How does the university allocate outside scholarship funds?
- If my teen receives outside monies, can he or she use them to offset student loans and/or my parent contribution?
- Can the financial aid package be negotiated?
- Can a family expect to receive the same financial aid package all four years?
- How is the family contribution index calculated?
- When does a student have to notify the college that he or she is coming to your school?
- If a student sends a deposit to your school and changes his or her mind, is it refundable?

Getting Through College: Questions for Academic Deans and Counselors at College

- Who should my teen call if he or she is having a problem with his or her roommate?

- Who should my teen call if he or she is having a problem with a professor?

- Does your school offer any diversity training to address issues of race, gender, and social class?

- How is your academic advising program structured?

- How often can my teen meet with his or her academic advisor?

- At what point does my teen choose his or her major?

- What is the retention rate of students in general?

- What is the retention rate of first-generation college students?

- Is the faculty actively involved in the lives of students on your campus?

- How would you rate the social and the academic experiences of first-generation college students on your campus?

- Can my teen speak to a few first-generation students on your campus?

- Can I speak to some of the alumni who were first-generation college students on your campus?

- In your opinion, what challenges do first-generation college students face on your campus, and how is the faculty and administration addressing those needs?

These are a sampling of questions that will jumpstart any discussion you as a parent want to have at the various stages of your teen's education up to and through college, starting with the high school years.

I hope this chapter has inspired you to motivate your teen to hold on to his or her dream. It can be realized with the right guidance, determination, and a bit of luck along the way.

In closing this chapter, I offer you some astute observations from a first-generation college graduate:

● ● ● ●

As a first-generation student, you must believe in yourself because at times you may be the only one. "It is the pleasure of Howard University to inform you that you have been accepted for the fall semester 1992..." Wow, this was my second acceptance letter in as many days—I was ecstatic! But, there was no excitement or encouragement from my dad when I showed him the acceptance letters. And, later that spring, when I announced that I had won a scholarship from our church in the amount of $700.00 to assist with my college expenses, there was still no positive response. Being the first in my family to go to college was a source of great pride for my mother who had always wanted more for her four daughters and two sons. On the other hand, my dad, having only attended grade school in rural South Carolina, seemed so far removed from the idea of a college education. Even the colonel at my summer job in DC was not excited to hear that I had decided to attend Howard University in the fall and not accept the offer of a full-time position at the Department of Army.

I thought to myself, "What is wrong with the male authority figures in my life? Don't they want to see me succeed in college?!" I was going to show them. Not only will I earn a baccalaureate degree, but a master's degree and a doctorate degree, too!

One day after classes in early December, my parents called me into their bedroom. My dad handed me an envelope and said, "This is from me and your mother for your college tuition." Inside the envelope were five $1000 bills. I was stunned and happy at the same time. He had dipped into his savings to ensure that I could return to college the next semester. Although he never said it, I knew he was proud of his oldest daughter. I felt a sense of pride as well, because I knew that I was setting the standard for my younger siblings and I would not let them down. Thank you, Daddy, for believing in me.

—Vera Faulkner

RESOURCES

Antonoff, S. (2008). *The college finder: Choose the school that's right for you!*, 3rd edition. Westford, MA: Winter Green, Orchard House Press.

Cushman, K. (2006). *First in the family: Advice from first-generation students; Your high school years.* Providence, RI: Next Generation Press.

—- (2006). *First in the family: Your college years; Advice about college from first generation students.* Providence, RI: Next Generation Press.

CHAPTER VII

FINANCIAL AID

During the college application process, I was informed that I would have to save some energy for applying for financial aid and that meant I had to complete the FAFSA and the CSS Profile. While most of my colleges only required the FAFSA, some of them required both. Because my mother was unfamiliar with the process, I asked my guidance counselor for help. Before meeting with my guidance counselor, I talked to my mother about the information I would need prior to the meeting, and I also told her the kind of information I would share and the kind of information that would not be discussed. Since there are many parents in this country who are uncomfortable with sharing financial information, I made sure that I asked my mother for her permission before talking to my counselor about her finances. Luckily, my mother was not afraid to share her household income and expenses with my guidance counselor, so when it came time to gather the information needed, my mother gave me her W-2 forms and any other documents I needed to complete the forms with my guidance counselor.

Interpreting the financial aid packages was a challenge for my mother and me, so I asked my guidance counselor for assistance and she helped me interpret the various packages. What I believed to be a $20,000 scholarship from a university in the Northeast was in fact a $20,000 loan that I would have to take out yearly if I attended that school. Without my guidance counselor's help, I wouldn't have chosen the school I am going to now. In the end, I chose to attend the University of Virginia (UVA) because their financial aid package was the best out of all other colleges, and I felt comfortable within UVA's environment both academically and socially.

—**Jasmine Drake**

WHAT IS THE FINANCIAL AID PROCESS?

The financial aid process is a systemic process designed to determine a student's eligibility, based on the parents' and student's income, assets, and financial resources for federal and institutional need-based aid resources.

The process begins with viewing the required financial aid applications and gathering the necessary financial documents needed to complete the application. There are two financial aid applications: the Free Application for Federal Student Aid (FASFA) and the College Scholarship Service Profile (CSS Profile). It is highly recommended that your teen complete both applications online although the federal application has a paper version. Depending on the college, your teen will be required to complete one or both applications. The Financial Aid offices at the colleges your teenager is considering will be able to tell you which financial aid application to complete and submit.

Your teen's current federal tax and bank statements, social security number, and W-2s are several items they will need in order to complete the financial aid application. Your teen may also need to collect documents related to your mortgage, business and farm records, untaxed income such as social security and welfare benefits, investments, and foreign tax returns.

THE FSA ID

Your child should register for an FSA ID (which has replaced the PIN number) before they start filling out the financial aid application. The FSA ID is a unique username and password combination created by the student and for at least one parent. This ID serves as a legal signature and will allow the applicant and a parent to sign the financial aid application electronically online. As a result, it spares the applicant and parent from having to download a signature page to mail in to the application processing center. Having an FSA ID will speed up your daughter or son's application process and give you access to a number of governmental student aid related websites. To register for an FSA ID, students must go to the following website: https://fsaid.ed.gov/

THE FEDERAL AID APPLICATION (FAFSA)

The FAFSA (Free Application for Federal Student Aid) is the federal financial aid application used to calculate an expected family contribution (EFC) based on the income, assets, and other financial resources information provided on the form by the student. The processing of the application is free and will allow the student to enter up to eight schools on a single application to receive the processed information.

Currently, the best time to complete the FAFSA is between January 1 and February 28 of each year. In most cases, this puts a student within the early priority deadlines for financial aid consideration by most colleges.

Beginning with the 2017-2018 financial aid application year, the FAFSA will require prior prior year tax information—which means the income information supplied for the 2017-2018 FAFSA will be from 2015 taxes. As a result, the timeline to begin completing the 2017-2018 FAFSA will be moved forward to October 1, 2016. Once prior prior year data is used, there should no longer be a need to estimate tax information to complete the FAFSA. Students should check with their college choices to find out the priority deadline dates.

The FAFSA is comprised of seven steps or sections:

- Step One: Student personal and background information

- Step Two: Student income, assets, and financial resources information

- Step Three: Student dependency questions

- Step Four: Parents' personal, background information along with income, assets, and financial resources questions

- Step Five: Independent student household size questions

- Step Six: School listing to send your information

- Step Seven: Student and parent signatures section

The FAFSA application can be accessed at www.fafsa.ed.gov.

THE STUDENT AID REPORT

The Student Aid Report is received after the FAFSA application is processed. This report contains information relevant to your child's eligibility for federal student aid. It also allows you and your teen to review the submitted processed data for any necessary corrections that might be needed for resubmission of the application. If corrections are needed, they can in most cases be done online with the FSA ID or via a phone by providing the Data Release Number (DRN) that will be located on the Student Aid Report. Lastly, the Student Aid Report will provide your daughter or son with a calculated Expected Family Contribution. The calculated Expected Family Contribution, once determined, will be reported to each school listed on the FAFSA.

THE COLLEGE SCHOLARSHIP SERVICE APPLICATION (CSS PROFILE)

The CSS Profile financial aid application is designed to determine a family's eligibility for nonfederal student aid funds. In order to use the CSS Profile, students must register online with a collegeboard.com account and debit card, credit card, or check. Students are encouraged to register at least two weeks before the priority application filing dates to meet the deadlines for scholarships and other aid programs.

Students should check to find out if the CSS PROFILE is required by the Financial Aid Office of the schools they are considering.

The CSS PROFILE can be accessed at https://student.collegeboard. org/css-financial-aid-profile.

Once they are registered, a personalized PROFILE application will be made available to complete. In order to complete the PROFILE, current year taxes for the parents and student, along with information on other financial resources, will be needed.

Once completed and processed, the PROFILE data will be sent to the schools listed on the application to determine eligibility for institutional financial aid, such as scholarship and institutional grants.

THE INSTITUTIONAL PROCESS

After the FAFSA and CSS PROFILE applications are processed and forwarded to the schools requested by the student, the different colleges will review the information received for financial aid eligibility. As part of the Financial Aid Office review process, each year the U.S. Department of Education randomly selects student financial aid applications for a process called "verification." Verification simply checks the information reported on the FAFSA against the tax documents used to complete the financial aid application. To verify tax information, your child will be required to complete a process titled "IRS Data Retrieval." This process allows the student and parent to access tax information submitted to the IRS through a hyperlink portal. This eliminates the submission of tax transcripts and speeds up the financial aid process. If you filed as married filing separately, married filing as Head of Household, filed a 1040x amended return, or filed a Puerto Rican or foreign tax return, the "IRS Data Retrieval" will not work in these cases.

Most colleges have their own institutional financial aid forms that are utilized in the verification process, so your teen may be required to fill out several of these documents. Institutional forms are used to verify and gather information on household size, minimal income, supplemental nutrition assistance program participation, student background information, previous colleges attended, and untaxed income.

The Financial Aid Office will send the student letters requesting the completion and submission of all institutional documents that normally are accessible online through the college's website.

COST OF ATTENDANCE

The cost of attendance is created by the Financial Aid Office and may vary from school to school; however, all "cost of attendance" lists will have the following major components:

- Tuition and fees
- Room and board
- Books and supplies
- Transportation
- Personal expenses

Schools may also include the fees associated with borrowing a student loan, a personal computer purchase, and other costs associated with a student with a disability.

When it comes to cost of attendance, the type of school your teen attends will have a significant impact on the amount they pay for a college education. Cost can vary tremendously among public colleges, private colleges, community colleges, vocational, technical, and trade schools. In most cases, financial need increases as the cost of attendance increases.

AWARD LETTER NOTIFICATIONS

The colleges that have accepted your teen for admission will begin sending out award letters normally in April. Your award letter notification may arrive in paper form or by email indicating that your award can be viewed online. This will allow your teenager to compare all of the offers of financial aid from the different schools based on their cost of attendance. Some of these letters will list only direct cost whereas other letters may list all college costs. For example, an award letter may reflect the cost of tuition, fees, room, and board; however, these costs may vary depending on a variety of meal plans to select from and whether your teen lives on- or off-campus. These are a few of the things to take into consideration when students are looking at the actual cost of the college. Don't forget about the cost of books and supplies because both can be expensive depending on the major and whether your teen chooses to buy new or used books.

There are two categories of financial aid that your teen's award notifications may offer. One category might be need-based that will consist of grants, scholarships, work-study, and some loans. With the exception of the loans, these are funds, if offered, that your teen will not have to repay. The second category of awards might be non-need based loan funds. Loan funds, if offered, will have to be repaid.

Your teen should also know that they have the option in most cases to decide which financial aid funds offered in the award letter they will accept or decline.

Lastly, they will need to be aware of the deadline to respond to the financial aid offer. If students fail to respond before the deadline, the offer will be rescinded and the funds redistributed to other waiting applicants.

If your daughter or son has any questions, they should contact the Financial Aid Office.

HELPING YOUR TEEN EVALUATE AND NEGOTIATE THE FINANCIAL AID AWARD OFFER

When it comes to evaluating the financial aid award offers, students will need to spread out the award letters so that they can compare the packages from the different colleges. This can be complicated because of the types and amount of financial aid that could be offered. An easy way to make the comparisons is to create a spreadsheet with the following headings and categories.

List all the colleges by name; then, make a list of the following items for each college:

- Cost of Attendance (tuition and fees, room and board, other expenses) = total cost of attendance

- expected family contribution

- Financial Aid Eligibility (scholarship and grants, student loans, work-study job, other financial aid offers) = total aid offer

Once your teen has the total cost and total aid, they will have a sense of what will be required in order to fill the remaining difference in what the financial aid covers and the college costs. Have your teen look at the amount or percentage of the financial aid offer that is need-based compared to non-need-based financial aid.

Saying, "I want to negotiate the financial aid offer I received with the Financial Aid Office," can be viewed as very strong words. Your teen should keep in mind that the Financial Aid Office professionals are simply stewards of the institution's and federal government's funds and their job is to make sure that those funds are disbursed fairly and go to the neediest students. If your teen chooses to talk with the Financial Aid Office about the need for additional funds, a better approach would be to ask that the financial aid offer be given a review or reconsideration or that they would like to appeal the offer due to specific reasons.

If the requested reason for an appeal of a financial aid offer is a good one, it does not hurt to make the request since the student could receive additional money. If the Financial Aid Office is unable to assist with your teen's present situation, they should stay in touch because the office might be able to help them in the future.

THE FEDERAL FINANCIAL AID PROGRAMS

The Federal Pell Grant

The Federal Pell Grant program is a federal student aid program administered by the college for students who have not earned a bachelor's degree. The program is designed to offer assistance to students with the greatest need. Students can receive funding for enrollments of full time, three-quarters time, half-time, and less than half-time. Pell Grant funds are one of the few aid programs where the funds are portable, which means that funding can move with the student to different colleges and is not based on availability of funds at any one school. Eligibility for the Pell Grant is determined by the expected family contribution (EFC), calculated by the FAFSA and the student's enrollment in college. The minimum and maximum under the program vary up to $5,775.

The Pell Grant has a lifetime eligibility unit (LEU) limit of six years of full-time enrollment. Students can track their use of the Pell Grant by accessing the National Student Loan Data System (NSLDS) through its website: https://www.nslds.ed.gov/npas/index.htm.

The Federal Supplemental Educational Opportunity Grant (FSEOG)

The Federal Supplemental Educational Opportunity Grant provides financial assistance to needy students who have not earned a bachelor's degree. If your teen qualifies for the Pell Grant, they will be given priority consideration for the FSEOG program. However, this program has limited funds, so it's important to make the financial aid deadline. FSEOG award amounts vary from $100 to a maximum of $4,000, depending on the availability of school funds.

The Federal Perkins Loan Program

The Federal Perkins Loan Program is a low interest loan (five percent). The loan is need-based and the interest is paid by the federal government while the student is enrolled in school at least half-time. Students with exceptional need are required to be given priority by schools. Funding is based on the availability of the funds from loans being repaid by previous borrowers and new loan funds being appropriated by Congress.

A student can borrow as much as $5,500 per year up to an aggregate maximum of $27,500 as an undergraduate. Repayment begins nine months after graduation or after a student ceases to be enrolled at least half-time. Repayment schedules are designed so that the loan is repaid within ten years. There is no penalty for repaying early the full amount of the loan or part of the loan to avoid interest payments.

This program was extended through 2016 but may eventually disappear if funding for new loans is not approved by Congress.

The Federal Work-Study Program

The Federal Work-Study Program is an employment program that allows students to work on-campus in administrative or academic offices and off-campus with community service organizations. The funds offered through the program are need-based and have no limit as long as the amount offered does not exceed the student's financial need. The hours per week vary from school to school; however, most will advise that a student work no more than twenty hours per week. The rates of pay will also vary depending on the type of work the student will be performing. The Federal Work-Study Program has limited funding, so it is important that students apply for financial aid before the deadline.

The Federal Direct Student Loan Program (FDSLP)

The Federal Direct Student Loan Program is composed of three federally guaranteed and low interest loans: the Federal Direct Subsidized Loan and the Federal Direct Unsubsidized Loan. Additionally, the Federal Direct Parent Loan for Undergraduate Students (PLUS) is a member of the federal guaranteed loans.

The Federal Direct Subsidized Loan is a need-based loan with interest paid by the federal government while the student is enrolled at least half-time in school. Six months after graduation, the student starts to repay the loan with interest. The amount borrowed may be limited by other financial aid offered to the student.

The Federal Direct Unsubsidized Loan is non-need based; the student is responsible for paying the interest while in school. The deferment of interest payments is available, but the interest will accrue if not paid while in school.

The student could receive either a Federal Direct Subsidized or Unsubsidized Loan or a combination of both loans.

The maximum amounts a student can borrow are based on grade levels:

- $5,500 per year for first-year students–$3,500 of this may be subsidized

- $6,500 per year for second-year students–$4,500 of this may be subsidized

- $7,500 per year for third-year students and beyond–$5,500 of this may be subsidized

The college's Financial Aid Office will normally have a simplified in-house application to apply for these loans. Direct Student Loan funds are made available through the federal government through the U.S. Department of Education, which eliminates having to use banks or other private lenders for these loans. Interest rates on direct loans were determined with the passage of the Bipartisan Student Loan Certainty Act of 2013. As a result, new federal student loan interest rates are to be set based on financial markets for all DIRECT student loans disbursed on or after July 1, 2013. As of July 1, 2016, subsidized and unsubsidized direct loans for an undergraduate have a fixed rate of 3.76 percent.

The Federal Direct Parent Loan for Undergraduate Students (PLUS)

The Federal Direct Parent Loan for Undergraduate Students (PLUS) is designed for the parents of an undergraduate student to borrow, if necessary, up to the cost of attendance of the student's educational cost, minus any other financial aid the student receives. The credit history of the applicant is checked for any adverse activity. The repayment of the loan begins immediately after the last disbursement.

The PLUS Loan funds are made available through the federal government via the U.S. Department of Education and, therefore, no banks or other private lending institutions are needed to apply for the loan. The college Financial Aid Office will normally have a simplified in-house application to apply for the loan. The interest rate is presently fixed at 6.84 percent.

SCHOLARSHIPS AND INSTITUTIONAL FINANCIAL AID PROGRAMS

Searching for scholarships can be a daunting task, but the Internet has made this process easier, and it is far better than paying someone for something your teen can do for free. If they decide to use the Internet to find scholarships, they should use the free scholarship searches.

Here are some tips for students interested in researching scholarships:

- Check with your employer about scholarships for children of employees.
- Consider scholarships through military and armed services.
- Look up professional associations, religious membership, civic, fraternal, and benevolent organizations.
- Check for scholarships on student and parental heritage.

- Research merit scholarships offered by state or national organizations.

- Join national competitions for scholarships.

- Talk with the high school counselor about local scholarships.

- Research schools that offer merit scholarships in your daughter or son's area of interest.

Scholarships do not have to be repaid and are considered need-based financial aid.

NCAA ATHLETICS AND FINANCIAL AID

While Chapter IV focused on the college athlete, I wish to stress again here the financial aid logistics and requirements for this special category of student. In order to be eligible to practice, play, and receive financial aid at a Division I school, students must be able to present 16 core courses.

To be eligible to practice, play, and receive financial aid at a Division II school, students must present 16 core courses.

Subject	Division I	Division II
English	4 years	3 years
Mathematics	3 years	2 years
(Algebra I or higher)		
Natural/physical science	2 years	2 years
(One must be a lab science)		
Years of additional English, math or science	1 year	3 years
Social studies	2 years	2 years
Years of additional core courses	4 years	4 years
(From any area listed above, or from foreign language, comparative religion, or philosophy)		

Effective August 1, 2018, student athletes must earn at least a 2.3 GPA in NCAA core courses along with the corresponding required test score to compete as a college freshman in Division I sports and a 2.2 GPA in Division II sports.

NCAA athletes are required to take the SAT or ACT test. Both tests have a writing component that is optional. Presently, the NCAA does not require the writing component. Additionally, information on test scores and how they are used by the NCAA can be obtained from your teen's high-school guidance counselor and at www.ncaa.org.

All student athletes are required to register with the NCAA Initial Eligibility Clearinghouse online.

Athletic scholarships are not plentiful, and full-ride scholarships are rare and highly competitive. The key to receiving one is for your teen to start the process early and to be an excellent athlete. They should contact the school, prepare to do well in the interview process, put together a good presentation of their talents and skills, be prepared to ask intelligent questions, and follow up with the coaches and school officials.

In the area of athletic scholarships, schools will offer two types. An institutional grant gives an athlete the flexibility to change her or his mind after signing with one college to change and sign with another college. The second type of scholarship is a conference grant, which will bind an athlete to a particular college once signed.

These scholarships could take the following forms:

- A full four-year ride covering all college expenses, room and board, tuition, and books.

- A scholarship for one year with a renewable contract. You and your teen should find out from the coach or recruiter the college's track record for renewing the scholarship if the athlete meets all the academic, athletic, and other standards set by the school.

- A one-year trial grant with a verbal agreement between the athlete and the school that it will be renewed at the end of the year based on academic and athletic performance on the team.

- A partial grant covering a portion of the college cost such as room and board or tuition and fees or books.

- The athlete could be offered a waiver of out-of-state fees that would allow the student to pay the same fees as an in-state student.

OTHER CONSIDERATIONS IN THE FINANCIAL AID PROCESS

Professional Judgment

Professional Judgment is a tool used in the Financial Aid Office to address special circumstances that may have occurred after the student files for financial aid. Some good examples of situations of this nature are divorce, loss of employment, death of a parent, hardship due to illness, or other unusual things that could and do happen. If any of these events happen to the student during the application process, they can only be addressed in the Financial Aid Office by requesting a professional judgment appeal.

If the Financial Aid Office reviews the student's changed circumstances and approves her or his appeal, the student's financial aid file will be reprocessed with the adjustments made by the Financial Aid Office. This reprocessing could change the student's eligibility for financial aid.

Selective Service

All males in order to be considered for federal financial aid must register with the U.S. Selective Service Board when they reach the age of eighteen. The selective service system is designed to create a database of eligible men to draft into the military in case of war. Parents should be aware that a draft is not likely in the near future. See http://www.sss.gov/ for how to register online.

THE AMERICAN OPPORTUNITY TAX CREDIT

The American Opportunity Tax Credit (AOTC) can be claimed in tax years 2009–2017 for certain qualifying educational expenses that you pay for tuition and certain fees and course materials for higher education for a dependent whom you claim as an exemption on your tax return. The credit will cover qualifying expenses for the first four years of a student's undergraduate education. Your teen can include tuition, student activity fees, and any expenses for course-related books, supplies, and equipment—only if the fees and expenses are paid to the college as a condition of the student's enrollment or attendance.

The following list is a quick look at expenses that do not qualify for the tax credit:

- room and board
- transportation
- insurance
- medical expenses
- fees not required as a condition of enrollment or attendance
- expenses paid with tax-free educational assistance
- expenses used for any other tax deduction, credit, or educational benefit

The AOTC credit is worth up to $2,500 credit per eligible student, and forty percent of the credit up to $1,000 is refundable even if you owe no taxes.

- The student must be pursuing an undergraduate degree or other recognized educational credential.

- The student must be enrolled at least half-time.

- The student cannot be convicted of a felony drug offense.

IRS Publication 970 has additional information on the AOTC.

THE LIFETIME LEARNING CREDIT

The Lifetime Learning Credit can be claimed for tuition and fees required for enrollment or attendance (including amounts required to be paid to the institution for course-related books, supplies, and equipment) at an eligible educational institution. The eligible student can be yourself, your spouse, or a dependent whom you claim as an exemption on your tax return.

Some highlights of the Lifetime Learning Credit:

- The credit is worth $2,000 per return.

- The credit is available for all years of postsecondary education and for courses to acquire or to improve job skills.

- It is available for an unlimited number of years.

- In order to qualify for the credit, the student does not need to be pursuing a degree or other recognized education credential.

- The student can be enrolled for one or more courses and still receive the credit.

- The student can qualify for the credit even if the student has been convicted of a felony drug offense.

For more information on the tax credits, view the IRS website: http://www.irs.gov/publications/p970/index.html.

HELPING STUDENTS REDUCE THE FOUR-YEAR COST OF COLLEGE

Freshman Year

- Leave the car at home.

- Live on campus.

- Decorate your college dorm with furnishings from home.

- Don't buy all new clothes. Buy a few new basics and take the others from your high school senior year.

- Cancel the paid Internet service and use the free wireless service on-campus.

- Purchase a cell phone and disconnect the landline in the dorm room.

- Purchase used books online by conducting a Google search for online bookstores or new and used textbooks.

- Purchase a meal plan that will not waste money. If you don't like getting up for breakfast, you should not buy a plan with breakfast meals.

Sophomore Year

- Investigate ways to pay in-state tuition if you are out-of-state.

- Prepare to take summer classes at the local community college and transfer the credits back to your school.

- Register and pay bills on time to avoid late fees.

- Sell used textbooks.

- Get a job on- or off-campus.

- Reduce the number of trips home.

- Skip expensive spring break trips.

Junior Year

- Avoid unnecessary purchases with credit cards.

- Move off campus and share an apartment or room.

- Drop the meal plan and cook food at home.

- Bring your car to school, but use public transportation or the shuttle system provided by the college as much as possible.

- Get a paid summer internship.

Senior Year

- Save summer job earnings to purchase an interview suit and the cap and gown. (Gowns usually are available as rentals.)

- Tutor students for a fee.

The financial aid process may seem daunting, but getting an early start will cut down on frustration by allowing enough time for your teen to avoid the rush. Planning for college is challenging enough without having to spend a lot of time worrying about how and if your daughter or son can afford the college of her or his choice.

● ● ● ●

Since this generation is so advanced in technology, it does not come as a surprise that almost all of the financial aid applications are online. In this respect, applying for financial aid is easier now than it has been in the past. Still, it is crucial to meet all of the deadlines to ensure that your daughter or son receives all of the aid that she or he can. If your daughter or son has questions about the financial aid process or applications, she or he does not have to rely solely on her or his guidance counselor. Your daughter or son can call the financial aid officer at one of the schools of interest.

Upon receiving the financial aid package, it should be read carefully as some of the aid may include loans. It is important that your daughter or son is aware of the differences in aid and, when in doubt, here again, not always rely on the guidance counselor but instead call the financial aid counselor at the respective college. Now that your daughter or son has been admitted, the financial aid counselor will have even more of an investment in making sure that your daughter or son comes to the school.

Finally, if your daughter or son is unhappy with the financial aid package, she or he should let the college know. The college may inform your daughter or son that it is willing to increase the scholarship allocation.

—Neferteneken Francis

GLOSSARY

American Opportunity Tax Credit (AOTC): This tax credit is worth up to $2,500 for tax filers. The credit is available only for expenses paid during the first four years of qualifying college education and forty percent of the credit up to $1,000 is refundable even if no taxes are owed.

Award Letter: A5n official document issued by the Financial Aid Office of the college. It will show the financial aid offered a student. The letter is normally mailed through the USPS or by e-mail.

Cost of Attendance: The total amount it will cost the student to attend a particular school. The cost of attendance includes room and board, tuition and fees, books and supplies, transportation, and personal expenses.

CSS Profile: A financial aid application with a processing fee used to determine eligibility for financial aid by some colleges. The application is usually a requirement of aid consideration by private colleges.

Dependent Student: An undergraduate student who is under the age of twenty-four, has no legal dependents, is not an orphan or ward of the court or a veteran of the United States Armed Forces.

Deferment: An entitlement provided through student loans that allows the borrower to temporarily postpone payments for several reasons, including employment, disability, returning to school, and personal hardship.

Eligibility: A term used when the calculated expected family contribution (EFC) is less than the cost of attendance (COA) of the educational institution.

Expected Family Contribution (EFC): The estimated amount (based on income, assets, and other contributions and calculated by the processed FAFSA) that the federal government says a family should be able to contribute to the cost of education.

Federal Pell Grant: A federal grant aid program. As such, the funds do not have to be repaid. Funds are awarded to students with exceptional need. Grant amounts depend on the expected family contribution (EFC).

Federal Perkins Loan: A federal loan for students managed by the college. Exceptional need is the first requirement, and interest is paid by the government while the student is enrolled at least half-time.

Federal Supplemental Educational Opportunity Grant: A federal grant aid program. Funds received from the program do not have to be repaid. Funds are awarded based on need and availability by the college.

Federal Direct Subsidized Loan: A federal need-based loan on which the government pays the interest while the student is enrolled in school at least half-time.

Federal Direct Unsubsidized Loan: A federal non-need based loan where the student is responsible for paying the interest on the loan from the date of disbursement. Deferment options are available.

Federal Direct Parent Loan for Undergraduate Students (PLUS): A federally guaranteed loan utilized by parents of dependent students to cover college education costs. The loan repayment begins immediately after the full disbursement of the loan.

Federal Work Study: A need-based employment federal aid program that provides part-time employment opportunities to the student on- and off-campus to assist with educational costs.

Free Application for Federal Student Aid (FAFSA): The federal form used to apply for financial aid and determine eligibility for all federal aid programs.

Forbearance: An agreement with the lender, at its discretion, to postpone payments when the borrower is having financial difficulty.

Grace Period: The amount of time allowed before the principal repayment of the loan must begin after the student graduates, leaves school, or drops below half-time enrollment.

Lifetime Learning Tax Credit: A credit designed to aid students in acquiring or improving job skills. The credit is equal to twenty percent of the first $10,000 of tuition-related expenses paid by a family. The maximum credit is usually $2,000 per year.

Merit-Based Aid: Financial assistance offered on the basis of personal achievement and individual characteristics without regard to financial need.

Need-Based Financial Aid: Financial aid resources awarded to the student based on eligibility showing that the expected family contribution (EFC) is less than the college's cost of attendance (COA). If subtracting the EFC from the COA yields a figure greater than zero, that equates to need.

No Need: A term used when the calculated expected family contribution (EFC) is greater than the cost of attendance (COA) of the educational institution.

Promissory Note: A document that a borrower signs before receiving loan proceeds. The note includes information about the terms and conditions of the loan. It establishes that the borrower has promised to repay the loan.

Section 529 Plan: Plans established by states as college savings programs/pre-paid tuition plans that allow families to set aside money to cover college tuition, fees, supplies, books, and certain room and board costs in a savings account that can grow federally tax-free.

Student Aid Report (SAR): A report sent to the student by the government to acknowledge that the FAFSA has been processed. The report allows the student to review the submitted information and make any necessary corrections needed for resubmission.

RESOURCES

"Federal student aid." Studentaid.ed.gov/sa (2015). United States Department of Education. Web.

"National Association of Student Financial Aid Administrators." (2015). Nasfaa.org. NASFAA. Web.

National Scholarship Research Service and Cassidy, D. (2008). *The scholarship book: The complete guide to private sector scholarships, grants, and loans for undergraduates.* Upper Saddle River, NJ: Prentice Hall.

Ragins, M. (2013). *Winning scholarships for college: An insider's guide.* New York, NY: Holt Paperbacks.

Tanabe, G. and Tanabe, K. (2016). *The ultimate scholarship book: Billions of dollars in scholarships, grants and prizes.* Belmont, CA: SuperCollege LLC.

CHAPTER VIII

COLLEGE: GETTING IN AND GETTING THROUGH

Entering college for the right reasons is key to a successful college journey. People enter college for a variety of reasons, but if the reasons do not match the student's ambitions and goals, it will not be as fulfilling. Many students enter college with a vague career field or desired job title post-graduation. Some let others directly or indirectly decide which path they should pursue, letting parents, friends, and faculty who influenced them along the way dictate their path out of a well-meaning sense of loyalty to their supporters; this, in turn, causes them to lose themselves, and throughout their college tenure, they function on automatic pilot just to finish. Therefore, enter college for the right reasons. If you do not know the right reasons, do some serious soul searching; come up with the final conclusion on your own, and take ownership of your college destiny.

In retrospect, when I think of what helped me get through college, two patterns come to mind. I needed to make sure I understood what the expectations were from each professor. I spoke with them often to gauge how I was doing in their classes, and I also wanted to know how I could be more successful. I demanded feedback on papers and projects and always wanted to know how I could actively get a higher grade.

Which brings me to my second point: all of my close friends had a similar mindset. They checked in with their professors and were constantly striving to do better. I feel that if you want to be a productive student, you have to make sure that you do not fall victim to negative outside pressure. Peer pressure can be both good and bad. You need to surround yourself with those who share your goals, i.e., being around those of like minds increases the chances of being successful—in this case, academic success.

—Helena Edwards

CONGRATULATIONS TO YOU AND YOUR family. Your teen has, with the support of family, friends, teachers, and counselors, been admitted to college. Your teen is in, but now, he has to stay in and be productive while there. Ideally, he will enjoy his new home away from home, and if he does, he most likely will become engaged in the overall undergraduate experience.

Colleges, too, have an investment in your teen doing well. After all, a high rate of student attrition negatively affects their rankings. Consequently, they pay close attention to students, particularly freshmen, since that is the transitional year, and that is where most students face challenges. Institutions vary, though, as to the kind and amount of attention they pay to transitioning new students to their campuses. Your teen will be integrating into a new community with a new set of rules and expectations. How well he will succeed in college will largely be determined by how well he can adapt to these new expectations.

Your teenager will experience an orientation either during the summer preceding his first year of college or over a week in the fall preceding the start of classes. During that time, your teen will meet several people representing various departments and programs. In general, the goal of this week is to orient the new student to the campus by identifying resources and key people associated with those resources. For example, he will meet professionals from academic departments, student support services, residential life, and financial aid, to name a few.

Please do not let your teen be so consumed with high school graduation and getting ready to pack and go off to college that he forgets to read this section. Some, if not all, of this information will be covered at your teen's freshmen orientation, but I also know from experience that the quality of that information can vary and some topics may not be addressed. It is better to have the information and not need it rather than to need it and not have it. What follows are some tips that will help your teenager stay in and do well while they are at college.

At any college or university, there are many divisions, but generally everything falls under two major areas: Academic Affairs and Student Affairs. Academic Affairs focuses on the academic areas of college while Student Affairs addresses more of the social aspects. I would like to offer you some tips under Academic Affairs and then Student Affairs separately. Please note that I am not suggesting that once your teen is on campus, these two departments should work separately; on the contrary, institutions that are successful do so through collaboration; therefore, you will see a joining of hands, so to speak, between the two. No longer is your teen's well being seen as the exclusive province of those who work in Student Affairs. Today, it is the responsibility of all administrators, faculty, and staff to make sure that the community is a safe and nurturing one so that all students can maximize their potential in being successful.

TIPS FOR YOUR TEEN: ACADEMIC AFFAIRS

Time Management

If you have not learned how to manage your time by now, you will definitely face challenges. Think about who you are and how you learn. Recognize your limitations, and seek support from an academic dean and/or a tutor or counselor to help you improve in this area. Set priorities, and make a schedule. Make sure that you stick to your schedule. Have a place for everything, and keep everything in its place. You don't want to waste time spending one hour trying to find something that you should be able to put your hands on in one minute. Remember that there are resources on campus that will help you with time management. You only need to ask your resident advisor, and if you can't find him, go see your academic dean. Hopefully, you will know who the contact person is and may have even met that person at the Freshmen Orientation.

Academic Deans/Advisors

Before you arrive on campus, you will most likely have already been assigned an academic dean, sometimes referred to as an "academic advisor." An academic dean is to college what a guidance counselor is to high school. This is the person who will help you choose classes and a major and may advise you on summer opportunities, internships, and summer abroad programs. If you are entering college with an undeclared major, you most likely will have two academic deans, one for your first two years, and one after you have declared a major for your last two years. Just as you established a relationship with your high school guidance counselor, you need to establish one with your academic dean. This is another resource available to you, should you be facing academic challenges. He may be able to advocate for you. If you are fortunate, he may even teach you some strategies that will enable you to advocate for yourself.

Also, when it comes time for applying to graduate or professional schools, this is the person that you will come to for guidance. You may also need to call on this individual to provide you with a character recommendation for a job, internship, fellowship, or graduate or professional school. Get to know the academic advisor before you need to see him. And stay in touch with him after he has helped you out.

Choosing Classes

Unless you are in engineering, nursing, business, dance, or education, what are referred to as the professional majors, you will have some freedom over what classes you will choose and, in some cases, when you can choose to take them. This is particularly the case at the more selective colleges where students are granted a great deal of academic freedom. Be careful not to over-extend yourself. Just because you were at the top of your class in high school does not necessarily mean that you won't face challenges in college. In fact, if you do not choose your classes wisely, you most likely will face some challenges.

Seek out the advice of your academic advisor and ask him to review your schedule. You should always at least consider the advice you receive although you may have a different opinion; sometimes, it may not be what you want to hear, but it may be what you need to hear. In these cases, you may want to consult others, e.g., your parents, and use your own judgment. You can assume that the academic advisors want you to be successful, and thus the advice that they provided is in your best interest, even if you can't recognize it at the time it is being offered.

Here is an example that might serve you well. If you are thinking about a pre-medicine major and you love science, your advisor may caution you not to take Calculus, two science classes, and Chinese the first semester of your freshmen year. He would caution you to think about how doing so could impact your achievement in the short run and impact your getting into medical school in the long run. He would recommend how you might best be served by taking one math and one science, a writing class, and something fun and entertaining, such as an Introduction to Film Studies. Furthermore, he would suggest that if you have never taken Chinese, you may want to audit the class at a local junior college during the summer after your freshmen year and enroll in Level I Chinese the first semester of your sophomore year. While offering sound advice in your best interest, a good advisor will be engaged and will insist that you are also engaged in the process.

Choosing a Major

If you are in the College of Arts and Sciences, sometimes called the College of Liberal Arts, you often do not have to declare your major until the end of sophomore year. Most students will fall into this category. If you think you have an idea of what you might want to major in, begin exploring those classes early. For example, if you have an interest in Psychology, you may want to take Introduction to Psychology in your freshmen year. If you decide it's not for you, you have not wasted your time since you can use that class to satisfy a distribution or elective requirement toward your graduation. You will have several people on campus who can help you explore major options: other students, juniors or seniors, who are majoring in a field in which you have an interest; your academic advisor; professors; and counselors in the Career Center.

At some point, you will want and need to know your career potential in a particular discipline. If you can, go with what will give you the greatest amount of pleasure. Choose a major that will give you the skill sets to engage a career that will be gratifying and rewarding. Hopefully, you will not choose one based solely on potential income.

Studying for Exams

Studying hard, and doing so for long hours, does not necessarily mean studying smart. People who study smart may study long hours, but they also study in groups. They have a routine study schedule, and they have chosen a space in which to study that optimizes their potential for focusing and allows them to process information that will be retained. Often, they have found that studying in a group can be to their advantage, but choosing the right group is key.

Choosing your group and the dynamics of the group is very important, or else, you could end up doing most of the work. Don't wait until the last minute to study for an exam. Pace yourself. You know yourself, and you should also know the group. Organize your reading schedule. If you have twenty-two books to read for one semester, determine how many pages you have to read over a four- or five-month period. In order to stay on top of your reading, you may only need to read seventy-five pages a day. That's better than waiting almost until the end of the semester when you may have to cram 7,000 pages in three weeks. Get help from a tutor and/or the professor sooner rather than later.

Decoding Your Professor

Understanding who your professors are and what they expect from you will maximize your performance in and out of class and help you do well on the exams, papers, and projects. Professors are also human: they want to know you; they like to be valued. If you are facing some personal challenges because of problems at home or on campus, you may want to share with your professors. If you have a learning disability and have an Individual Educational Plan that specifies special accommodations to which you are entitled, you may want to seek advisement from your professor, who may decide to refer you to counseling depending on the severity of the problem. When it comes to grading your performance, your professors could be more sympathetic and give you the benefit of the doubt. However, you won't know that if you don't know your professors, and your professors can't help you if they don't know you.

Speak to other students who have studied under your professors and ask your fellow students if they can share past exams with you. At some schools, previous exams are kept in the library and serve as guides for new students. In addition, it may be in your best interest to learn something about the temperament of your professors; students who know the professor can yield some insights in this area as well. If you feel uncomfortable with any material, go see your professors early in the semester rather than wait until the last minute. Be proactive, not reactive, in managing your needs and concerns within a particular class.

Writing Research Papers

No doubt, by now you have already written several research papers. If you have, you have a competitive advantage over those students who have not. Independent of their major, most students will have to write several research papers while in college. A research paper presents and argues a thesis. When you write a research paper, you use outside evidence to persuade the readers that your argument is valid or at least is worthy of serious consideration. Knowing how to write a good research paper is an essential skill for success in college. Make sure to ask your professors how they want you to give credit to those you may be quoting in your papers. You can be expelled from college for plagiarizing. Here are the basic steps you will need to complete as you write and research a paper:

- Select and narrow a topic

- Begin your research

- Evaluate your sources

- Take notes

- Outline

- Begin writing your first draft, including the thesis statement

- Document sources (Speak to your professor about how this should be done as citation styles vary across disciplines.)

- Share with your professor

- Find more resources if necessary

- Revise your first draft

- Share your second draft with your professor

- Re-write
- Proofread (You may want to seek out staff from the Writing Lab.)
- Write the final draft

TIPS FOR YOUR TEEN: STUDENT AFFAIRS

Time Management

Earlier tips about time management appeared under Academic Affairs, but students should also think about managing their time when thinking about the social aspects of college life. While, typically, the main reason why students go to college is to earn a degree and, by extension, receive an education, we also recognize that much is learned outside of the classroom. Knowing how to balance your time so that your social life does not trump your academic responsibilities is crucial to determining your success. You have to know yourself and know what your limitations are. You have an academic schedule already, and now you need to include your social schedule, creating one schedule for the week.

Remember that your schedule is your own and not your friend's. While your friend may have facility with math and not need to review at length, you may need to study three hours for a math exam because your foundation in math is weaker and math was not your favorite subject. Or, you may not be able to go to the party on Thursday evening because you have an economics exam at 8 a.m. on Friday whereas your roommate had his exam Thursday afternoon.

Make sure you have fun, and enjoy the social aspects of campus. Maintain a social schedule, and leave room for some spontaneity, but don't forget that the main reason for attending college is to receive an education and earn your degree. Seek out a counselor on campus if you are having problems managing your time.

Financial Management

Most students do not know how to manage money because they have never had to do so. If you have learned how to manage your funds, then you are one of the lucky ones. You have to develop a budget for yourself and, just as you have to know yourself in terms of your academic and social limitations, you have to know your financial self. By creating a budget, you will have a general sense of what you need and how much it will cost to take care of these needs over a specific period of time. If you have difficulty delaying gratification, you might be better served by asking your parents to send you an allowance once a month or to deposit the money in small sums in your bank account. If, on the other hand, you are not likely to spend your entire semester's budget in one week, then you are in a safe position and won't run out of money. Whether or not you manage money well, you would be best served to buy in bulk everything you need at the beginning of the school year. Here are some items you don't want to forget when you make a budget:

- **Personal essentials:** These include shampoo, toothpaste, mouthwash, razors, and shaving cream.

- **Clothing:** Your budget does not need to include clothes since you will have purchased them before you leave for college. Remember that students usually bring too many clothes.

- **Books and supplies:** You cannot buy books for the year as you will need new books each semester, but you might be able to buy supplies, e.g., pens, pencils, notebook paper, computer paper, ink cartridges for your printer, highlighters, etc.

- **Hair Grooming:** Research these services in your school community to find out the cost, and estimate how many times a school year you think you will need these services.

- **Laundry:** Most students wash their clothes in the dorm. So, you can buy your detergent in bulk for the year. However, you will have to budget your money over the academic year to pay for the washer and dryer fee. Inquire about this fee before you enroll in the college so that you include it in your budget prior to coming to school.

- **Entertainment:** Your room and board will be paid for, but you may want to enjoy a dinner out once a semester; or, rather than rent a video, which you will have to include in your budget if you watch lots of them, you may want to go out to a movie from time to time. This, too, will have to be included in your budget as entertainment.

- **Transportation:** This will be based on how far you live from school and how often you plan to return home.

There is a lot to think about, but it does help to know yourself and what your needs are. Use your common sense when spending money. If you are at college with little or no money, you will be stressed out, and it will impact negatively on your academic performance.

Identity Formation

When you leave college, you will not be the same person you were when you entered. You will experience new people, ideas, and situations that will challenge some of your values and beliefs in both positive and nega-tive ways. Through your negotiations of these challenges, you will incor-porate new ways of thinking about old ideas, and you will also invite new ideas in. You will also begin to look at your parents in different ways, in some ways more objectively. You will see qualities in yourself that you see in your parents that you may not like, and you will see many qualities that you have inherited that you do like. You may identify with certain causes and certain groups that your parents may not approve of and you may even face challenges coming to terms with the new you. Coming to terms with who you are as you move through the transition from being neither fully dependent on your parents but not quite fully independent of them is both exciting and can be sometimes scary, but it is a phase that is necessary and, in the final analysis, rewarding.

For example, a Jewish student informed me that he had fallen in love with a Catholic woman and that he did not know how to share this with his parents. A gay student who was financially dependent on his father was questioning if he should reveal to him his sexual orientation. Do not hesitate to seek out the advice of a counselor. The counselor can certainly help you process the issues that you may confront as you come to terms with your identity.

Diversity

Independent of who you are or where you go to school, you are go-ing to experience something foreign, and that is not necessarily a bad thing. After all, if you are going to go away to college for four years and come back the same way that you left, what would have been the point? Depending upon where you go to school, diversity will be defined ei-ther quite broadly to include all kinds of differences or very narrowly to include only some. For example, in college, you can be influenced by geographical, racial, cultural, religious, and socio-economic as well as gender factors. You can also discuss diversity from the perspective of the student body and/or the make-up of the administration and the faculty. Diversity can also be seen from the perspective of the curriculum. If you have a chance to experience all of the above, do so. The more you know about and are able to relate to and communicate with people who bring different perspectives, the more educated you will become. Moreover, you will be able to relate to and identify with a variety of groups both na-tionally and globally. An important point for students—particularly those of you who are first generation—to remember is that you will bring a very important perspective to the college so do not underestimate your value, particularly to what it can bring to a diverse campus. Finally, many colleges hold diversity training workshops for students and staff so that people are encouraged to embrace rather than be intimated by diversity. You are fortunate if you have chosen one of those schools.

Sexual Harassment

Colleges have very strict policies concerning sexual harassment, and they do everything they can to protect you from being harassed or violated. However, in the final analysis, you the student have the ultimate responsibility to govern your own behavior so that you will not be accused of sexual misconduct. Equally important, you have the responsibility to conduct yourself in a dignified manner and to exercise sound judgment so that you do not to put yourself in a vulnerable position and fall prey to aggressive individuals. Using common sense can carry you a long way when you are at social functions or traveling to, from, and through campus, particularly if you are alone. In your orientation, the Campus Police—or Campus Security, which is what they are sometimes called—will provide you with the skill sets to be safe on and near campus. However, they cannot be everywhere; so, once again, it is up to you to take care of yourself.

Drugs and Alcohol

Unfortunately, one can find drugs and alcohol on all campuses. For students who are of legal age and who drink responsibly, there is no problem. However, in too many situations, this is not the case. One can find upperclassmen drinking irresponsibly while also encouraging underage drinkers to do the same. Most colleges have very strict policies against drugs and underage drinking on campus. If you have a roommate who is engaging in illegal behavior, consult the Resident Advisor and/or the Dean of Students so that you will not be implicated because, sometimes, if drugs and alcohol are found in your room, it can be difficult to determine to whom they belong. This situation can become particularly problematic if you live in a suite with several roommates, and the alcohol is found in a common area. You could also contact the Dean of Housing to petition for a room change to avoid conflict, as well as avoiding implication in a situation over which you had no involvement and no control. The Dean of Housing and/or the Dean of Students may give you some advice on how to handle such situations. You can be assured that they have had these types of complaints before and can offer assistance to you. Don't wait until the situation becomes a pattern and gets out of control before you act.

Roommates

When thinking about your roommate or roommates, there are several recommendations. Be willing to negotiate: it's not always about you or them. Be considerate and don't pre-judge. Never claim a bed or a space until your roommate or roommates have arrived. Be respectful: don't play your music late in the evening if you know your roommate has an early class and needs to get to bed early. Communicate: maybe you can play the music late and loudly; it may not be a concern for your room-mate. Be responsible and be reasonable. Give the relationship time, and give your roommate some space. Even under the best of circumstances, it is refreshing to come back to your room and have the space to yourself for three or four hours.

Don't assume that your roommate is going to become your best friend. In this instance, you are setting your expectations too high. All you can hope for is that you get along with your roommate and that there exists mutual respect. If you do become best friends with your roommate to whom you're assigned your first year of college, you are one of the fortunate students. Finally, try to avoid rooming with your best friend from high school. Usually, it does not work out. You might want to find out what the roommate change policy is during freshmen orientation. At some schools, because of a housing shortage, it is sometimes difficult to change rooms. In any case, your Resident Advisor and eventually the Director of Housing are the contacts who would advise you, should you have a conflict with your roommate.

Town-Gown Relationship

Know the community around you. After all, most students do not spend all of their time on campus, unless of course their campus is the town. Many colleges try to establish relationships with the surrounding commu-nity through employment opportunities and/or through service learning programs whereby students go into the community and provide tutorial services for young children or other support services for senior citizens. One can also find local school children visiting the campus for sponsored activities. You should be familiar with the community in which your col-lege is located. If the college has established a positive relationship with the surrounding community, you can assume, for the most part, that stu-dents can move freely within and around that community without hav-ing to be pre-occupied with safety issues. Conversely, if the college has a contentious relationship with its neighbors, students may have problems in those neighborhoods. In all cases, be alert, be aware, and be respectful.

Dating In College

Relationships in college can be wonderful when they are working, but when they are not, the situation can be quite overwhelming. If you have a class with and/or live in the same dorm as your "ex," this can be quite emotionally unsettling. This problem is further exacerbated if you are attending a small college where you are running into your former partner and his or her friends several times a day. To help you work through this separation, seek comfort from your friends. Or, if you need more help, seek counseling from the University Counseling Center; don't try to go it alone. In time, the sun will shine again.

Returning Home

Remember that when you return home, you may have changed, but your parents and other people in your circle will not have. You have to be patient and let them adjust to the new you. If you are lucky, they will be excited by what you have learned and how it has offered you some new perspectives. You might even become a change agent for them. On the other hand, if you come from a conservative family, you may have to suppress some of your new ideas so that the family can simply just get along. Most likely, you will know your family and know what they can and cannot accept. Be patient. In time they may grow, as you have, and be able to at least respect some, if not all, of your newfound wisdom that now informs your identity.

Your family will expect you to come back a changed person; a healthy family will even welcome that change. The new wisdom and knowledge that you bring home cannot only become a change agent for your family, but for your community at large.

● ● ● ●

College is especially different from high school because, unlike typical high school teachers, college professors are not as likely to be as involved in assuring that each individual student is doing everything necessary to succeed in the class. More bluntly, college professors are not as likely to hold your hand as you complete the work required for the course. During college, the burden of being responsible for succeeding in the class rests more with the student: you must initiate contact with your professor when there is a question or concern. College professors tend to treat their students as adults and, as such, they expect students to be responsible for addressing with them any issue that needs to be addressed to succeed in the class.

—Justin Silvey, Brandeis University

GLOSSARY

Academic Dean: Sometimes called an "academic advisor," the administrator at a college or university who advises students on class schedules, majors, and various academic programs.

Alma Mater: The school, college, or university from which a person has graduated. The term is Latin for "dear mother."

Alumni: Graduates of a specific school or college.

Associate Degree: A degree that is granted by most two-year colleges and some four-year colleges at the end of two years of study.

Bursar's Office: Also called "Student's Accounts Office." The office that is responsible for the billing and collection of colleges'/universities' charges.

Catalogue: A college or university publication that gives information about cost, courses, faculty, administration, admissions, and governance.

Class Load: The number of class units that a student takes within any given term or semester.

Commencement: Graduation ceremonies.

Community Colleges: Two-year regional colleges that offer an Associate Degree for part-time or full-time study.

Consortium: A voluntary association of colleges and universities that provides joint programs and services to enrolled students.

Convocation: An official ceremony commemorating the opening of the academic school year.

Core Courses: Classes that every student must take to qualify for graduation.

Credit Hour: A measure of completed college work. Usually, colleges give one credit hour for each hour of class time during the week.

Default: Failure to repay a loan according to the terms agreed to when a student signed the promissory note. Defaulting on the student loan may affect the borrower's credit rating for a long time.

Double Major: A course of study in which a student completes the requirements for two major degrees simultaneously.

Drop/Add: Revision of program of courses when a student wants to drop, change, or add a course.

Elective: Any course that is not required for a major field or general education requirement.

General Education Requirements: A group of basic courses for all students in a course of study at a college or university. Usually, these courses cover broad subjects in the arts, social sciences, and natural sciences.

Greek Life: A system of fraternities and sororities (consisting of a group of male students for the fraternities and female for the sororities) organized in a club for social, professional, and academic reasons.

Honors Program: Special academic programs for exceptional students.

Independent Study: A course or course of study that allows a student to do all or part of the required course work on his or her own.

Intercollegiate: Activities between colleges and universities; often athletics, but it can mean any activity.

Intramural Sports: Informal programs run by the athletic departments on a college campus. Competition is limited to students of that college or university.

RESOURCES

Chickering, A.W. and Schlossberg, N. K. (2001). *Getting the most out of college*, 2nd edition. Upper Saddle River, NJ: Prentice Hall.

Groccia, J.E. (1992). *The college success book: A whole-student approach to academic excellence.* Centennial, CO: Glenbridge Publishing.

Savage, M. (2009). *You're on your own (but I'm here if you need me): Mentoring your child during the college years*, 2nd edition. New York: Touchstone.

Tyler, S. (2008). *Been there, Should've done that: 995 tips for making the most of college.* East Bath, MI: Front Porch Press.

Woodacre, M.E.B. and S. B. Carey. (2015) *I'll miss you too: An off-to-college guide for parents and students*, 2nd edition. Naperville, IL: Sourcebooks.

FOR THE TRANSFER STUDENT

I started college at a four-year school where I excelled academically and where I had declared a major in International Studies. My GPA was 3.1 on a 4.0 scale, and I was involved in a few clubs on campus where I was able to develop and sustain a small group of friends. I was both happy and productive, and I feel that all those close to me—both family and friends—would agree.

During my freshmen year, I balanced my days with class, study, exercise, and good eating habits and, of course, rest, though when I look back on it, maybe I could have used a bit more rest. What I never cut corners on were my studies and my exercising. In fact, it was my exercising combined with my healthy eating habits that directed my interest toward the field of nutrition. The only problem was that the college I was attending did not offer a major in Nutrition.

After some soul searching and speaking with my parents, I realized that what I wanted to do with my life is help people by encouraging them to live healthier lifestyles through eating well and getting good exercise. It was working for me and I knew it could work for others, but I wanted to become an expert in the field, and I knew that having a degree in Nutrition, at least for my first degree, would give me some credibility.

Once I was clear about my major, it did not make sense to stay at a college that did not offer my major and yet cost my family thousands of dollars for me to attend it.

At the end of my sophomore year, I transferred to a local two-year public school in my state and enrolled in a couple of nutrition classes, and I am really enjoying them. Also, since it is a state school, my Pell Grant is covering most of the cost of my schooling. I am researching four-year colleges that offer my major, and I plan to transfer back to a four-year college by next year.

—Alejandra Quezada, Silver Spring, Maryland

179

ARE YOU A STUDENT WHO is matriculating at a two-year college and plans to transfer to a four-year college? Or, are you a student who is already enrolled in a four-year school and plans to transfer to another four-year school? Or, are you someone who faced some challenges at a four-year college and now finds it necessary to attend a two-year college in order to re-enroll in a four-year school?

Whatever the reason, you are not alone.

According to the National Student Clearinghouse Research Center (2012), one third of all students transfer at least once in five years. Further, of those students, more than one-fourth transfer to an institution out of state, and they tend to do so during their second year of college. In other cases, students transfer after two years at a community college, thus entering a four-year college with junior standing.

Presently, public two-year colleges educate about forty percent of all undergraduates. Enrollment in this sector is increasing in part because the tuition is typically much cheaper than that of a four-year public or private college. Also, community colleges are often the convenient local college; most students commute to the community college from home, thus defraying room and board expenses at a four-year college.

Increasingly, students enter community colleges not only as a stepping stone towards a bachelor's degree but also as a place where they can inexpensively take courses that will earn them credits towards their bachelor's degree (Horn and Skomsvold 2012).

Because the transfer student market continues to increase, it is important for students and their families to know how to plan their education if they see themselves either wanting to or needing to transfer from one school to another.

Moreover, since the admissions policies can vary across states, across public and private colleges, and across some four-year and other four-year colleges, it is important to know what questions to ask and what answers to look for. In addition to knowing the whats, the hows, and the whens with respect to transfer admissions, equally important is which and how many credits can be transferred towards the degree at the college to which they are transferring. Finally, once admitted, transfer students have to consider the financial support available to pay for the schooling and make sure that there are appropriate resources to guarantee success once enrolled.

TRANSFERS: WHO ARE THEY?

The traditional definition of a transfer student has been one who starts at one school and transfers to another. While today that definition still holds true, there is another term that is used as frequently in higher education:

it is called "Swirling" to define the "Swirling Student." Swirling students are those who are moving back and forth between and amongst institutions, both two- and four-year schools, sometimes enrolling at multiple institutions simultaneously. Increasingly, then, these students embody our understanding of the transfer student. For the purposes of this chapter, we will use the more traditional term "transfer."

There are far too many examples of transfer scenarios to present each in this chapter, but for the purposes of the discussion, I have provided a few for your consideration. Far more important to the discussion is not that students transfer but why they do. Some transfer because they want to, and others transfer because they need to.

TRANSFER BY DESIGN OR BY DEFAULT

During my first years as a guidance counselor in the late seventies, I found myself working with a talented group of seniors who were college-bound. While most were prepared for a four-year college, there were always a few at the bottom of the class who wanted to go away and attend a four-year school, but because of poor academic performance, needed to consider a two-year school. This decision was informed by nothing other than poor grades. In a word, they could not qualify for most of the four-year schools nationwide, and the few into which they could be offered admission their families did not want them to consider.

Then, unlike now, the two-year college, its name whispered in the halls of secondary schools, was considered to be the last stop. Today, the tide has changed, and for many, the two-year college has become the first stop. Unlike the aforementioned example, these families have students with good grades who can be admitted to a four-year college, but their parents cannot afford four years of a four-year college and thus opt for the "two and two plan," whereby the student will spend two years at the two-year public school, for example, and then transfer to a four-year public school or private school for two years, thereby reducing the cost of the education considerably.

There are those students who enroll in a four-year college directly from high school and, after a year, decide that they have made the wrong choice for a number of reasons. Some of these students come to this revelation sooner than later and transfer out after the first year while others transfer out after the second. A student could start at an all-women's college and decide that the institutional culture with respect to cross-gender education is narrow and choose to attend a coeducational school. Or, the student might start at a predominantly white school and find that the institutional response to the needs of students of color is insufficient for their needs and thus want to transfer to a historically black college. In both of these examples, the students were maintaining strong GPAs and pro-actively made the decision to leave; the decision was not made for them.

Unfortunately there continue to be students who start at a four-year college and, due to a poor academic performance, are asked to take a year off. In some of these cases, students are advised to attend a two-year college, where they enroll in general education classes and where their goal is to improve their skills and grades in order to transfer back into their current school. In this case, these students work out an agreement with the Academic Dean. A student's ability to show academic progress at the two-year school will most likely inform the decision towards re-enrollment at the previous college.

For those late bloomers, whether in high school or in your first year of college, I stress: it is not how you start the race; it is how you finish. For others whose parents cannot finance an education for four years, I would advise that few will know about or care where you studied the first two years; all they will see is your bachelor's degree from the four-year college. Finally, for those students who seemingly make the wrong decision on the first, four-year college choice, don't beat yourself up. It is part of your journey in life, and you need to experience it in order to be able to advance to the next level.

ASSURING SUCCESS FOR THE TRANSFER STUDENT

The challenges of the transfer transition process can be divided into three phases: the Prospective Applicant Phase, where you are researching one or more colleges to determine if they can meet your needs; the Transfer College Application Phase, where you have submitted your application and supporting documents and you are simply waiting to hear the decision from the admissions office; and the Enrolled Student Phase, where now your focus is on taking advantage of those opportunities that you know exist from your upfront research so that you can be a successful student. As a prospective applicant, you should first research to determine if there exists a Transfer Agreement and Articulation Agreement between the two-year college in which you are currently enrolled and the four-year college or colleges to which you hope to apply.

TRANSFER AGREEMENTS AND ARTICULATION AGREEMENTS

Two very important agreements between two- and four-year colleges as well as between four-year colleges are Transfer Agreements and Articulation Agreements. While most of the aforementioned agreements exist between two-year and four-year public schools within a given state, they can exist across states at both public and private institutions. A Transfer

Agreement program, then, is one in which a student is guaranteed admissions under certain conditions agreed upon by the school out of which a student is transferring and the one into which they are transferring. For example, some four-year public schools will offer a student guaranteed admission if they have a particular GPA from the two-year public school within their state.

An Articulation Agreement is defined as those courses from a two-year college that are transferable towards a student's bachelor's degree at a four-year college. While a student can expect that these relationships generally exist and are easy to navigate within a given state between a two-year and four-year public school, where they exist across states and between two-year public and four-year private schools, the policies may not always be as welcoming.

What is important to keep in mind is that these policies can vary within states between two- and four-year public schools, vary within states between two-year public and private schools, and vary across states and also across departments within a particular college. For example, the English department at a four-year college may accept all credit for entry-level courses from a two-year college, but the Computer Engineering department may not accept any credit.

Becoming aware of admissions transfer policies and the applicability of transfer courses are of primary importance as you transfer into a four-year institution. Therefore, it is incumbent on you to ascertain if these arrangements exist and how you can access them to leverage your chances of getting into the four-year college. While doing this, you should also assure that, once enrolled, you will receive some if not all of your credits earned from the previous college.

THE ADMISSIONS PROCESS FOR TRANSFERS

As soon as you know that you are going to transfer, develop a plan. For some students who enter a two- or four-year college with the intention of transferring, you can start your plan as soon as you enroll in college. For those of you who end up deciding later, for whatever reason, you can begin your plan at that point. Your plan should begin with two important meetings. You should speak to the advisor at your outgoing school and speak to an admissions officer or a pre-advisor at the incoming school.

PROSPECTIVE APPLICANT PHASE

Planning Questions for the Admissions Officer

As is the process for high school seniors, by contacting the Admissions Office transfer students have to research the school and/or schools in which they have an interest. Understanding what is expected of you earlier rather than later in the process will enable you to put your best foot forward, and you will be able to position yourself as a competitive student from the start. Below are a few sample questions that you might want to ask when speaking with an admissions officer at the colleges to which you are considering applying.

- What is the application deadline date?
- Are applications accepted in both fall and spring semesters?
- Does your school use the Common Application?
- Do you require an essay or essays?
- Do you require recommendations, and if so, how many?
- Are interviews required?
- Do you have an Admissions Officer who reviews transfer applications?
- What is the average GPA for admitted transfer students?
- If one is applying with less than 30 semester hours, does one have to submit a high school transcript and SAT or ACT scores?
- What percentage of transfer students come from community colleges?
- As an athlete, can I be considered for one of your sports programs?
- Do you require auditions for performing arts students?
- Do you require portfolios for visual arts students?

These are some basic questions that you need to find answers to as you think about transferring schools. However, the above questions only address one side of the equation. They inform the admissions process with the requisite deadline dates and polices, but they do not address the question of earned credit accepted by the incoming college. Here, you most likely will have to speak with a separate administrator where you would ask another set of questions.

Planning Questions for the Pre-Academic Advisor

- Does your school offer Academic Advising for transfer students prior to enrollment?

- Under what conditions does your school accept credit earned from previous colleges?

- Can one find out prior to enrolling how much credit will be transferred?

- Are there certain levels of courses that will be off limits to one as a transfer student, potentially coming in with junior standing, e.g., introductory level classes usually offered only to freshmen or sophomores?

- Do you only accept credit for general education courses, or would you accept course work completed in a particular major?

- Is there a limit on how much credit your school will accept for a particular major?

- If I received credit for AP and IB classes at my previous school, can I be guaranteed that the credit will transfer at your school?

It is worth repeating that, when possible, the above questions should be addressed at the planning stage, which should begin sooner rather than later. The sooner you can find the answers to the above, the sooner you can plan with confidence for the transfer process. You can develop your plan that will consist of the appropriate courses you should take and when. You can also develop a timeline so that you can stay on track to meet your target goals. If you are working, you also need to calibrate that schedule into your plan and, of course, the plan should consist of a routine schedule for study. Finally, your plan might consist of routine meetings with your advisor at the community college to make sure you are on track as well as some contact with the Admissions Office and pre-academic advisor at the school or schools to which you are applying.

Transfers Are Welcomed

As you are researching colleges in which you have an interest, please do so with self-confidence. Know that you are valuable and that you will bring qualities to the college that will be seen as noteworthy. Will you meet some students who will look down on students who come from a two-year college? Yes. Will you meet or hear about an occasional professor who is suspicious of the academic preparation of students coming from a two-year college? Of course. Will you hear about students who look down on students who come from a less selective four-year college? Unfortunately, you will encounter a few. However, do not be intimidated. Know yourself and know your self-worth. Moreover, whether a first-generation college student, student of color, student from an economically disadvantaged background, or a veteran, know how your unique experience adds value to your new college community, and be proud of the unique role you play.

In some cases, you will add to diversity. While some colleges address diversity when enrolling their freshmen class, others depend on their transfer student population to enhance their diversity. Other colleges are facing fiscal challenges because their numbers are low. As a transfer student, you contribute to increased enrollments, which enhance the dollars for that institution. Finally, you are coming in often already with one or two years of college, which also means you are more mature and, in some cases, you may have worked, supported your birth family, or may have started one of your own. In all cases, you have had some life experiences that render your background impressive and as such would add value to any college environment.

Applying to Selective Colleges

When thinking about colleges to which to transfer, think selectively. If you are a student who has performed exceedingly well at a two-year college, you will have lots of choices available to you. Don't assume that because you are coming from a two-year college, you will not be admissible to a selective four-year school. Nor should you assume that you will not be welcomed. Moreover, do not be intimidated by the high price tag that generally accompanies competitive schools. If you have stellar grades, you stand a good chance of being admitted, perhaps even being offered a transfer scholarship. You are coming from a unique experience that will add diversity at schools that may have diversity but not necessarily the kind that you are bringing. Furthermore, many of the selective colleges continue to seek creative ways to enhance their diversity by admitting greater numbers of students who mirror the demographics of students coming from two-year colleges.

Finally, if your family has a low income so they cannot afford a $60,000 price tag, since your expected family contribution will be low, your need will be high. That being said, selective colleges can more often than not satisfy one hundred percent of a family's demonstrated need, meaning you will be offered a full ride and not have to worry about financing your education.

THE TRANSFER COLLEGE APPLICATION PHASE

With any application process, one has to conduct some research to acquire baseline data before completing applications. By meeting with your academic advisor at your current school and having spoken with the admissions officers at the schools you are considering for transfer, you can focus more earnestly on the application process when the time comes. If the time is now, you need to develop a timeline listing each college in order or the deadline dates along with the information needed by each. Also, make sure you give those who are writing recommendations enough lead time so that they have more than sufficient preparation time to represent you in the best light. Do not wait until the last minute to complete your applications and essays because a last-minute application looks like a last-minute application.

Essays

Give yourself ample time to craft an impressive essay. This is your time to shine above and beyond your GPA. For those students who are applying with less than 30 semester hours, you most likely will need to submit your SAT and/or ACT scores in addition to writing one or more college essays. You are more than a number, and if there is something that you feel the committee needs to know to leverage your standing in the application pool, use an essay and/or any additional piece of writing to let them know who you are beyond a GPA and test scores (if test scores are part of your application).

Make sure you ask someone to proofread your drafts, ideally an English teacher or someone who has some experience reviewing essays for college applications. For a more detailed outline on how to write your college essay, I recommend that you not only refer to Chapter II to provide more detailed tips, but also, please take some time to read a number of the essays that are contained in this book. Both will provide you with some insights into how you might approach your essays.

Visiting Colleges

If you can, it is always better to visit the colleges to which you are applying. If you are applying to colleges locally, it is a no-brainer: you need to get in your car or access public transportation and visit the colleges where you can take advantage of the standard information sessions and a tour. In some cases, you may have already visited at the planning stage one or two years earlier, but for other colleges, you may have only connected with staff by phone or email and never paid a formal visit to the campus.

There is nothing like a visit where you can witness and interact with the students on campus. As a transfer applicant, you should call the Admissions Office and request to visit. If they don't ask, let them know that you are a transfer applicant so that they can design a visit that meets your specific needs.

Questions that you might ask at this stage would be the following:

- What support services are available to transfer students to assist them with the transition, particularly from a two- to four-year college?

- Are there specific organizations for transfer students?

- Is there a specific Transfer Student Advisor?

- Are transfer students guaranteed student housing?

- What kind of housing is available for students with families/ children?

- Are there opportunities for transfer students to become involved with academic research and/or study abroad programs?

- Is there an office for commuting students?

- Are there workspaces for commuting students to use in between classes?

The Common Application

When you research colleges, you will be able to determine if the college is part of the Common Application Program or whether it uses its own application or both. By using the Common Application, you can save yourself some time in that, if you are applying to more than one school and they are all part of the Common Application program, you only need to complete one application and write one principal essay for all of the schools. However, some Common Application schools require a supplement. Be sure that you are aware if a particular school requires a supplement. For schools that do not use the Common Application, make sure you pay attention to their application process and complete all of the appropriate essays should they require any. As does the Common Application, some of these colleges may also require one or more recommendations. Pay attention to what you are expected to do and by when. An incomplete and/or late application will not be considered. Generally, there are no exceptions, particularly at those schools that receive more qualified applications than they can admit.

Fee Waiver

If you have received a Pell Grant under the aegis of the FAFSA program, you are also eligible for a Fee Waiver that you can obtain from the National Association of College Admissions Counseling (NACAC). Google NACAC, obtain their contact information, and a staff person will inform you as to how you may access the Fee Waiver. In addition to the NACAC Fee Waivers, several colleges will waive the application fee for students from economically challenged backgrounds; however, you must ask. You know what they say… If you don't ask, you know what the answer will be.

Financial Aid

When visiting each college, make sure that you make time to visit the Financial Aid Office and, if possible, meet with a Financial Aid Counselor. If you need to make an appointment and come back another time, do so. Minimally, you should have a telephone conversation with an official in the Financial Aid Office. During your discussion, make sure you discuss both types of financial aid: need-based and merit-based. If you have applied for financial aid to date, you are already familiar with the Free Application for Federal Student Aid (FAFSA), which is a need-based financial aid program.

Whether attending a two- or four-year college, all students applying for financial aid are required to complete the FAFSA. Unlike two-year colleges, some four-year colleges will require that students complete the College Scholarship Service (CSS) Profile in addition to the FAFSA. The CSS Profile is financial aid application that is administered under the aegis of the College Board. There is a fee associated with the CSS Profile, but if you are eligible, the fee will be waived. Once you complete the form, you will know if you qualify for a fee waiver. For more information about the CSS Profile, go to www.collegeboard.org. When visiting colleges, be sure to ask what financial aid applications are due and by when.

There are occasions where you will need to complete the FAFSA to also qualify for merit-based aid, but, generally, merit-based aid is reviewed under separate applications submitted to you by the sponsoring agency. It is advised that you ask the college about both internal merit based scholarships–those earmarked by the college–and external merit based scholarships–those outside of the college. You will want to know if there are scholarships specifically for transfer students. Be sure you understand how the Office of Financial Aid allocates external scholarships, i.e., monies coming from private sources outside of the university.

Financial aid is very time sensitive, so be sure to you have all of your documents completed correctly the first time on time. If you are late or a document is incomplete, you will lose time, and losing time in this case can cause you to lose some free money. Give yourself the opportunity to receive all of the financial aid for which you are eligible to receive by completing all forms the first time on time.

Follow Up

Once both your college applications and financial aid forms have been completed, make sure that you follow up. It is not the responsibility of the admissions office to call you and inform you that one of your recommendations is missing; nor is it the onus of the financial aid office to contact you instructing you to send in a missing tax form that you overlooked. These are your applications, and it is your responsibility to stay front and center throughout the process to assure that all documents are in the right hands, completed correctly, and on time.

You might first start by checking with the school out of which you are transferring to make sure that your transcripts have been forwarded to the colleges to which you are applying. Secondly, you need to check with the professors who have agreed to provide you with a recommendation. Once you are assured that those items have been completed, you can proceed to follow up with the colleges where those documents have been sent. When doing so, you can ask if your application is complete with all of the supporting documents. You might then ask them to send an email confirmation from both the admissions and financial aid offices, assuming that both are separate offices. In some cases, they both will be under the same umbrella, in which case, one email confirmation will be sufficient.

ENROLLED STUDENT PHASE

Once enrolled, your success depends on two factors: a college or university that offers a welcoming culture for transfer students through communication, engagement, and intentional orientation programs to ensure transfer students' success; and your willingness to self-advocate and intentionally take advantage of all the resources available. You play a key role in contributing to your own success. In other words, you need to have ownership in the process and, ideally, you should be pro-active: try to stay ahead of the process and take control over it; do not let it control you. There are several ways you can develop strategies to guarantee your success, and central to those are orientation programs, mentoring programs, tutoring services, and counseling.

Student Orientations

There are several indications that inform an institution's commitment to your success, and one is a formal orientation program prior to course registration. You can expect that all four-year colleges will offer orientation programs to assist you as you integrate into a new community which has its particular policies and procedures. Your first obligation is to attend the entire orientation. Here is where you will be introduced to the key players of the college/university and learn where you go for what and by when. It is important that you have access to this information pro-actively and not re-actively. Strategically, it would be in your best interest to develop and sustain relationships with key administrators and faculty before you are in a crisis.

Mentoring

During the orientation, you may be introduced to a mentoring program: either a Transfer Student Mentoring Program or a Faculty Mentor Pro-gram, or both. If such programs exist, I would highly recommend that you consider one of them. It is not uncommon for universities to offer mentoring programs for their students. In your case, one that is designed specifically for transfer students would be ideal. If the school does not have a formal mentoring program, you might speak with a staff in the Student Affairs Office and request a mentor. Of course, you can always seek a mentor from your community outside of school, but you would want a mentor who has a professional relationship with the college and, more importantly, an individual who had been a transfer student dur-ing his/her undergraduate schooling. In this way, your mentor would be more able to identify with the challenges you might encounter and to be a greater resource as you manage those challenges.

Academic Advising

During your orientation program, you will be introduced to the advising system of your college, and, most likely, within your first few days of col-lege you will learn to which advisor you have been assigned, the pairing to be determined by the major you have selected. Recall that if you had entered a four-year college as an undeclared major, you would have had two years before deciding on your major. Thus, if you are transferring with junior standing, you will also need to have a major. Your academic advisor will help you map out your course of study for the next two years. He or she most likely will be one of your professors in your ma-jor. In that meeting, you might inquire about internships and scholarship opportunities.

Rather than wait for your advisor to call you to schedule a subsequent meeting, it is highly recommended that you structure time to meet with him or her four or five times during an academic year. It might also be in your best interest to meet with your advisor in the dining hall for meals where they may get to know you outside of a formal academic setting. This scenario will give your advisor more information to draw from should you ever need a recommendation for employment, graduate school, or professional school.

Tutoring

While transfer students have had at least one, often two years, to experience higher education, attending a four-year college, particularly a selective one, could introduce some new challenges, particularly in the academic areas. Here is where students need to be pro-active since it will be expected that, if they are having academic challenges, they will meet with the professor or one of the professor's graduate student assistants, someone who most likely is working on their Ph.D. In large universities, students could get lost in the numbers and thus will have to make the professor aware that they are in need. In smaller colleges with often smaller classrooms, students are less likely to be able to hide or to get lost. In all cases, when students are feeling overwhelmed with the material, even if it is the first two weeks, they should reach out for help, and that help could result in tutoring services.

Counseling

The Counseling Department (usually under Student Affairs) will offer the students both individual and group counseling. Students could be referred to counseling by a professor, an academic advisor, a residence hall advisor, or all three. Of course and most importantly, students can self-refer and are encouraged to do so if they are feeling overwhelmed with any issue that could be impacting their success in or outside of the classroom. If you are living on campus, your first point of contact could be the Resident Advisor or the Dorm Counselor, but it might also be one of your professors, particularly if you are having difficulty in his or her class. Sometimes, your first point of contact may be a parent or an extended family member.

To whom you reach out first is largely informed by the nature of the problem. In all cases, it is important to reach out to someone, to know that you are not alone, and to always know that colleges have wonderful support staff in their counseling centers to assist you with most of the problems you could encounter. As in managing your academic challenges, don't wait until the last minute to handle your personal ones. Usually, the personal challenges can negatively impact your academic performance, and that is what you want to avoid. While there is a range of services provided by colleges to ensure a student's success, the four mentioned here are key and thus ones I would advise students to utilize if necessary.

CONCLUSION

When choosing an ideal school to which to transfer, look for schools where the best practices ensure transfer success, retention, and graduation rates. There should exist a strong partnership between institutions that share students. Students planning to transfer need early access to advising at the school where they eventually plan to earn their degree. Programmatic offerings allowing transfers to transition smoothly from one school to the other and to be part of a community are also important. Institutions that identify curricular barriers for transfers, mismatches in course alignment, potential duplication of course content, and grading and repeat policies—and resolve these matters—enable students who transfer in to experience success. Those schools where collaboration exists between academic and student affairs to accommodate the needs of the transfer students are ones in which the transfer student will experience the most success.

● ● ● ●

In high school, I spent my summers at Phillips Academy in Andover, Massachusetts, as a student of the rigorous math and science program, (MS)2. I had such a wonderful time during my summers at Andover that I sought to recreate that experience in college. I applied to sixteen colleges, twelve of which were in New England. My mother, seeing that I had a serious case of tunnel vision, recommended a school that a cousin of mine graduated from in North Carolina, but at the time, I was determined not to go to school down South. Either I'd go to college in New England or a college in my hometown. After hearing back from all of my prospects, I decided to attend Mount Holyoke College. I had a great time there. The campus was beautiful, and I felt a true sense of empowerment being surrounded by so many intelligent, independent women.

I came home after the end of my first year excited to share my experiences with my friends. I spoke to one friend who would start college that year and listened to her talk about how she narrowed her choices down from schools up and down the East Coast, and even some in the Midwest. It wasn't until I spoke with this friend that I realized how many possibilities I overlooked in my own college application process simply because I wanted to recreate an experience that honestly couldn't be recreated. I wasn't unhappy at Mount Holyoke, but as I sat and thought about it, I knew that I was missing something from my college experience. I spent that summer looking at other schools, especially in the South, since I had been so adamant in ignoring it the first go around.

I decided that I wanted to visit the University of Virginia and the University of North Carolina at Chapel Hill, which surprisingly was the very school in North Carolina that my mother suggested when I first applied to college. What was even more surprising was that my supervisor for my job that summer was a graduate of Chapel Hill. After visiting both schools, I found that UNC really left an impression on me, but even so, I was still unsure as to whether or not I truly wanted to transfer.

I went back to MHC in the fall and continued to enjoy myself. When I went home for winter break that year, I decided to look up UNC again. I saw some pictures on their website of students donning their UNC paraphernalia at a recent basketball game. That's when it struck me that transferring would allow me to experience something I never did in all my years of school-ing—school spirit. I went to a small high school where school spirit was nonexistent, and school spirit wasn't big at Mount Holyoke either. I decided to apply to UNC, and if I didn't get in, I would just stay at Mount Holyoke.

Well, I got in, and I couldn't wait to go to my first college football game. That morning when I stepped out of my dorm, I saw hordes of people sporting their Carolina blue, walking towards Kenan Stadium. I saw families tailgating across the campus, mothers carrying their small children who also donned Carolina paraphernalia, elderly couples with pom-poms and seat cushions in hand and even those select few individuals who covered themselves in body paint. In that moment, I realized that I was a part of something big. I pictured myself years later walking with my own family to the stadium dressed in all of our Carolina blue glory. In that moment, I realized that I was starting a legacy that I truly wanted to continue and becoming a part of a true community. I went to every football game that year, bought a drawer full of Carolina clothing items and became an avid fan of a sport I never truly paid attention to before—basketball.

Do I regret going to Mount Holyoke? Absolutely not. I truly enjoyed my time there and have encouraged several young women, including my younger cousin, to apply. There was just something I realized I needed and wanted out of my college experience that Mount Holyoke couldn't give me, and, as many people mistakenly assume, that "something" was not more interaction with the opposite sex. As much as we like to say we have a plan for our future and we like to see things go according to that plan, some things really do just happen by chance. Had I not spoken to my friend about their college application process that summer after my first year, I never would've thought about transferring. That one conversation truly changed the course of my life, and because of it, I am one of the proudest Tar Heels you'll ever meet.

—Courtney Grispy, Washington, DC

GLOSSARY

Articulation Agreement: An agreement each institution makes with the transfer student, assuring the student that a certain number of credits will be accepted by the institution to which the student is transferring.

The College Board: An American non-profit organization that was formed in 1900 as the College Entrance Examination Board (CEEB) to expand access to higher education. The College Board develops and administers standardized tests, e.g., the SAT, SAT Subject Tests, PSAT, Advanced Placement Test, and the Accuplacer. It also develops curricula used by K-12 and post secondary institutions.

Common Application: An universal application used by a number of colleges allowing students to complete one application and one essay that they can submit simultaneously to several schools. Some schools under this program may require students to submit a supplement which, in most cases, is an additional essay.

Fee Waiver: A waiver of the application fee, provided by the College Board, the National Association of College Admissions Counseling (NACAC), or the college to students from low-income families.

NACAC: The National Association of College Admissions Counseling, established in 1937, is an organization of more than 15,000 members from around the world dedicated to serving students as they make choices about pursuing higher education.

Pre-Advisor: An administrator from whom a student can seek academic guidance prior to being admitted and/or enrolled in that particular school to which the student seeks to transfer.

Prospective Student/ Applicant: A name given to a student who is considering submitting an application to a particular college.

Supplement: A term associated with the Common Application, which means that, in addition to the one essay required for the Common Application, some colleges require an additional essay and/or writing sample.

Reverse Transfer: Students who start at a four-year college and transfer to a two-year college.

Swirling: Defines multiple types of student enrollment patterns and where students can attend multiple institutions in pursuit of their degree.

Transfer Agreement: Generally an agreement between a two- and four-year public school within the same state where guaranteed admission is offered to a student who satisfies a particular competitive GPA.

Transfer: Any student who transfers from one college to another, usually a two-year to a four-year or a four-year to another four-year.

RESOURCES

Horn, L., and Skomsvold, P. (2011). *Community college student outcomes: 1994–2009* (NCES 2012- 253). Washington, DC: U.S. Department of Education, Institute of Education Sciences, National Center for Education Statistics.

Hossler, D., Shapiro, D., Dundar, A., Ziskin, M., Chen, J., Zerquera, D., and Torres, V. (2012). *Transfer and mobility: A national view of pre-degree student movement in postsecondary institutions* (Signature Report No.2). Herndon, VA: National Student Clearinghouse Research Center.

CONCLUSION

I INVITE YOUR TEEN TO enjoy the high school years. This guide aimed to present a comprehensive menu of how your teen should prepare for college, those considerations that influence how they choose an institution, along with those factors that need to be considered to influence their staying power. Whether in a public, private, parochial, charter, exam, independent day, or boarding school, I am hopeful that you and your teen will find this guide to be useful and innovative.

Remember that educational planning is part of the college placement process and that the last minute is definitely too late. With that caveat, do not wait until your teen is in the middle of high school to look at this guide. Don't delay until they are a senior in high school to read Chapter II on The College Application Process. The lessons I learned over the years are incorporated here for you and your teen's use, so take advantage of them to ensure that your teen is positioned to be a competitive high school student who will have multiple options available when they are ready to apply to college.

One of those options may need to be a two-year college, and, to that end, this second edition of *Dream College* has included a chapter for the Transfer Student. As part of their plan, some choose to start at a two-year and transfer to a four-year institution while others start at a four-year and have to transfer to a two-year institution before transferring back to the original or a different four-year institution. And then, there are those who start at a four-year and for a number of reasons, find that this was not a good fit and thus choose to transfer to another four-year institution. Years ago, the two-year college used to be frowned upon; as such, it was the last stop. Today, for many it has become the first stop, and there is nothing wrong with that. Simply know that one's journey from point A to point B can take on many forms and many directions. In the final analysis, it is not how or where students start their higher educational journey; it is where and how they finish it.

Your teen will also find it useful to take a moment away from the excitement of high school graduation, college admissions, and award letters to read Chapter VIII, which addresses what they need to know now that they are getting ready to attend college. It will admittedly be a challenge to sit down with your teen and take in even more information after graduation, but it will assuredly be worth your while. After all, this statement deserves repeating: Getting into college is achieving one milestone, but staying in and getting through is achieving another. I know you have an investment in your teen getting through successfully, and I have the same investment. Good luck.

APPENDIX A

STUDENT SELF-EVALUATION FOR COLLEGE EXPLORATION

YOU KNOW YOURSELF BETTER THAN anyone else, so your input is extremely important as you begin to explore colleges. Providing specific anecdotes where possible is particularly helpful in answering the list of questions below:

1. What are your greatest strengths and weaknesses? Your answer should include both academic and personal.

2. How would you rate your academic success? Does your transcript (do your evaluations) accurately reflect your abilities?

3. Have you been involved with any community service? If so, please describe the nature of the service and the extent to which you have been involved.

4. Outside of your academic classes, what other interests do you have? Examples might include sports, travel, religion, art, etc.

5. Are there academic or other qualities about you that make you particularly proud?

6. How do you spend your free time?

7. Are there any particular events that you see as turning points in your life? Please explain why you view them as such.

8. What is the best thing that has happened to you during your teen years (or high school years)?

9. What has been the most challenging or difficult thing about your teen years?

10. Do you have a job during the school year? How many hours per week do you work?

11. Describe your family. Comment on family background, language of household, important relationships, and educational background of your parents.

12. What words would you use to describe yourself?

13. Describe your ideal college.

14. Are there any particular colleges you would like to consider? Why?

15. Are there any special factors that will influence your decision about college, i.e., religion, distance from home, family pressure, work, etc.?

16. What aspect of the college application process concerns you most?

17. What aspect, if any, of getting through college concerns you most?

18. Is there anything else about you that will help you find the best college or university to match your skills and interests?

APPENDIX B

COLLEGE APPLICANT PROFILE

Name: _____

Birthdate: _____ Email: _____

Address: _____

_____

Cell: _____ Home: _____

High School Name: _____

Counselor's Name and Phone #: _____

Profession: Mother _____
             Father _____
             Guardian _____

High School Course Information

	Course (Title, Honors/A.P.)		*Grade/Mark*
Math:	_____	(9)	_____
	_____	(10)	_____
	_____	(11)	_____
	_____	(12)	_____
English:	_____	(9)	_____
	_____	(10)	_____
	_____	(11)	_____
	_____	(12)	_____
Science:	_____	(9)	_____
	_____	(10)	_____
	_____	(11)	_____
	_____	(12)	_____
History:	_____	(9)	_____
	_____	(10)	_____
	_____	(11)	_____
	_____	(12)	_____

High School Course Information

	Course (Title, Honors/A.P.)	Grade/Mark
Language:	_____	(9) _____
	_____	(10) _____
	_____	(11) _____
	_____	(12) _____
Electives:	_____	(9) _____
	_____	(10) _____
	_____	(11) _____
	_____	(12) _____

Class Rank: _____ of _____

Cumulative Grade-Point Average (unweighted/weighted): _____

Standardized Test Scores

TEST	ATTEMPT	GRADE	DATE	MATH SCORE	EBRW SCORE	ESSAY (optional)
PSAT:	(1st attempt)	_____	_____	_____	_____	_____
	(2nd attempt)	_____	_____	_____	_____	_____
SAT:	(1st attempt)	_____	_____	_____	_____	_____
	(2nd attempt)	_____	_____	_____	_____	_____

SAT Subject Test:	TEST TITLE	GRADE	DATE	SCORE
	_____	_____	_____	_____
	_____	_____	_____	_____
	_____	_____	_____	_____
	_____	_____	_____	_____
	_____	_____	_____	_____

TOEFL:	TEST FORMAT	GRADE	DATE	SCORE
	_____	_____	_____	_____

AP:	TEST TITLE	GRADE	DATE	SCORE
	_____	_____	_____	_____
	_____	_____	_____	_____
	_____	_____	_____	_____
	_____	_____	_____	_____
	_____	_____	_____	_____
	_____	_____	_____	_____

ACT:

GRADE	DATE	MATH	SCI	ENG	READ	WRIT	COMP
_____	_____	_____	_____	_____	_____	_____	_____
_____	_____	_____	_____	_____	_____	_____	_____

Activity	In and/or Out of School	No. of Years	Leadership

Summer Enrichment Programs

Freshman _____

_____

_____

Sophomore _____

_____

_____

Junior_____

_____

_____

Senior _____

_____

_____

Awards

Academic

_____
_____
_____

_____
_____
_____

_____
_____
_____

_____
_____
_____

_____
_____
_____

_____
_____
_____

Athletic

_____
_____
_____

_____
_____
_____

_____
_____
_____

_____
_____
_____

_____
_____
_____

_____
_____

Community

_____
_____
_____
_____
_____
_____
_____
_____
_____
_____
_____
_____
_____
_____
_____

Potential Schools

School Name	Applied	Accepted	Rejected	Wait-listed/ Deferred	Application Deadline

Do you fall into any one of the following categories?

❏ Athlete　　❏ Under-represented Groups　　❏ Special Talent

❏ Child of an Alumnus/a

Have you accomplished any of the following?

❏ Counselor Recommendation　　❏ Teacher Recommendation

❏ Essay　　❏ On-campus Interview　　❏ Alumni Interview

Have you or do you plan to apply to any schools through an early action/early decision program? _____

If so, what school? _____

Notes

_____

_____

_____

_____

_____

_____

_____

_____

_____

_____

_____

_____

_____

_____

_____

_____

_____

_____

_____

_____

COLLEGE INFORMATION REQUEST LETTER

Malika Wilson
1334 ABC St. NW
Washington, DC 20011
malikawilson@abcmail.com

August 15, 2016

Mr. Sammie Robinson
Director of Admission
Williams College
Williamstown, MA 34566

Dear Mr. Robinson:

I am a senior at Wilson High School. I plan to enter college in the fall of 2017. I am interested in learning more about Williams College. I would appreciate it if you would send me the following materials:

● Information outlining summer opportunity programs for high school students

● Fly-In Programs for students who may not otherwise have funds to visit your school

● General financial aid information and any scholarship programs for students in general as well as specifically for women, students of color and/or first-generation college-bound students

● Special information related to your special interest groups, e.g. students of color, students with learning disabilities, and athletes

● A video or CD-Rom, if available

I will access your website to learn about the application process, college cost, majors, and course offerings.

Thank you very much for your consideration.

Sincerely,

Malika Wilson

APPENDIX D

SAMPLE THANK-YOU LETTER

Maria Reyes
4545 ABC Street, SE
Washington, DC 20011

October 1, 2016

Ms. Denise Walden
Associate Dean of Admissions
Colby College
Waterville, ME 40799

Dear Ms. Walden:

It was nice meeting you during your visit to Wilson High School.
I also wanted to say thank you for taking the time to grant me a
personal interview. I felt very comfortable during our conversation
and you provided me with some helpful information about Colby
College.

I will be completing my application by December and sending it to
you before Christmas. I hope you had a safe trip back to Colby.

Sincerely,

Maria Reyes
Wilson High School
Class of 2017

APPENDIX E

COLLEGE APPLICATION PROCESS CHECKLIST

COLLEGE INFORMATION	College #1	College #2	College #3	College #4	College #5	College #6
Admissions contact person, phone, email address						
Information and application requested (date)						
Financial Aid forms requested (FAFSA)						
Scheduled campus visit						
APPLICATION DEADLINES						
TESTING DATES						
ACT completed (SCORE)						
SAT completed (SCORE)						
Number of SAT Subject Tests required						
Other tests taken (i.e. TOEFL)						
INTERVIEW						
On-campus: during visit to the school						
College representative high school visit (date)						
Thank-you notes						
APPLICATION						
Form completed and signed						
Essay completed						
Teacher recommendations requested						
Teacher recommendations mailed						
Other recommendations requested						

COLLEGE INFORMATION	College #1	College #2	College #3	College #4	College #5	College #6
Transcript mailed						
Fee or fee waiver mailed						
Photograph (only if requested)						
Any other information requested by college						
Entire application copied for your records						
MID-YEAR						
7th-semester grades sent						
ADMISSION DECISIONS						
Accepted, wait listed, denied						
FINANCIAL AID OFFER						
Scholarships						
Grants						
Loans						
Work-Study						
FINAL DECISIONS						
Enrolling						
Deposits paid						
Not enrolling						
Courtesy notification completed (phone, postcard, email)						

APPENDIX F

TRANSCRIPT

Walker Jones High School
188 58th Street, New York, NY 10056

Kara L.
123 72nd Street
New York, NY 10043
212.888.8888

Expected Date of Graduation: June 2017
Class Rank: 32/547
Weighted GPA: 3.5/4.0
Un-Weighted GPA: 3.4/4.0
SAT Scores: Math-620 EBRW-640 Writing-3/4/3

Grade 9	**2013–2014**		**Grade 10**	**2014–2015**	
Courses	*Grade*	*Credit*	*Courses*	*Grade*	*Credit*
English 1	B+	1	H-English 2	B+	1
Algebra 1	B	1	Geometry	A-	1
Biology	B	1	Chemistry	A-	1
History W	B+	1	US History	B+	1
French 1	A	1	French 2	B+	1
Art	A	1	Writing	A-	1
Credits: 6			Credits: 6		
GPA: 3.3			Current GPA: 3.5		
			Cumulative GPA: 3.4		

Grade 11	**2015–2016**		**Grade 12**	**2016–2017**	
Courses	*Grade*	*Credit*	*Courses*	*Grade**	*Credit*
AP English 3	A	1	AP English 4	B	
Alg2/Trig.	B+	1	Pre-Calculus	B+	
Physics	A	1	AP Biology	B	
US Gov't.	B-	1	Thesis	C	
French 3	B+	1	AP French	A	
Psychology	A	1	Comp. Sci.	B	
Credits: 6					
Current GPA: 3.5			Current GPA:		
Cumulative GPA: 3.4			Cumulative GPA:		
			*First Quarter Senior Grades		

Signature of Registrar _____ Date_____

APPENDIX G

SAMPLE RESUME

PENONE F.
341 ABC Street, NW
Washington, DC 20001 202.888.1345
pfowler@abcmail.com

High School
Woodson Senior High School
3214 North ABC Street, NW
Washington, DC 20079

Academic Honors and Awards
2015–2016	National Honor Society
2015–2016	Spanish Honor Society
2015–2016	Honor Roll
2013–2016	Perfect Attendance
2015–2016	Eagle Scout

Athletics
2012–2013	Junior Varsity Basketball
2013–2016	Varsity Basketball
2014–2015	Captain-Basketball Team
2014–2015	Spring Track

Activities
2012–2013	Student Government-Class Representative
2015–2016	Treasurer of Junior and Senior Class
2015–2016	President, Business Club
2015–2017	Community Service-Davis Senior Citizens Home

Work Experience
2012–2013	Assistant to Accountant-Future Quest, Inc.
2005–2016	Cashier-Giant Foods

Summer
2014	The Lead Program. Kellogg School of Business Northwestern University. Evanston, IL.

APPENDIX H

INTERNET SCHOLARSHIP RESOURCES

www.scholarships.com

www.supercollege.com

www.collegequest.com

https://bigfuture.collegeboard.org/scholarship-search

www.collegescholarships.com

www.smexpress.com

www.scholarship-page.com

www.collegenet.com

www.uncf.org

www.college-scholarships.com

www.collegefund.org

www.ajm.org

www.iefa.org

www.rhodesscholarship.com

www.gmsp.org

www.marine-scholar.org

www.jackierobinson.org

www.iie.org/cies

www.scholarships-education.com

scholarships.berkeley.edu

www.collegescholarships.org

www.act.org/goldwater

ABOUT THE AUTHOR

DR. KPAKPUNDU EZEZE IS THE founder and President of Future Quest, Inc., a consulting firm that specializes in educational planning and college placement for high school students. Over the past thirty years, Dr. Ezeze has developed a number of partnerships nationwide that have helped thousands of students to prepare for college. In the Washington, DC, metropolitan area, these partnerships include Urban Alliance, College-Bound, The Ionia Whipper Home for Girls, the College Information Center at the Martin Luther King Memorial Library, Mentors, Inc., Jack & Jill, and Upward Bound programs at Howard and Catholic Universities. Most recently, Dr. Ezeze has been involved with designing and implementing college advising programs for charter schools.

For over six years, Dr. Ezeze was the director of the Washington Tennis & Education Foundation's Center for Excellence (CFE), an educational planning and college placement enrichment program which brings young tennis players together from under-resourced communities and introduces them to a range of competencies in public speaking, writing, interviewing skills, computer skills, and career opportunities.

Before coming to Washington, Dr. Ezeze served as a college consultant to students in Boston, Philadelphia, New York, Miami, and Princeton, New Jersey. Some of his clients included The Boys Choir of Harlem, New Jersey Nets Basketball Academic Camp, Salomon Brothers, Inc., Prudential Securities Adopt-a-School Programs, I Have a Dream Foundation, and The 92nd Street Y in New York. His professional career includes experience as a guidance counselor in three school systems: Lexington, MA, Wellesley, MA, and Arlington, VA. He has served as Assistant Dean in the College of Arts and Sciences at the University of Pennsylvania, Associate Program Director with the College Board Educational Testing Service, Academic Advisor at Wellesley College, Director for Upward Bound at Worcester College, and Admissions Associate for the Graduate School of Education at Harvard University.

Dr. Ezeze holds a bachelor's in fine arts from Howard University, a master's in education from Tufts University, and a doctorate in education from Harvard University.